MAKE IT EASY

VEGETABLE
COOKBOOK

KNACK

VEGETABLE
COOKBOOK

Savory Gourmet Recipes Made Easy

Mary Beth Crain

**Photographs by Peter Ardito and Susan Byrnes,
Ardito + Byrnes Photography**

KNACK
MAKE IT EASY

Guilford, Connecticut
An imprint of Globe Pequot Press

Copyright © 2010 by Morris Book Publishing, LLC

Editorial Director: Cynthia Hughes
Editor: Lara Asher
Project Editor: Tracee Williams
Cover Design: Paul Beatrice, Bret Kerr
Interior Design: Paul Beatrice
Layout: Joanna Beyer
Cover Photos by: Peter Ardito and Susan Byrnes, Ardito & Byrnes Photography
Interior Photos by: Peter Ardito and Susan Byrnes, Ardito & Byrnes Photography

Library of Congress Cataloging-in-Publication Data
Crain, Mary Beth.
  Knack vegetable cookbook : savory gourmet recipes made easy / Mary Beth Crain ; photographs by Peter Ardito and Susan Byrnes.
     p. cm.
  Includes index.
  ISBN 978-1-59921-919-6
  1. Cookery (Vegetables) 2. Vegetables. I. Title. II. Title: Vegetable cookbook.
  TX801.C77 2010
  641.6'51--dc22
                    2010001559

The following manufacturers/names appearing in *Knack Vegetable Cookbook* are trademarks:
Anna's Ginger Thins, Better than Bouillon, Boboli®, Bundt®, Burger King®, Calphalon®, Campbell's®, Carr's® Table Water® Crackers, Flatout®, I Can't Believe It's Not Butter!®, "JIFFY"®, Knorr®, Mama Mary's®, McDonald's®, Microplane®, Old El Paso®, Pepperidge Farm®, Philadelphia®, Pillsbury®, Pyrex®, Rice-A-Roni®, TABASCO®, V8®, Wheat Thins

Printed in China

10 9 8 7 6 5 4 3 2 1

Acknowledgments

A cookbook is never a one-person endeavor. There are always those special dishes from bygone days and places that have a hallowed place in memory; a few million variations for every recipe in cookbooks and online, which I checked and tested against my own; and plenty of people to provide suggestions, resources, support, and bravery, if they've volunteered to test taste a new creation! So, special thanks to:

My sister-in-law, Deb Gersten, for loaning me her *Cook's Illustrated* collection, cheerfully bouncing ideas around with me, sharing her own recipe tidbits, and providing a welcome source of ongoing support.

My best pal, John Spalding, who was instrumental in getting me this assignment, and who got the benefit of my "Best Borscht Ever" in return (see recipe, page 74). Barb and Francis Bray of Applewood Kennels, for helping me to meet my deadline by housing and pampering my Chihuahua, Truman, who hates it whenever I'm paying attention to my computer instead of him.

My dear friend Linda Hunt, an excellent cook who grew up on good old Louisiana cookin' and had lots of advice and recipes to share.

Larry Miller, who demonstrated his simple but so delicious technique for grilling eggplant and other vegetables fresh from his garden, and invited me to eat the results, too!

Brenda Bont, who provided me with some great cookbooks and took Truman off my hands for sleepovers with her beagle, Molly, when I was ready to change the title of my book to *1,000 Ways to Cook a Chihuahua*.

Maurice Toulemon, former executive chef at, among other prestigious institutions, Los Angeles's Beverly Wilshire Hotel, who bequeathed to me some of his rarest and most treasured cooking treatises.

And finally, my dad, Emil Gersten, from whom I inherited my love of cooking, eating, and entertaining, and from whom I also inherited too many extra pounds as a result. Daddy passed away many years ago, but I'm sure he's beaming down from heaven in fatherly pride and, if he could, would order every copy of this book. Hmmm. Is there a celestial discount???

CONTENTS

Introduction...viii

Chapter 1: Buying Vegetables
What Is Fresh?.. xii
Buying Local.. 2
Storing Fresh Vegetables............................. 4
Washing Vegetables................................... 6
Fresh, Frozen & Canned............................... 8
Eat Seasonal...10

Chapter 2: Cooking Techniques
Steaming...12
Blanching..14
Roasting...16
Grilling...18
Sautéing & Stir-Frying...............................20
Frying...22

Chapter 3: Raw Vegetables
Why Eat Raw?...24
How to Eat Raw.......................................26
The Best Raw Vegetables..............................28
Going Organic..30
Juicing Raw Vegetables...............................32
Getting Off to a Raw Start...........................34

Chapter 4: Appetizers
Baby Artichokes with Aioli...........................36
Vegetable Wontons....................................38
Asparagus Tempura....................................40
Vegetable Spread Supreme.............................42
Pesto Bruschetta.....................................44
Cheesy Spinach Squares...............................46

Chapter 5: Salads
Artichoke Avocado Caesar Salad.......................48
Pea & Radish Spring Salad............................50
Asparagus Potato Salad...............................52
Tailgate Three-Bean Salad............................54
Grilled Mediterranean Salad..........................56
Roasted Green Bean Salad.............................58

Chapter 6: Side Dishes
Bacon Hollandaise Asparagus..........................60
Green Beans Paprikash................................62
Zucchini Boats Provençal.............................64
Red Cabbage with Bacon & Wine........................66
Sweet & Sour Roasted Beets 68
Carrot & Parsnip Gratin..............................70

Chapter 7: Soups
Creamy Thyme Asparagus Soup 72
Best Borscht Ever 74
Creamy Carrot Ginger Soup............................76
Roasted Tomato & Barley Soup.........................78
Kicked-up Mushroom Leek Soup.........................80
Curried Butternut Squash Soup........................82

Chapter 8: Sandwiches & Pizza
Cucumber & Pork Pitas................................84
Portobello Ciabattas.................................86
Vegetable Po'Boys....................................88
Broccoli Carrot Potato Burritos......................90
Vegetable Bacon Caesar Wraps.........................92
Veggie Medley Pesto Pizza............................94

Chapter 9: Pasta Dishes
Pea & Mushroom Tortellini............................96
Broccoli Mushroom Alfredo............................98
Vegetable Noodle Kugel..............................100
Spinach Lasagna.....................................102
Gnocchi with Spinach Béchamel.......................104
Creamy Veggie Pasta Salad...........................106

Chapter 10: Rice & Grain Dishes
Vegetable Fried Rice................................108
Spanish Rice with Green Beans 110
Risotto with Summer Squash 112
Tomato Carrot Rice Pilaf............................114
Shiitake & Wild Rice Casserole......................116
Tabbouleh...118

Chapter 11: Potatoes & Yams

Mexican Scalloped Potatoes 120
Broccoli Mashed Potato Bake .122
Sherried Vegetable Potato Skins 124
Coconutty Sweet Potatoes. 126
Roasted Teriyaki Sweet Potatoes 128
Brandy Yams Mousseline. 130

Chapter 12: Vegetarian Entrees

Casserole of Spring Vegetables. 132
Red Pepper Eggplant Parmesan. 134
Mushroom Stroganoff 136
Coconut Vegetable Curry 138
Tomatillo Enchilada Pie 140
Vegetable Tofu Lo Mein 142

Chapter 13: Vegetables & Eggs

Spinach & Leek Frittata. 144
Mixed Vegetable Soufflé 146
Broccoli & Bacon Quiche. 148
Asparagus Timbales 150
Baked Eggs with Artichokes 152
Cabbage & Chicken Egg Foo Young. 154

Chapter 14: Vegetables & Seafood

Thai Asparagus & Scallops 156
Green Beans with Salmon 158
Shrimp with Spring Lettuces. 160
Cajun Trout with Broccoli Rabe. 162
Braised Sea Bass with Fennel. .164
Vegetable Seafood Newburg 166

Chapter 15: Vegetables & Chicken

Chicken Caprese. 168
Crusted Chicken with Greens 170
Chicken with Morels & Madeira 172
Coq au Vin Magnifique 174
Three-Pepper Sizzling Chicken 176
Zucchini-Stuffed Chicken Legs. 178

Chapter 16: Vegetables & Meat

Spiked Baby Carrots with Pork 180
Spring Vegetables with Lamb. .182
Green Bean & Beef Stir-Fry 184
Corned Beef & Cabbage 186
Shepherd's Pie. 188
Creamed Spinach with Veal. 190

Chapter 17: Stuffed Vegetables

Stuffed Eggplant Barquettes 192
Potato & Veal Stuffed Pumpkin 194
Stuffed Artichokes. 196
Spinach-Stuffed Mushrooms. 198
Athenian Cabbage Rolls 200
Christmas Stuffed Peppers 202

Chapter 18: Pancakes & Fritters

Corn Fritters with Chile Relish .204
Indian Vegetable Fritters 206
Sweet Potato–Carrot Croquettes. 208
Zucchini Latkes 210
Eggplant Pancakes Milanese 212
Mushroom & Spinach Crepes .214

Chapter 19: Breads & Desserts

Zucchini Bread 216
Tomato Herb Bread. 218
Chile Cheese Corn Muffins. 220
Winter Squash Cognac Pie 222
Cream-filled Pumpkin Roll 224
Oh My God Carrot Cake. 226

Chapter 20: Resources

Farmers' Markets, CSAs & Vegetable Festivals 229
Books & Magazines 230
Cooking Shows, Videos & Web Sites. 232
Find Ingredients 234
Find Cookware & Accessories .235
Cooking Hotlines & Help Sites. 236
Metric Conversion Tables 237

Glossary 238
Index 240

INTRODUCTION

One of the most famous cartoons in the history of *The New Yorker* dates from 1928. It shows a mother and her little girl at the dinner table, arguing over a plate of vegetables. The mother is saying, "It's broccoli, dear." The scowling little girl replies, "I say it's spinach, and I say the hell with it!"

It's still funny, even today, because it's the ultimate scenario of childhood rebellion and maternal defeat. When I was growing up, vegetables were one of the most frequently employed items in the arsenal of parental weaponry. "Eat your vegetables or no dessert!" "You're not leaving this table until you finish those brussels sprouts and I don't care if you sit there until the Second Coming!" "For your information, young man, there are plenty of starving children who would be grateful for even one bite of that eggplant!"

How things have changed, for us grown-ups, anyway. Maybe it still takes Popeye and a crowbar to make kids eat their spinach, but in today's world of designer recipes and health-conscious eating, the versatile vegetable has at last come into its own. As a result, there's absolutely no excuse anymore for not eating your vegetables—and loving them.

Because many people, however, still tend to confuse vegetable cooking with vegetarian and health-food cuisine, let us state here and now that this is neither a vegetarian nor a health-food cookbook. The *Knack Vegetable Cookbook* is simply that: a guide to the endlessly creative, amazingly delicious, and beautifully simple things you can do with vegetables. In it you'll find appetizers, entrees, sides, soups, stews, and other types of dishes, made with and without meat. You'll discover how to choose the freshest vegetables; what's in season in your area; the wacky, wonderful world of vegetable festivals; when it's acceptable to use frozen and yes, even canned, vegetables; how to store vegetables; the pros and cons of different cooking methods; and much more.

As a cook and caterer, I've spent a good part of my life creating and developing recipes, and as far as I'm concerned,

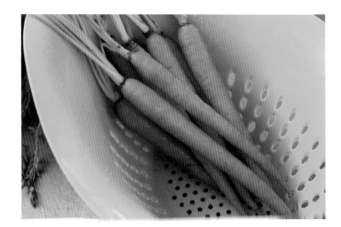

when it comes to cooking, it all boils down (no pun intended) to two basic tenets. One: It's just as easy to cook well as it is to cook badly. Two: The best recipes are generally the simplest. And nothing holds truer for vegetables. Cooking them well is just as easy as, if not easier than, cooking them badly, and the tastiest and most nutritious vegetable recipes value simplicity over complicated preparation.

This doesn't mean, however, that vegetables have to be served without grace or imagination. All too often, our typical vegetable experience consists of a fried or boiled mess that passes for a vegetable. On the other end of the offending spectrum, there are those "healthy" restaurants that serve steamed vegetables in their naked,

unaltered state—completely plain, without any seasonings to enhance their palatability. This book will show you how to serve vegetables simply, but with flair. Instead of fried asparagus, how about the great light, greaseless alternative of asparagus tempura? Steam that zucchini by all means, but dress it up with some butter, lemon, pepper, thyme, and garlic, accessorize with a little grated Gruyère, and you're ready for the summer squash ball!

The inimitable Will Rogers observed that "An onion can make people cry, but there has never been a vegetable invented to make them laugh." That may be true, but the recipes in this book are intended to bring you plenty of joy. You won't be crying over the onions in roasted tomato and

barley soup or zucchini boats Provençal. Your taste buds will be laughing when you treat them to vegetable pesto pizza, carrot and parsnip casserole with mustard and Gruyère, or lamb shanks with early spring vegetables. There's really no end to the happiness that great vegetable dishes can bring to the table, the palate, and the psyche. When you find yourself getting this joy from cooking and transmitting it to others through healthy, inspiring dishes, you become, in essence, a spiritual cook.

The idea of cooking as a spiritual calling has been explored in lots of movies. *Like Water for Chocolate, Babette's Feast, Chocolat,* and *Eat Drink Man Woman* are some of the film classics that explore the power of food to transmit

love and transform lives. But it isn't just the food itself that does the transforming. It's the cook, whose good intentions inspire the alchemistic miracle. When food is prepared with love and grace, with the pure motive of nourishing others, it becomes a blessing for all concerned.

In my cooking experience, one book in particular has made an indelible impression: *The Sri Chinmoy Family Vegetarian Cookbook.* Sri Chinmoy taught people what I call "transcendent cooking" for years. As India's Consul General in San Francisco and head of spiritual meditation centers throughout the United States, the late philosopher/teacher looked at food from the standpoint of higher consciousness. "The most important aspect of cooking," he maintained, "is its life-energizing reality."

Did you know that food has a consciousness? That vegetables have awareness? That you, as a cook, have the power to either positively or negatively impact others on a spiritual level through the food you prepare and serve? According to Sri Chinmoy, the consciousness of food and the consciousness of the cook go hand in hand. "The cook can transform the consciousness of food," he said. In adopting attitudes of joy, peacefulness, and compassion while preparing dishes, we can actually contribute to the well-being and enlightenment of those who consume them.

I gave Sri Chinmoy's advice a try some years back, when I decided to cook a "higher consciousness" Indian meal. Now, I am, if I say so myself, fairly accomplished in the art of Indian cookery. Once, during a period of culinary fanaticism, I even made my own garam masala (curry powder), grinding up about twenty different spices by hand with a mortar and pestle. For this particular meal, I used a few tasty recipes from the *Family Vegetarian Cookbook,* along with some of my own. And for the first time in my life, I cooked with not only love, but with gratitude and humility as well.

Whereas before, cooking had been both a pleasure and an ego trip, for this meal I left my ego behind. I concentrated on my breath until I achieved a peaceful rhythm in the chopping of the vegetables. I thanked God for the food, and the food for giving us nourishment and new life. I worked not at my usual bustling pace, but with a happy serenity.

I had never had so much fun preparing a meal. The kitchen seemed to be glowing along with me. Energy filled the room, along with scents both exotic and intoxicating. Everything went so smoothly that the dishes seemed to prepare themselves.

And the proof was in the rice pudding. My guests wolfed down the potato and pea samosas, the cauliflower curry, the homemade apricot chutney, the chicken makhani, the yogurt raita, and the dal pakora. The table seemed to pulsate with something more than simple gustatory satisfaction—something like unconditional love. Even though several people had brought friends whom I'd never met, a peculiar warmth overtook us, the feeling that we were all one.

"This is the best Indian food I have ever had!" exclaimed Daniel, an authority on ethnic cuisine.

"This is the best meal I have ever had!" said his wife.

And I think it was the best dinner I ever made. Even though it took place twenty-one years ago, I have never forgotten it. The memory still pushes my bliss button.

And I hope this book pushes yours.

WHAT IS FRESH?

A fresh vegetable is like a gorgeous fall day—bright, crisp, and colorful

When vegetable shopping, follow the Fresh Vegetable Golden Rule: If it smells good and looks good, it will taste good.

Just because a vegetable has come directly from the farm to the supermarket, farmers' market, or roadside stand, it is no guarantee that it's fresh. It might be underripe or overripe. It may have been treated with gases in a warehouse and stored in a temperature-controlled environment for days. It may look okay on the outside but be over the hill on the inside. How can you tell?

Look for bright, natural color and firm, healthy skin. An overripe vegetable will be darker and softer than it should be. If

Fresh Test Equipment

- Eyes: Examine the vegetable closely.

- Nose: Vegetables smell either fresh or "off."

- Ears: Ask questions about vegetable sources and shipments.

- Hands: Feel the vegetable for soft spots and give.

- Brain: Know what's in season.

- Bags: Protect vegetables with the plastic bags available in the produce section.

Signs of Freshness

- Always look closely at fresh produce before buying it. Don't be afraid to pull back the leaves of a corncob to make sure the kernels are bright or to examine a cabbage for worm holes.

- Root vegetables should be firm to the touch. If they're flexible or rubbery, they're past their prime.

- Lettuce and other fresh greens should have no limpness or discoloration.

- Broccoli and cauliflower should have tight, close flowers with no dirt spots, which can indicate pests or disease.

a vegetable has bruises, cuts, holes, or spotting, avoid it; all of these are breeding grounds for rot and mold. Underripe vegetables, on the other hand, will be too tough and green or pale (if that isn't their natural color).

For top quality and price, buy vegetables at the peak of their season. And don't overload your shopping cart just because something looks like a good buy. It's no savings if you buy more vegetables than you can store or use before they spoil.

•••••••••••••••• RED ● LIGHT ••••••••••••••
Be vigilant with prepackaged and bulk bagged vegetables, which are often plagued by hidden rot that can spread quickly. If you notice any bad odors, black areas, or softness in bags of potatoes or onions or white cotton-like growths on packaged tomatoes, zucchini, and other vegetables, be afraid. Be very afraid . . .

Buying Supermarket Vegetables

- Scan the entire produce area. Signs of spoilage are a trusty indicator of how the store maintains its produce section.

- Find out where the store's vegetable shipments come from. The farther vegetables travel, the more their freshness is compromised.

- Find out shipment frequency. Stores with shipments six days a week are better bets than those with weekly shipments.

- For substantial savings, ask for a vegetable box, which will have very ripe vegetables at a discount.

Roadside Stands

- Roadside stands can be good bets for vegetables fresh off the vine or stalk.

- Roadside stands are also excellent places to get in-season vegetables, which means higher quality and better prices.

- Fresh doesn't necessarily mean pesticide free. Always wash fresh-picked vegetables carefully.

- Check through boxed vegetables to make sure each piece is fresh. All it takes is one spoiled specimen to infect the others.

1

BUYING LOCAL

Buying local produce benefits your health, your budget, your community, and the environment

Did you know that most produce in the United States is picked anywhere from four to seven days before it comes to you in the supermarket? And that it's shipped an average of 1500 miles? And we're not even talking about imported produce from Mexico, Asia, Canada, South America, and other countries.

When you buy from your local growers, you are taking advantage of vegetables that are in season—at their peak in freshness and at their best price. These vegetables will not only taste better—they'll have more nutritional value. In the vegetable world, it doesn't take long for starches to turn to sugars, plant cells to shrink, and produce to lose its vitality and flavor.

Questions for Your Local Growers

- Do they do all direct marketing, i.e. "farm to fork," eliminating a middleman and affording the consumer the freshest produce possible?

- What are their farm goals?

- What vegetables do they grow?

- Is their produce organic?

- Do they grow everything they sell?

- How do they deal with weeds, insects, and diseases?

- What fertilizers do they use?

- Do they welcome visitors to their farms?

Farmers' Markets

- At farmers' markets, local growers convene to sell their goods to residents of the community, providing a direct link between farmer and consumer.

- Incorporate a "market day" into your week, where you can buy the freshest produce and meet and talk with local growers.

- Prices aren't rock bottom at farmers' markets. Unlike grocers, however, vendors aren't locked into a price and will often negotiate.

- Shop after lunch, when vendors are ready to leave and may sell at a discount.

2

Buying local produce also cuts down on energy waste and other practices harmful to the environment. And it supports small farmers who struggle against government-subsidized agribusiness. When you consider that only 18 cents out of every dollar spent on produce at a large supermarket goes to the grower, and 82 cents to middlemen, it's obvious how buying directly from your local farmer is an investment in your community.

ZOOM

Community Supported Agriculture (CSA) has enjoyed increasing popularity over the last 20 years. The farmer offers a certain number of "shares," which may consist of a box of vegetables or other farm products, to consumers who purchase their shares via membership or subscription and receive weekly deliveries of seasonal produce throughout the farming season.

Community Supported Agriculture

- Community Supported Agriculture, or CSA, is a cooperative venture in which members purchase a share of a farmer's crop before it's planted.

- CSA farmers typically use organic or biodynamic farming methods.

- CSA produce has been harvested as recently as the morning of pickup.

- Each week, the farmer delivers fresh produce to designated drop-off spots. Or members may pick up the share directly from the farm.

Vegetable Festivals

- Vegetable festivals are great ways to buy in-season vegetables, promote local produce, sample fresh vegetables and recipes, and participate in fun activities.

- Michigan's National Asparagus Festival features fresh asparagus, an asparagus food court, arts and crafts, music, and a parade led by Mrs. Asparagus.

- Pumpkin festivals offer fresh pumpkins and winter squash, sample dishes, and fun pumpkin-oriented activities.

- Check the Resources chapter for a festival near you.

STORING FRESH VEGETABLES

Some fresh veges respond well to refrigeration, while others do not

When it comes to storing fresh vegetables, there are a variety of methods, depending on the vegetable. Some should be refrigerated, while others require room-temperature storage. Some vegetables freeze well; others don't. While your refrigerator's fruit and vegetable bins are designed to keep produce fresh as long as possible, there are still some vegetables that are better kept in dry, cool areas like root cellars, basements, or enclosed porches.

Following a few simple rules can maximize your use of fresh vegetables. First, buy only what you'll use within a week to ten days. That's about the longest you'll want to refrigerate most fresh produce, although there are exceptions like cabbage, celery, and carrots, which may keep for several weeks. Second, never chop vegetables until you're ready to use them, as exposure to air and light speed nutrient loss. Third, plan weekly menus that incorporate the vegetables you've

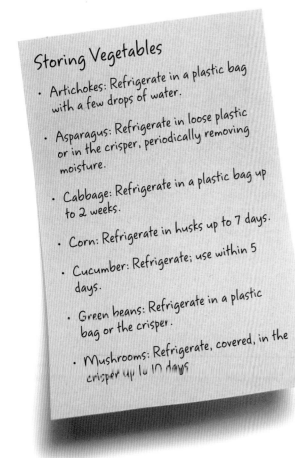

Storing Vegetables

- Artichokes: Refrigerate in a plastic bag with a few drops of water.

- Asparagus: Refrigerate in loose plastic or in the crisper, periodically removing moisture.

- Cabbage: Refrigerate in a plastic bag up to 2 weeks.

- Corn: Refrigerate in husks up to 7 days.

- Cucumber: Refrigerate; use within 5 days.

- Green beans: Refrigerate in a plastic bag or the crisper.

- Mushrooms: Refrigerate, covered, in the crisper up to 10 days.

Storing Potatoes

- Place potatoes in a plastic, burlap, or brown paper bag with holes in it.

- Store up to a month in a cool, dry place at about 45–50°F.

- Avoid storing potatoes with onions; when close together, they produce

gases that spoil both.

- Check the potatoes periodically and remove any that have become soft or have sprouted. If rot has set in— and you'll know it by the memorably horrible odor— you may have to discard all the potatoes.

bought, whether fresh or reheated. All of these suggestions will cut down enormously on food waste.

In general, root vegetables should be stored in a cool, dry place. Pumpkins, winter squashes, and tomatoes should be stored at room temperature, as refrigeration can damage their flavor. Vegetables like artichokes, leeks, greens, spinach, summer squash, mushrooms, and peas should be refrigerated.

··········· RED ● LIGHT ·············

Never rinse or wash potatoes before storing them, as this may lead to mold and rot. And never store potatoes in the refrigerator, as the starch will convert to sugar and the potatoes will become too sweet.

Storing Leafy Vegetables

- Rinse lettuce, spinach, kale, parsley, and other greens to remove dirt and other impurities.

- Pat leafy vegetables dry with paper towels or spin them in a salad spinner. Too much moisture will accelerate rot.

- Wrap dry vegetables in paper towels and place them in separate plastic bags in your refrigerator crisper.

- Set your fridge to the middle of the temperature scale and keep the humidity setting at low. This will keep the greens from freezing or turning mushy.

Freezing Raw Vegetables

- Celery: Clean stacks and freeze stalks whole; use only for cooked dishes.

- Mushrooms: Wipe with a damp cloth and place in dated plastic freezer bag.

- Peppers: Wash, dry, cut in half, and remove stems, seeds, and membranes.

Quick-freeze by freezing on a flat sheet and then transferring to freezer storage bags, removing extra air.

- Tomatoes: Wash and dry, place in a single layer on a tray and quick freeze. Transfer to a plastic freezer bag, seal, and use within 8 months.

WASHING VEGETABLES
What's the best way to wash fresh produce?

With pesticides and other toxins an unfortunate part of our daily lives, it's vitally important to wash fresh vegetables. Opinions differ as to the best way to remove surface contamination. Some people advocate plain old everyday tap water, while others swear by vegetable washes and even chlorine bleach solutions. Some say it's okay not to wash vegetables with inedible peels, while others insist that all vegetables must be washed. What's the real scoop?

Based on the evidence, it seems wise to wash all fresh vegetables—even those you intend to peel. The reason: As you peel vegetables, contaminants like pesticides or bacteria can get on your hands and be transmitted to the edible parts.

All produce should be carefully washed before you eat it. The risk of contamination is highest for crops like radishes,

Vegetable Cleaning Equipment

- Colander or sieve
- Swivel peeler
- Vegetable scrub brush or mitt
- Sink spray nozzle attachment
- Paper towels
- Salad spinner
- Paring knife for cutting out bad spots

Wash by Hand

- Take all the vegetables to be washed and place them on a counter near a sink.

- Wash your hands thoroughly with soap and water.

- Rub the vegetables with your hands under cool, not warm, running water to remove dirt and impurities. You can use a colander if you like.

- Some people advocate washing vegetables in a bowl of cool soapy water. Just make sure they're completely rinsed afterward.

carrots, mushrooms, and leafy vegetables, where the edible parts come in contact with the soil. Washing with clean water and peeling will remove most harmful contaminants.

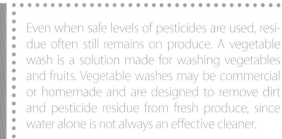
Scrubbing Vegetables

- Produce scrubbers include plastic bristle brushes, scrubbing gloves and pads, and plastic scrubbers that suction-cup to your sink.

- Use a stiff brush to scrub thick-skinned produce such as potatoes, which can pick up a lot of dirt.

- When scrubbing softer vegetables, be gentle so as not to tear the skin.

- Delicate mushrooms may either be washed and wiped with a cloth or paper towel, or simply scrubbed with a special soft brush.

Make Your Own Organic Wash

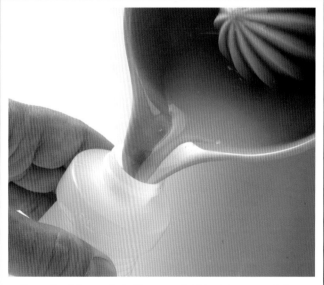

- Slice a fresh lemon in half.

- Squeeze 1 tablespoon of lemon juice into a spray bottle. It acts as a natural disinfectant and will also leave fruits and vegetables with a nice scent.

- Add 1 tablespoon of vinegar to 1 cup of water and pour into the spray bottle. Shake vigorously.

- Spray all of your vegetables with the wash and rinse it off, rubbing the vegetables clean with your hands.

FRESH, FROZEN & CANNED
When it comes to vegetables, fresh is usually—but not always—best

Most people believe that fresh vegetables are always superior and preferable to the frozen and canned alternatives. This isn't always true. Frozen vegetables, for instance, have some advantages over fresh ones. They're available when their fresh counterparts are out of season, they have a very long shelf life, and since they're already cooked and will likely be cooked more, they're probably more sanitary than fresh vegetables.

Then, consider that fresh supermarket produce is actually not so fresh, having most likely spent days in transit, causing many of the original nutrients to be leeched out. Frozen vegetables, on the other hand, are frozen at their freshest, maintaining their nutrients.

As for canned vegetables, generations were brought up to believe that they were not only great for you but in some

Good to Have on Hand

Frozen vegetables:

- Artichokes
- Broccoli
- Corn
- Green beans
- Peas
- Spinach

Canned vegetables:

- Artichokes
- Beets
- Black, kidney, and pinto beans
- Chickpeas
- Whole kernel and cream-style corn
- Pumpkin
- Sweet potatoes
- Tomatoes

Fresh Is Best

- While frozen, and sometimes canned, vegetables have good nutritional value, nothing beats fresh vegetables for flavor.

- Vegetables like cabbage, eggplant, cucumber, lettuces, and radishes are only available in their fresh state. You won't find them frozen or canned, with the exception of sauerkraut.

- Frozen and canned carrots, potatoes, onions, and green beans lack the flavor of their fresh counterparts.

- With rare exceptions, salads should only feature fresh vegetables.

cases a miracle drug. Who isn't familiar with that iconic image of Popeye the Sailor popping open a can of spinach and downing its contents in the midst of a crisis to be transformed into the world's strongest man? Today we know that canned vegetables are generally a poor alternative to fresh and frozen. But there are times when it's acceptable to use them.

GREEN ● LIGHT

According to the Food & Drug Administration (FDA), frozen fruits and vegetables provide the same essential nutrients and health benefits as fresh, because they're nothing more than fresh produce, picked at its nutritional peak, that has been blanched (cooked for a short time in boiling water or steamed) and frozen within hours of being picked.

Frozen Alternatives

- Frozen corn and peas are fine to use in place of fresh in cooked dishes or as a side dish.

- Frozen spinach has the equivalent flavor and nutrients of fresh spinach.

- Frozen broccoli and cauliflower can be substi-

tuted for fresh, although their texture is sometimes tougher. Avoid using them in anything but cooked dishes

- Frozen winter squash and okra are excellent for soups and stews.

Acceptable Canned Substitutes

- Canned tomatoes are fine for sauces, soups, stews, and casseroles.

- Use canned corn and cream-style corn in casseroles, Mexican dishes, and corn breads.

- Canned beets are great in soups like borscht or

as a snack. You can also get away with using the julienned, sliced, or pickled varieties in a salad.

- Canned pumpkin and sweet potatoes are acceptable in pies, cakes, and other baked items.

EAT SEASONAL
Vegetables are at their absolute best when they're in season

Eating seasonal is the natural way to eat. In ecological terms, the seasons are a source of natural diversity. As growing conditions change from spring to summer to fall to winter, the earth's resources and life forms are balanced accordingly.

So, to enjoy the full nourishment of vegetables, you should start with a seasonal menu. Of course, this isn't always possible. As previously mentioned, eating local vegetables—the best place to get seasonal produce—should be a priority. But what's seasonal in one part of the country isn't necessarily seasonal in another, so if you want a certain vegetable that isn't in season, what do you do? You might learn the art of canning, which isn't all that difficult, so that you can enjoy seasonal vegetables all year round. And there are some universal rules of seasonal eating you can follow.

Checklist for Seasonal Eating

- Local seasonal produce chart

- Seasonal vegetable recipe book

- Names and phone numbers of local grocers, growers, and produce managers

- Locations of local farmers' and produce markets

- Visit www.sustainabletable.org/shop/eatseasonal to find out what's currently in season in your area

Spring Vegetables

- Tender, leafy vegetables like Swiss chard, spinach, new lettuces, and parsley signal the fresh new growth of the season.

  Purple sprouting broccoli is a unique spring vegetable that's delicious steamed and tossed with oil, sesame seeds, and garlic.

- Asparagus is unbeatable for taste, nutritional value, and versatility.

- Other early spring vegetables include sugar snap peas, baby carrots, new turnips, spring onions, baby spinach, radishes, and new potatoes.

Summer Vegetables

- Arugula, collard greens, beets, cucumber, eggplant, okra, bell peppers, and tomatoes are summer favorites.

- According to Chinese medicine, summer is the time for light, cooling foods like summer squash, broccoli, cauliflower, and corn.

- Summer squashes include zucchini, yellow squash, and pattypan squash.

- Go summer mushroom hunting for porcinis, chanterelles, and hen-of-the-woods varieties.

Fall and Winter Vegetables

- Fall brings the desire for more warming autumn harvest vegetables, including carrots, turnips, parsnips, sweet potatoes, pumpkins, onions, and garlic.

- Belgian endive, also known as chicory or witloof, peaks in November and is a great source of fiber and vitamins A and C.

- Although available all year round, brussels sprouts are at their peak in the fall.

- Enjoy sweet, hearty winter squashes like acorn, butternut, banana, and kabocha.

STEAMING

Steaming vegetables allows them to retain their color, texture, flavor, and nutrients

In steaming, foods are cooked by moist heat on a rack or in a steamer basket in a covered pan over boiling water. The gentle heat keeps vegetables crisp without overcooking them.

There are various utensils that work for steaming. Steamer pots and baskets are designed especially for steaming, although a colander and a pot with a lid will do the job as

well. Microwave steaming is a convenient option, requiring little or no water; just place the vegetables in a microwave-safe bowl and cover them with plastic wrap, leaving one corner open to vent. Cooking time is anywhere from 1–2 minutes for peas to 7–8 minutes for brussels sprouts and zucchini.

Steaming Equipment

- Steamer pot

- Steamer basket

- Several sizes of saucepans with lids

- A large skillet with a lid

- A colander

- Microwave-safe bowls

- Plastic wrap

Steamers, Baskets, and Colanders

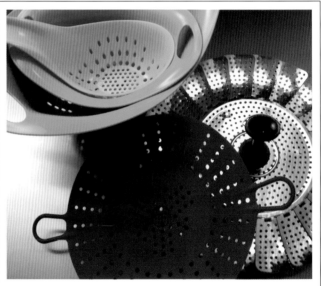

- In a steamer pot, a perforated pot holds the vegetables and stacks on top of a solid pot that holds the water.

- Steamer baskets are folding metal baskets that can be adjusted to fit most pots.

- A colander and a pot make a good DIY steamer.

- Fill the pot with only enough water to reach the basket or colander (about an inch). When the water is boiling, add the vegetables and cover them with a loose-fitting lid to let some steam escape.

Skillet Steaming

- Skillet steaming allows you to cook and season vegetables in the same container.

- Place the vegetables in a single layer in about an inch of water in the skillet.

- As soon as the water boils, place the lid loosely over the vegetables, checking them periodically to make sure they don't burn.

- If there's only a little liquid left in the skillet, don't drain the cooked vegetables. Just add some butter or olive oil and seasonings and you have the finished dish.

Steam Boiling and Braising

- To steam boil vegetables, place them in a saucepan with a tight-fitting lid and cook them over moderate heat with just enough water to keep them moist.

- Braising involves browning followed by steaming. Sauté the vegetables in a small amount of butter or oil until they're browned. Add cooking liquid, such as broth or stock, wine, or a combination of both—to cover the vegetables halfway. Cover and simmer on medium-low heat until they are tender. Raise the heat until the liquid boils off and the vegetables are nicely glazed.

BLANCHING
Blanching partially cooks vegetables for finishing later or for freezing

Blanching is an easy technique that many cooks use to keep vegetables crisp and tender. This method makes skins easier to remove, reduces strong odors, and sets the color of vegetables.

There are three main reasons for blanching. One is par-boiling—cooking vegetables way ahead of time, for quick finishing later. Another is color fixing: When a green vegetable like broccoli is blanched, green gases expand and escape from the cells, bringing out the chlorophyll. So, green vegetables are at their brightest after blanching. And the third is freezing. Blanching destroys the enzymes that cause the loss of nutritional value and flavor. Onions, peppers, and herbs

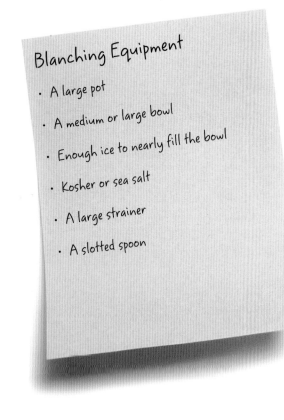

Blanching Equipment

- A large pot

- A medium or large bowl

- Enough ice to nearly fill the bowl

- Kosher or sea salt

- A large strainer

- A slotted spoon

Prepare the Ice Bath

- Fill a medium bowl about ¾ full with ice.

- Add enough cold water to come just to the top of the ice.

- You can also use very cold water without ice, but wait to fill the bowl until the vegetables are ready to come out of the boiling water.

don't require blanching, and squash, sweet potatoes, and pumpkin should be fully cooked before freezing. All other vegetables, however, should be blanched.

The trick to blanching is to boil the vegetables as briefly as possible. This can range from 30 seconds for greens to 3 minutes for broccoli and 7 minutes for artichokes. Blanching starts as soon as the vegetables hit the water, even if the boil stops temporarily.

Boil the Vegetables

- Bring a large pot of salted water to a rapid boil over high heat. Liberal salting results in even seasoning and also helps maintain the chlorophyll's brightness.

- Trim the vegetables to the size you need. It's best to trim them just prior to cooking so they won't oxidize or dehydrate.

- Add the vegetables to the boiling water in batches to ensure that the water doesn't lose its boil.

- Boil the vegetables only until they're barely cooked through.

Shock the Vegetables

- Shocking the vegetables in ice water is essential. Otherwise they'll overcook in their own steam.

- Test for doneness by removing one vegetable from the boiling water, putting it in the ice bath for a few seconds, and eating it. It should be very crisp.

- Scoop out the vegetables with a strainer, or pour the hot water through a strainer.

- Plunge the strainer into the ice bath for the same amount of time used to blanch the vegetables.

ROASTING

It doesn't get more delicious than crispy roasted vegetables tossed with butter and seasoned with fresh herbs

Roasting is a dry heat method of cooking that's similar to baking, but faster because the vegetables are tossed with a light coating of oil or butter, which speeds cooking while giving them a crisp brown outer surface.

When you roast, you need to start with more vegetables than you would for other methods of cooking because, since vegetables have such a high water content, they cook down substantially during the roasting process.

And because of the larger amounts of vegetables you'll be dealing with, you'll need large pans. Your pans should be shallow—no more than 2 inches deep. 13 x 16, 13 x 18, and 11 x 17 baking dishes or sheets are good sizes. You can

Roasting Essentials

- Large shallow roasting pan
- Half sheet pan
- Large bowl
- Rubber spatula
- Olive oil
- Butter
- Fresh and dried herbs
- Kosher or sea salt
- Freshly ground pepper

Oil the Vegetables

- Cut all the vegetables to the same size, generally ¼–½ inch sliced or diced (1-inch wedges for potatoes). Large chunks tend to cook unevenly.

- Coating the vegetables with oil or melted butter gives them a crispy outer crust that seals in flavor.

- Good oils to use include olive, canola, grapeseed, and flavored oils.

- In a large bowl, toss the vegetables with a rubber spatula in the butter or oil until they're lightly and evenly coated.

16

also use two smaller pans, placing them side by side on the oven rack.

A roasted vegetable is browned, caramelized, and crisp; a delight to the senses. They look beautiful, smell tantalizing, and taste fabulous. And best of all, roasting is as easy as 1, 2, 3.

ZOOM

Different vegetables require different roasting times and temperatures. Baby artichokes roast in 20 minutes at 425°F. Beets can take anywhere from 45 minutes to 2 hours at 350°F, depending on their size. Allow 20 to 25 minutes at 400°F for sliced egg-plant, 15 minutes at 425°F for fennel, 30 minutes at 375°F for winter squash, and 20 to 30 minutes at 425°F for carrots and turnips.

Season the Vegetables

- After the vegetables are coated with oil, toss them with kosher salt, freshly ground pepper, and herbs of your choice.

- Or sprinkle the vegetables with the seasonings after you've spread them out on the baking dish or sheet.

- Be creative. Mix and match garlic, basil, chervil, oregano, rosemary, parsley, tarragon, and other herbs.

- Fresh herbs are usually pref-erable to dried, but if dried is all you have, they will still deliver flavor, as long as they're not too old.

Roast the Vegetables

- Roast vegetables in single layers; if they're stacked on top of one another, they'll steam and get mushy.

- Roasting time depends on factors like the age of the vegetables, the amount of water in them, how evenly they're cut, and the depth of the roasting pan.

- Stir cubed vegetables periodically with a metal spatula. If roasting round vegetables like asparagus or green beans, shake the pan.

- The vegetables are done when they are fork-tender with a browned, not burned, crust.

GRILLING
In the vegetable realm, grilling can be thrilling!

At first thought, grilling seems like a pain. Isn't it a big outdoor affair, with all sorts of expensive equipment, charcoal or tanks of propane, labor-intensive prep and time-consuming techniques?

Naw! Grilling can be easy and quick, and it's performed both indoors and out. You don't need a lot of fancy equipment. And when you taste your first grilled vegetable, you'll know it was worth it. Grilled veggies have a wonderful smoky edge and an intensified sweetness. They're delicious marinated or just lightly oiled and seasoned with salt and pepper.

Grilling is a fast, dry method of cooking with radiant heat directed from below or from above. Its chief benefit is that it provides for the maximum amount of browning. While many vegetables grill well, some aren't cut out for it. You

Grilling Equipment

- Stovetop grill pan or outdoor grill
- Metal and bamboo skewers
- Tongs
- Metal spatula
- Marinade brush
- Chef's knife
- Paring knife
- Cutting board

Prepare the Vegetables

- Wash vegetables and pat dry with paper towels.

- Cut into slices, chunks, strips, or wedges, depending on the vegetable. Grill ꞁꞁꞁꞁ ꞁꞁꞁꞁꞁꞁ ꞁꞁꞁꞁꞁ

- Use a prepared marinade, or combine ⅓ cup each

extra-virgin olive oil and lemon juice with ¼ cup chopped fresh basil. 2 tablespoons fresh chopped parsley, 1 teaspoon chopped garlic, salt, and ꞁꞁꞁꞁꞁꞁ

- Marinate the vegetables for at least 30 minutes.

wouldn't want to grill celery, cucumber, or lettuce or other leafy greens. Delicate vegetables like tomatoes require a grill basket or mat. Tough root vegetables like carrots, turnips, and potatoes must be blanched or parboiled before grilling. But raw vegetables like asparagus, eggplant, onions, peppers, corn, zucchini, mushrooms, and even cabbage can be placed directly on the grill and transformed into mouthwatering side dishes, sandwiches, and wraps, salads, and kebabs.

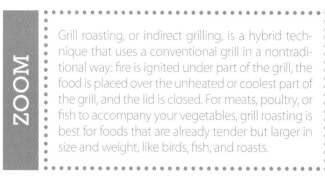

ZOOM

Grill roasting, or indirect grilling, is a hybrid technique that uses a conventional grill in a nontraditional way: fire is ignited under part of the grill, the food is placed over the unheated or coolest part of the grill, and the lid is closed. For meats, poultry, or fish to accompany your vegetables, grill roasting is best for foods that are already tender but larger in size and weight, like birds, fish, and roasts.

Outdoor Grilling

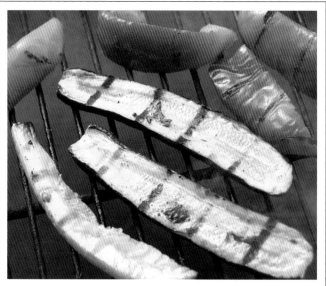

- Preheat a gas grill to high heat or light coals and wait until they're evenly covered with light or white ash.

- Place marinated vegetables directly on the grill or on skewers. Cook most vegetables approximately 3 minutes per side, brushing frequently with the mari-

nade. Vegetables are done when they're fork-tender.

- For grilled corn, husk, rinse, and securely wrap each ear in an aluminum foil packet with 3 tablespoons crushed ice and 1 tablespoon salted butter. Grill for 30 minutes, turning after 15 minutes.

Pan-Grilling

- In pan-grilling, vegetables are cooked directly on the stove on a heavy cast-iron pan or ridged griddle pan.

- The cooking surface should be seasoned to avoid sticking.

- Marinate vegetables or toss with olive oil,

salt, and pepper.

- Lightly oil the grill pan and cook the vegetables over medium heat to minimize smoking and spattering. When done, the vegetables will be browned on the outside and fork-tender on the inside.

SAUTÉING & STIR-FRYING

Sautéing and stir-frying are similar methods of quick-cooking bite-size vegetable pieces

Sautéing is a form of dry-heat cooking that uses a very hot pan and a small amount of fat to cook the food very quickly. Like other dry-heat cooking methods, sautéing browns the food as it cooks and develops complex flavors and aromas.

A key element to sautéing is the toss. In French, *sauter* means "to jump," and sautéing keeps the food jumping in the pan by tossing it, allowing it to cook evenly while keeping the pan hot. Sautéing works best with food that's been cut into small pieces, making it an excellent cooking method for vegetables. To facilitate tossing, some sauté pans have sloped sides that make it easier to flip the contents within the pan and not all over the kitchen.

Sautéing and Stir-frying Equipment

- Several sizes of sauté pans, preferably nonstick or cast iron
- A large wok
- Wooden spoons
- Metal and plastic spatulas
- Chef's knife
- Cooking oil

Use the Right Pan

- A good sauté pan has a wide flat bottom so that heat is evenly distributed; straight or sloped sides and a long handle for tossing; and a secure lid.

- Handles should be attached with heavy screws or rivets and lids should be tight-fitting.

- Frying pans should be made of fairly heavy material like cast iron to prevent problems with scorched food in "hot spots"

- The Calphalon wok is made of anodized aluminum and gets the highest consumer rating for durability, heat conduction, and size.

Stir-frying is basically the Asian version of sautéing. A traditional round-bottomed cast-iron or carbon steel pan called a wok is heated to a high temperature. A small amount of cooking oil is then poured down the side of the wok, followed by onion, ginger, and dry seasonings. As soon as the seasonings emit an aroma, the vegetables are added, stirred, and tossed out very quickly, usually within 1 to 2 minutes.

MAKE IT EASY

Stir-frying requires some prep. Because there's little actual cooking time due to the high heat, assembling all your ingredients beforehand is critical. So, keep your stir-fry ingredients separated in bowls based on how much time they need in your wok. Chop veggies and meat into bite size pieces for two reasons: they're appealing and easy to eat, and similar size pieces will cook at the same time.

Sautéing Vegetables

- Dice and slice vegetables into small pieces, mincing items like garlic, onion, shallots, and ginger.

- Heat 1–2 tablespoons of oil in a sauté pan over medium to high heat.

- Place the hardest vegetables into the pan first and allow them to caramelize or brown for several minutes. Add the rest of the vegetables, moving or tossing them frequently to prevent burning.

- Most vegetables will take 3–5 minutes and should be crisp-tender when done.

Stir-frying Vegetables

- Cut the vegetables into bite-size pieces.

- Heat 2–3 tablespoons peanut, canola, or other vegetable oil in a wok or frying pan. If using a wok, drizzle the oil in so that it coats both the sides and the bottom of the wok.

- Season the oil with a few pieces of garlic and ginger, making sure not to let them burn.

- Add the vegetables according to density and fry quickly, stirring continuously until they're crisp-tender. Add sauce and seasonings to taste.

21

FRYING
Contrary to popular belief, properly fried foods are high in nutrition and low in fat

Fried foods tend to get a bum rap in our fat-phobic society. We blame them for everything from obesity to high cholesterol to just about every disease. And yet, when prepared correctly, fried foods should not be excessively greasy or fatty. In fact, as that revered cooking authority Marion Rombauer Becker observes, "A serving of French fried potatoes properly cooked may have a lower calorie count than a baked potato served with butter."

The secret is in heating the oil to the correct frying temperature, between 350 and 375°F. This high temperature in turn heats the water within the food, steaming it from the inside out. The moisture in the food naturally repels the oil,

Frying Equipment

- Deep fryer or deep, flat-bottomed kettle or saucepan
- Wire basket
- Slotted metal spoon
- Frying thermometer
- Long-handled tongs
- Paper towels
- Mixing bowls for breading and batter
- Peanut, sunflower, or canola oil

Choose the Oil

- Choose an oil with a high smoke point, meaning it won't break down at deep-frying temperatures.

- Peanut oil is often used in deep frying. Be aware, however, that it can impart a peanutty taste to the food.

- Sunflower oil is high in the essential vitamin E and low in saturated and trans fats.

- Canola oil is one of the healthiest cooking oils. It's low in saturated fat, rich in omega-3 acids, and considered superior for high-heat cooking.

confining it to the outer surface. If you're eating greasy fried food, you can bet that the oil it was cooked in wasn't hot enough or the food was immersed in the oil for too long.

Deep-frying and pan-frying vegetables is a quick cooking method that seals in flavor and nutrients and gives the added appeal of a crunchy, tasty batter coating.

Pan-Frying

- Bread or batter cut up vegetables.

- Let the coated vegetables sit on a wire rack for 20–30 minutes so that the coating sets and dries.

- Add oil to a cold frying pan, leaving a 2-inch safety margin at the top of the pan for the oil to bubble up as the food is added.

- When the oil reaches 350°F, add the vegetables in batches so as not to overcrowd the pan. Cook quickly until browned, then drain on paper towels.

Deep-Frying

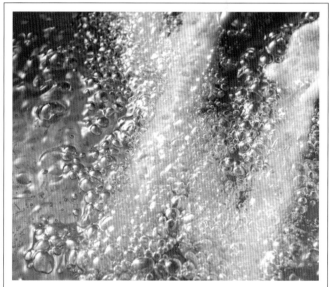

- In a deep fryer, kettle, or deep pot, measure enough oil to immerse the vegetables. If using a deep fryer, check for a "max" line.

- Set the temperature to 350°F. Check with a frying thermometer or drop a bread cube into the hot oil. If it browns within 60 seconds, the oil is ready.

- Place the battered or breaded vegetables in a wire basket or lower them into the oil with a slotted spoon.

- Fry the vegetables quickly, remove from the oil, and drain.

WHY EAT RAW?

Raw vegetables provide many benefits for both our health and the environment

In recent years, raw food diets have received more and more attention. Those who advocate "going raw" cite many advantages to this radical departure from the normal Western diet. Raw foods, they maintain, are better quality than processed or cooked food, as they're more likely to be organic and the heat of cooking sometimes depletes vitamins, damages proteins and fats, and destroys beneficial digestive enzymes.

Raw foods require very little preparation, so meals are quick and everyone, including children, can easily throw them together. In addition, eating raw is a natural cure for obesity and lowers the number of free radicals in your cells,

Reasons to Eat More Raw Vegetables

- Lose weight naturally
- Get more fiber naturally
- Food budget friendly
- Environment friendly
- Boost immune system
- Cure and prevent disease
- Save kitchen time
- Save on health-care costs

Minimum Prep

- Food shopping is simpler. You'll be spending more time in one area—the produce section—and less money.

- Eating raw vegetables requires very little prep time. You basically just wash your vegetables, peel and seed them if necessary, and cut them up.

- Menu planning is simple but can also be creative as you learn how to do more with less.

- Cleanup is a breeze. No dirty pots and pans, and dishes and silverware can be quickly washed and rinsed.

possibly stopping or even reversing the spread of many chronic diseases.

Since this book is concerned with vegetable cooking, we obviously don't advocate a completely raw vegetable diet. First of all, not all vegetables should be eaten raw. And secondly, studies have shown that cooked vegetables are by no means always nutritionally inferior to their raw counterparts.

Yet while an extreme back-to-Eden philosophy may be too idealistic and unrealistic for most of us, simply eating more raw vegetables is not. It's easy to prepare them in many tasty ways, and they can have many health benefits.

Nutritional Advantages

- Raw vegetables have the best balance of water, nutrients, and fiber to meet your body's needs.

- Raw vegetables are extremely rich in minerals, vitamins, trace elements, enzymes, and natural sugars.

- Raw vegetables have no cholesterol or fat, making them naturally low-cal and high energy.

- Raw vegetables are an important source of antioxidants, which aid in the prevention of chronic and life-threatening diseases like diabetes and cancer.

Helping the Environment

- Eating more raw foods saves natural resources used to provide energy and supplies for the food industry.

- Raw food requires little or no electricity, gas, or oil to prepare.

- Raw food consumption reduces the amount of carbon dioxide released into the atmosphere from cooking.

- Orchards and gardens produce oxygen through the process of photosynthesis, helping to reverse the greenhouse effect.

HOW TO EAT RAW
Raw vegetables should be part of a varied, balanced diet

As I mentioned earlier, we don't advocate a raw food diet per se. We think it makes more sense to include more raw vegetables in your diet without giving up the delicious and healthy cooked vegetable, dairy, meat, poultry, and fish dishes featured throughout this book. Going raw shouldn't mean going overboard.

Expanding your raw vegetable repertoire means being more creative in menu planning and recipe creation, and paying even more attention to buying and washing vegetables. While overripe vegetables are okay for stews and casseroles, always choose the freshest vegetables for raw eating. Wash all vegetables, including the organic variety, thoroughly. The point of eating raw vegetables is to enjoy the best nature has to offer, but that doesn't include pesticides and fertilizers,

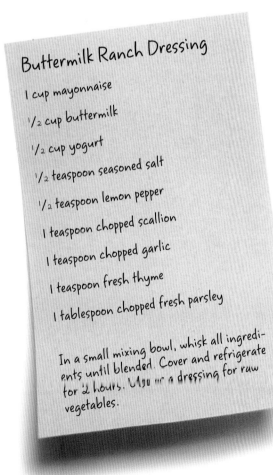

Buttermilk Ranch Dressing

1 cup mayonnaise

1/2 cup buttermilk

1/2 cup yogurt

1/2 teaspoon seasoned salt

1/2 teaspoon lemon pepper

1 teaspoon chopped scallion

1 teaspoon chopped garlic

1 teaspoon fresh thyme

1 tablespoon chopped fresh parsley

In a small mixing bowl, whisk all ingredients until blended. Cover and refrigerate for 2 hours. Use as a dressing for raw vegetables.

Choose the Freshest

- Leafy greens should be crisp and bright with no wilted or brown leaves. Root vegetables should be firm and blemish-free.

- Cabbage, winter squashes and other large globular vegetables should be firm, bright, and heavy for their size.

- Asparagus, broccoli, and cauliflower should have tight, firm stalks, tips, and flowers.

- Fresh herbs like parsley, sage, rosemary, thyme, tarragon, and dill enhance the flavor of raw vegetables.

even if they're composed of natural ingredients.

Get creative with dressings and sauces. There are so many delectable ways of preparing vinaigrettes, dips, creamy dressings, and light sauces that you'll never be at a loss for ways to accessorize your raw veggies.

Try chilling vegetables. Even vegetables you might normally prefer cooked can prove to be just as flavorful when served cold. And use lots of fresh herbs, which boost taste and reduce salt intake.

YELLOW LIGHT

The "rawer" you go, the faster you'll fulfill that daily 5 servings of vegetables and fruits requirement, because that's about all you get on a raw foods diet. But eating totally raw definitely isn't for everyone. For instance, if you eat out a lot, it probably isn't practical. Bottom line, going raw doesn't necessarily mean eating a 100 percent raw foods diet. The main goal is to eat more vegetables than you're eating now.

Be Colorful

- Use colors to create a visually appealing meal or snack.

- Red, yellow, green, and purple bell peppers, sliced carrots, radish rosettes, chickpeas, and fresh snap peas make a colorful, super healthy salad.

- Bright green zucchini, yellow crookneck, orange pattypan squash, and red and yellow grape tomatoes, all tossed with crumbled goat cheese, and vinaigrette make a radiant salad

- Snack on bright, crunchy fresh vegetables served with hummus or a creamy dip.

Eat a Balanced Diet

- If you're thinking about or embarking on a raw food diet, you'll want to pay special attention to nutrition.

- Vegetables, fruits, and nuts compose the bulk of a raw food diet. You will also want to include grains and seeds.

- Soy, avocado, and nuts are good sources of both fat and protein.

- You might want to begin with a semi–raw food diet that includes some lightly cooked vegetables along with a little dairy, fish, poultry, and meat.

THE BEST RAW VEGETABLES

One of the most common misconceptions about vegetables is that if it's raw, it's edible

Not all vegetables were meant to be consumed in their raw state. Most people don't realize that raw vegetables are only beneficial if you can digest them. And there are a number of raw vegetables that must always be cooked before eating.

Because raw vegetables are rich in enzymes, they're assumed to be one of the best sources of enzymes that aid in digestion. In reality, however, many people have digestive systems that are too weak to process raw vegetables. If you've ever experienced gas, bloating, abdominal cramping, or diarrhea after eating raw vegetables, you might be one of them. While raw vegetables contain beneficial enzymes, they also contain cellulose, a fiber that humans often have difficulty

A Safe Raw Vegetable Snack Bar

- Baby spinach
- Bell peppers
- Carrots
- Celery
- Cucumbers
- Jicama
- Lettuces
- Summer squashes
- Tomatoes

Go Green

- Virtually all lettuces and greens are meant to be eaten raw

- Romaine, butter, and iceberg lettuce are water- and nutrient rich and easily digested when well chewed.

- The slightly bitter taste of red and green leaf lettuce makes this variety a little less digestible but still acceptable.

- Celery and bok choy are highly alkaline and digestible. Baby spinach is better than mature spinach.

digesting. If you don't have trouble digesting raw vegetables, you can safely choose from a wide variety of them. Or, you may have difficulty with some vegetables and not others, which you can test by trial and error. And finally, there are a number of vegetables that must always be cooked before eating.

····· YELLOW ● LIGHT ·····

There is some controversy as to whether you should eat green bell peppers raw. Some sources maintain that, unlike yellow, orange, and red bell peppers, the greens are actually "unripe," and should be avoided in their raw state. Since people eat raw green bell peppers all the time and they're frequently featured in salads and on platters of crudités, the best idea is to go ahead and eat them. Just watch how they affect you.

Best to Digest

- Tomatoes, cucumbers, and bell peppers are considered optimal foods, rich in water and nutrients. Eat all you desire, especially if you want foods that are nutritious and juicy but low in sugar.

- Carrots deliver in taste, fiber, and vitamin A departments.

- Add raw grated or julienned beets to salads.

- Sweet, crunchy jicama is a less familiar vegetable that is only eaten raw and is excellent as a satisfying snack or in salads.

Be Careful of These

- Tubers like potatoes and turnips are high in starch and cellulose and must be cooked before eating.

- Potatoes contain toxic compounds called glycoalkaloids, and, when not cooked, can cause headaches, diarrhea, and cramps.

- Winter squashes like acorn, butternut, spaghetti, and pumpkin must be cooked to make them palatable and digestible.

- Eggplant is high in cellulose and too bland and dry to be palatable in a raw state.

RAW VEGETABLES

GOING ORGANIC
When buying organic produce, know the source

In new-age food terminology, organic has become synonymous with healthy. But is this always true?

To be labeled organic, food must meet a rigorous set of requirements. Chemicals and hormones cannot be involved; the food needs to be harvested and raised sustainably; irradiation and sewage sludge are prohibited; and farmers cannot raise genetically modified organisms.

In a perfect world, we could trust organic produce. But with big agriculture having become a player in the organic market, the lines have become blurred. A food labeled "organic" isn't necessarily free of fertilizer and other toxins, isn't always locally grown, and isn't always cultivated without the use of illegal labor or under safe working conditions. Organic certification doesn't always mean higher quality; produce that's

Questions for Your Grocer

- Where did the vegetables come from?

- Are they certified organic?

- If not certified organic, are they pesticide-free?

- What can you tell me about the farm's growing practices?

- May I contact the farmer with questions?

When to Buy Organic

- Because of the high price of organic food, you'll want to be savvy in your shopping habits.

- Your local farmers' market or CSA can be great places to buy organic or pesticide-free produce because seasonality and competition keep prices down.

- Because organic produce has no pesticides or preservatives, it has a short shelf life. For best value, buy vegetables that are not quite ripe.

- Opt for organic when buying vegetables known to have the highest pesticide ratings.

labeled organic might be picked, chilled, and shipped thousands of miles from its source, making it inferior to a locally grown counterpart.

And, as the *New York Times* has reported, organic certification technically has nothing to do with food safety.

This is not to say that organic food isn't better for you. It is, when it's grown responsibly and safely. Knowing whether or not an organic vegetable is a good choice depends on how well informed you, the consumer, are about its origins.

Watch for Pesticides

- Today, most vegetables contain more pesticides than you want to know.

- Vegetables most affected by pesticides include celery, kale, lettuces, carrots, green beans, sweet bell peppers and hot peppers, collard greens, spinach, cucumbers, and potatoes.

- Onions, cabbage, cauliflower, broccoli, asparagus, sweet potatoes, and winter squash contain the least pesticides.

- Always wash your produce—organic or nonorganic—thoroughly.

Choose Organic Soup

- Soups are one of the best sources of vegetables and all-around nutrition.

- While it's easy enough to make healthful and delicious homemade soups, organic soups are the best bet if you're looking for absolute convenience.

- In addition to using organic vegetables, organic soups have no preservatives and a much lower sodium content than nonorganic soups.

- You can also use an organic vegetable soup as a base for your own homemade soup.

JUICING RAW VEGETABLES
Fresh vegetable juice is an incredible source of nutrients and energy

Mention vegetable juice and V8 immediately comes to mind. Or carrot juice, green juice, and other health-food concoctions. But there are actually no limits to how versatile and flavorful fresh vegetable juice can be.

Unlike fruit juice, which is high in sugar and calories and not recommended as a dietary staple unless it's cut with water, vegetable juice doesn't raise insulin levels and is substantially lower in calories and higher in nutritive value.

Why juice vegetables, you might ask? Why not just eat them? Of course it's great to eat vegetables; otherwise we wouldn't be bothering with this cookbook. But because many people have relatively compromised intestines as a result of poor food choices over many years, their bodies' ability to absorb all the nutrients from vegetables has also been

Some Benefits of Juicing

- Juicing breaks up the cell walls of whole foods, aiding absorption of vegetables and fruits.

- Because your body absorbs juice quickly, your digestive system expends less energy.

- Juicing is a great way to get your recommended five cups of vegetables per day.

- Fresh vegetable juices are one of the best sources of enzymes, which are essential for digestion and absorption of food, conversion of food into body tissue, and production of energy at the cellular level.

Types of Juicers

- There are four basic types of juicers. Masticating juicers are low-speed juicers that can juice anything from vegetables and sprouts to citrus fruits and melons.

- Pulp-ejecting juicers will juice pulpy fruits and vegetables, ejecting the pulp into a separate container.

- Citrus juicers are for citrus juicing, period.

- Centrifugal juicers hold the pulp in a basket while spinning the juice into a holding container below the basket.

compromised. Juicing tends to facilitate this absorption.

Vegetable juice is used in fasting and cleansing, and it is much healthier than a fruit juice cleanse because the mixture of vegetables provides a better balance of minerals, vitamins, enzymes, and other nutrients.

And if you just want to enjoy a glass of vegetable juice as a morning waker-upper or afternoon or evening snack, making your own juice or smoothie is a handy talent to acquire.

Make a Veggie Smoothie

- Trim and chop 4–5 stalks of celery into 1-inch pieces.

- Chop 2 cups of romaine lettuce and ½ bunch of cilantro or parsley (stems removed).

- Core but don't peel a Granny Smith apple.

- Fill a blender with 3–4 cups of filtered water. Add the celery, lettuce, apple, juice from half a lime, and half a large avocado. Puree until smooth.

About Carrot Juice

- For years, carrot juice was the stereotypical symbol of health-food consciousness.

- Carrot juice provides a big dose of beta carotene, which changes to vitamin A in the body and is thought to improve eyesight, promote healthy skin, and prevent certain cancers.

- Drinking too much carrot juice can cause the skin to turn orange.

- Because it's high in sugar, undiluted carrot juice is not recommended for people with diabetes.

GETTING OFF TO A RAW START
Raw vegetable recipes can incorporate meat, dairy, and other nonraw items

Raw vegetables don't have to be confined to salads and crudités. We regularly use raw vegetables in everything from coleslaw to sandwiches, tacos, and wraps. Raw vegetables can complement meat and other dishes. There are recipes for raw stuffed peppers and tomatoes, cold soups, and vegetable salsas.

Think of eating raw as adding raw foods to your diet. You don't have to go cold turkey on anything. Be versatile, creative, and open-minded.

The following recipes illustrate how simple and tasty raw vegetables can be.

Salmon, Tomato, and Vege Salad

2 cups fresh tomatoes

1 cup diced cucumber

³/₄ cup sliced red onion

³/₄ cup blanched green beans, cut into 1¹/₂-inch pieces

¹/₂ cup diced celery

¹/₂ cup grated carrots

¹/₄ cup sliced or chopped black olives

3 hard-boiled eggs, chopped

12–14 ounces canned salmon, drained, or fresh cooked salmon

2 tablespoons mayonnaise

Salt and pepper

Salad dressing of choice

In a large bowl, toss all ingredients until well mixed. Serve chilled on a bed of shredded lettuce. Yield: 6 servings

Crunchy Garden Salad Tacos

- Combine 1 cup grated carrots, 2 cups iceberg lettuce, 1 diced tomato, 1 cup diced cucumber, 1 cup diced green bell pepper, and ½ cup diced zucchini.

- Blend ¼ cup mayonnaise, ½ cup plain yogurt, ¼ cup buttermilk, 1 tablespoon olive oil, and 1 tablespoon lime juice. Whisk in ½ teaspoon tarragon, ¼ teaspoon seasoned salt, ¼ teaspoon lemon pepper, and 6 drops Tabasco.

- Toss the dressing with the vegetables. Fill the taco shells with the mixture and top with shredded cheddar cheese. Yield: 8–10 tacos

• • • • RECIPE VARIATIONS • • • •

Fruity Veggie Salad with Bacon: Brown, drain, and crumble 6 slices of bacon. In a large bowl, combine a mixture of raw broccoli florets, chopped celery, shredded carrots, peas, cranberries, green onions, green and red grapes, and almonds. Toss with the bacon and a dressing of your choice.

Super-sized Layered Veggie Salad with Bacon: In a big glass salad bowl, layer: one head iceberg lettuce, chopped; 1 head cauliflower, chopped; 1 red onion, chopped; 16 ounces sharp cheddar cheese; 2–3 pounds tomatoes, chopped; 6 large grated carrots; 1 pound raw baby peas; and 10 ounces cooked, crumbled bacon. Drizzle a blue cheese or Caesar dressing over the salad.

Fennel, Tomato, and Chicory Salad

- Finely chop 1 head of fennel, 1 small head of chicory, and 8–10 fresh basil leaves.

- Dice 2 large, firm tomatoes.

- In a small bowl, whisk together 6 tablespoons extra-virgin olive oil, 2 tablespoons balsamic vinegar, ½ teaspoon chopped fresh rosemary, 1 teaspoon minced garlic, ¼ teaspoon salt, and ¼ teaspoon lemon pepper.

- Combine the vegetables in a mixing bowl and toss with the dressing. Yield: 4 servings

Ginger Citrus Slaw

- Shred half a small head of purple cabbage.

- Combine the cabbage with 1 cup grated carrots, 1 cup diced cucumber, and ½ cup chopped Bermuda onion.

- Peel, seed, and chop half a fresh orange; remove zest.

- In a blender or food processor, combine 6 tablespoons extra-virgin olive oil, 2 tablespoons red wine, 1 teaspoon chopped garlic, 1 teaspoon freshly grated ginger, and the orange and zest. Process until smooth. Toss with the vegetables. Yield: 6 servings

RAW VEGETABLES

35

BABY ARTICHOKES WITH AIOLI

Tender baby artichokes are steamed, drizzled with a lemon-Parmesan dressing, and broiled to perfection

With its prickly, tough leaves and fibrous, inedible choke, a fresh artichoke bears no slight resemblance to the man-eating plant in *Little Shop of Horrors*. Maybe that's why so many people avoid the vegetable!

That's a pity, because there's nothing quite like a velvety cooked artichoke leaf or heart dipped in mayonnaise or melted butter and lemon. Artichokes are easy to cook, filled with nutritional value, and a boon to dieters because they contain virtually no calories and are immensely satisfying.

This recipe for baby artichokes is simple and delicious. *Yield: 4 servings*

Ingredients

12 baby artichokes

1 tablespoon plus 1 cup olive oil, divided

1 tablespoon Italian seasoning

1 teaspoon salt, more to taste

$1/2$ teaspoon freshly ground black pepper

6 garlic cloves

2 large egg yolks

1 lemon, juiced

1 teaspoon Dijon mustard

1 tablespoon balsamic vinegar

White pepper, to taste

Parmesan, shredded

Baby Artichokes with Aioli

- Prepare the artichokes (see technique).

- Cover the artichokes with water until they are fully submerged in a large pot with 1 tablespoon olive oil, the Italian seasoning, 1 teaspoon salt, and the black pepper. Steam until tender, about 25 minutes.

- Prepare the aioli (see technique).

- Using tongs, remove the artichokes from the water. Place on a lightly oiled baking sheet. Drizzle with the aioli, sprinkle with the Parmesan, and place under broiler for 5 minutes.

Sautéed Baby Artichokes: Prepare the artichokes as you would for Baby Artichokes with Aioli. Slice them into ¼-inch cross sections and sauté them in olive oil and butter until brown. Add some chopped shallots and garlic and sauté 30 seconds. Remove from heat; toss with salt, cracked pepper, and fresh lemon juice; and sprinkle with shredded Parmesan.

Pasta with Roasted Baby Artichokes: For a quick and easy pasta dish, combine roasted baby artichokes, sautéed mushrooms, and browned garlic and onions with a cooked bite-size pasta such as rotini, penne, or tortellini. Toss with olive oil, butter, chopped fresh basil, shredded cheese (Parmesan, Romano, or Asiago), a little kosher salt, and freshly ground pepper.

Prepare the Artichokes

- Baby artichokes should have tight, compact heads and fresh-cut stem ends.

- Pull off and discard the tough outer leaves.

- With a paring knife, trim the stem, keeping it as long as possible.

- Cut off the prickly leaf tips with kitchen scissors and slice the artichokes in half with a large knife.

Make the Aioli

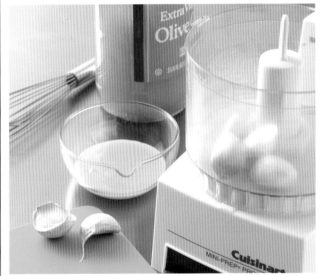

- Puree the garlic cloves in a food processor or blender.

- In a small bowl, whisk the egg yolks until smooth.

- Add the yolks, lemon juice, mustard, vinegar, and salt and white pepper to taste to the pureed garlic.

- While the processor is running, add 1 cup olive oil to the mixture in a slow, steady stream. Blend until the sauce is thick and shiny. The aioli can be refrigerated for up to 4 hours.

APPETIZERS

VEGETABLE WONTONS
Crisp wontons are filled with fresh vegetables in a spicy soy sauce

When I was an editor at a west coast magazine, I had to come up with a snappy headline for a story on an adventurous new Asian fusion restaurant. Suddenly it came to me: "My Wild Wonton Ways!"

Wontons are marvelously versatile. They lend themselves to all sorts of fillings and make perfect appetizers and side dishes, Asian and not. One of my friends likes to serve them

with nacho filling, as a sort of Mexican dim sum.

Wonton skins—paper-thin sheets of dough, made from flour, eggs, and salt—are the same as egg roll skins. When fried in hot oil, wontons won't be greasy, and vegetable wontons make a healthy addition to any meal. *Yield: 6 servings*

Ingredients

6 ounces mushrooms

6 scallions

$^1/_2$ cup fresh green beans

$^1/_2$ cup grated carrot

1 tablespoon peanut or vegetable oil used in the wok

$^1/_2$ cup corn kernels

$^1/_2$ cup bean sprouts

2 eggs, beaten

2 tablespoons soy sauce

2 tablespoons teriyaki sauce

2 tablespoons brown sugar

1 teaspoon ground ginger

$^1/_2$ teaspoon salt

$^1/_4$ teaspoon pepper

40 prepackaged wonton skins

Vegetable Wontons

- Chop the mushrooms, scallions, and green beans.

- Stir-fry the mushrooms, scallions, green beans, and carrot in the peanut oil in a large wok for 1–2 minutes. Stir in the corn and bean sprouts and move to one side of the wok.

- Pour beaten eggs into wok and scramble. Mix with vegetables, and add soy and teriyaki sauces, sugar, ginger, salt, and pepper.

- Fill the wontons and deep-fry until golden brown. Serve hot with Chinese mustard, chili sauce, or plum sauce.

Chipotle Pecadillo Wontons: Feeling bold? Fuse Asian and Mexican in a wonton filled with ground pork, raisins, garlic, scallions, chopped mild chiles, chipotle pepper sauce, cinnamon, and cloves.

Crab Rangoons: Rangoons are fried wontons filled with cream cheese and usually seafood (crab, lobster, or shrimp). To make crab rangoons, combine 8 ounces of cream cheese with 8 ounces fresh or imitation crabmeat. Add ¼ cup chopped red onion, 1 teaspoon Worcestershire sauce, 2 teaspoons soy sauce, 1 teaspoon sherry, 1 finely sliced green onion, 1 teaspoon minced garlic, and salt and pepper to taste. Fill the wonton wrappers with the mixture and fry until golden brown.

Make the Wontons

- Place the wonton skins in a pile. Put 1 teaspoon of the filling in the center of the top skin.

- Brush the skin's edges with beaten egg and fold in half diagonally to make a small triangular package. Repeat with the remaining skins and filling.

- Heat enough oil for deep-frying in a wok or skillet. Add the packages in batches and fry 3–4 minutes.

- Remove wontons from the oil with a slotted spoon and drain on paper towels.

Offer Choice of Condiments

- Guests will enjoy trying different condiments on their wontons. You can buy a wide variety in any large supermarket.

- Chinese sweet and sour sauce offers a tangy twist. Add crushed pineapple or apricot jam to the sauce for a fruity effect.

- The unique spicy heat of Chinese mustard is a perfect complement to the sweet-salty wonton filling.

- Asian chili sauces can range from slightly hot to sizzling in intensity.

APPETIZERS

ASPARAGUS TEMPURA

A fluffy tempura coating and a tangy herbed dipping sauce give asparagus a new aspect

I live in Oceana County, Michigan, aka the asparagus capital of the United States. In late spring and early summer, the favorite local delicacy is deep-fried asparagus. This appetizer can be quite delicious with a ranch or garlic mayonnaise dip.

For a lighter, less greasy alternative, I like asparagus tempura. Tempura is the Japanese method of deep-frying

vegetables and meats. The batter is made with flour, eggs, and ice water and is traditionally mixed for only a few seconds in small batches. The lumps in the mixture and the cold batter temperature create the uniquely fluffy and crisp tempura structure when cooked. *Yield: 4 servings*

Ingredients

1½ pounds fresh asparagus

1 egg

½–1 cup ice water

1 tablespoon sake (Japanese rice wine)

¾ cup all-purpose flour

¼ cup finely ground cornmeal

Oil (for frying)

½ cup mayonnaise

¼ cup plain yogurt

3 tablespoons white wine

¼ cup minced fresh chives

1 tablespoon minced fresh thyme

1 tablespoon fresh lemon juice

1 teaspoon fresh dill weed

Salt and pepper to taste

Asparagus Tempura

- Wash and dry the asparagus and cut off the thick ends.

- Beat the egg, then add the ice water, beating until the mixture is light. Add the sake.

- Mix the flour and cornmeal together and sift them into

the egg mixture. Stir until blended.

- Heat the oil to 340°F. Dip the asparagus, a few stalks at a time, into the batter and fry 3–5 minutes, until golden brown. Drain on paper towels and serve with chive mayonnaise as a dipping sauce.

Tempura Platter: Japanese restaurants offer a choice of shrimp tempura and various deep-fried vegetables. To make your own tempura medley, use whole mushrooms, yams or sweet potatoes cut in ½-inch crosswise slices, eggplant cut in ½-inch crosswise slices, zucchini cut into 1-inch sticks, onions cut into rings, and whole shelled and deveined prawns.

Tempura Dipping Sauce: This is the traditional sauce for tempura. Combine ¼ cup rice wine, ¼ cup dashi (traditional Japanese soup stock) or Thai fish sauce, ¼ cup soy sauce, 2 tablespoons finely grated ginger, 1 teaspoon wasabi powder, 1 tablespoon brown sugar, and 2 tablespoons chopped green onion. Serve in small dipping dishes.

Make the Tempura Batter

- Be sure to use ice water when making the batter. This will prevent the batter from absorbing too much oil.

- Don't overmix the batter. A few lumps here and there are fine, but a sticky or doughy batter will result in heavy and soggy tempura.

- Before frying the asparagus, drop a little batter into the oil. If the batter drops halfway to the bottom, then rises back up, the oil is the right temperature.

- The fried asparagus should be fluffy and crispy, not greasy.

Prepare the Chive Mayonnaise

- Use real mayonnaise, not light or fat free. The low-fat and fat-free alternatives tend to have an oily consistency and unpleasant aftertaste.

- You can, however, use light or nonfat yogurt, which has all the flavor of regular yogurt.

- Fresh chives, dill weed and thyme are a must. The dried versions have a dull, subdued flavor, in contrast to the sharp, bright taste of their fresh counterparts.

- Combine the mayonnaise, yogurt, wine, chives, thyme, lemon juice and dill. Add salt and pepper to taste.

APPETIZERS

VEGETABLE SPREAD SUPREME

This herbed cream cheese and yogurt spread features a tasty variety of chopped vegetables

We're all familiar with those cream cheese spreads made with packaged French onion soup or Knorr dry vegetable soup mix. They aren't bad, but I haven't yet found anything that comes close to this amazing vegetable spread, which uses broccoli, fresh mushrooms, water chestnuts, onion, and two kinds of olives, along with yogurt, cream cheese, mayonnaise, and seasonings.

This spread is sort of like a magic act. As soon as it appears, as an appetizer or hors d'oeuvre, it disappears. The blend of flavors is irresistible, and although the spread seems rich, it's really very light and goes down quickly—too quickly! *Yield: 3 cups*

Ingredients

8 ounces onion and chive or garden vegetable cream cheese

$^1/_4$ cup plain yogurt

$^1/_4$ cup plus 1 tablespoon mayonnaise

1 cup cooked broccoli florets

Half a medium onion

4 medium-size fresh mushrooms

1 teaspoon chopped garlic

1 tablespoon butter or margarine

$^1/_3$ cup sliced water chestnuts

3 tablespoons chopped canned black olives

2 tablespoons chopped Spanish olives

$^1/_2$ teaspoon paprika

$^1/_2$ teaspoon seasoned salt

$^1/_4$ teaspoon coarsely ground black pepper

Vegetable Spread Supreme

- In a medium bowl, combine the cream cheese, yogurt, and mayonnaise.

- Cook the broccoli and cool in the freezer for about 10 minutes.

- Chop the onion and mushrooms and sauté them with the garlic in the butter or margarine until soft. Cool in the refrigerator for 10 minutes.

- Chop the cooled broccoli. Add with the onion, mushrooms, chopped water chestnuts and olives to the cream cheese mixture with the paprika, salt, and pepper. Refrigerate ½ hour.

42

Carrot Salad: Leftover or extra grated carrots can instantly be turned into a delicious carrot salad. Just combine 3–4 cups of grated carrots with ½–1 cup of raisins, 1 apple (cored and chopped), and ¼–⅓ cup of mayonnaise. You can substitute pineapple chunks for either the raisins or the apple.

Cucumber Sandwiches: This spread makes a perfect base for cucumber tea sandwiches. Toast 5 slices of whole grain bread and cut off the edges so that the slices are square. Spread each slice with a layer of the vegetable spread. Then, cut the slices into quarters and top each quarter with a thin slice of cucumber and a sprig of watercress.

Fresh or Frozen Broccoli?

- Both frozen or fresh broccoli work for this dish.

- If using frozen, choose either chopped broccoli or broccoli florets and follow package directions to reheat.

- For fresh broccoli, remove leaves, wash, and trim the tough stems to within an inch of the bouquets. Cut through the bouquet stems to make florets.

- Microwwave 1 cup of the florets with 2 tablespoons water 4–5 minutes, until crisp-tender.

Present a Bread Platter

- A variety of crackers and breads go well with this spread.

- Crisps might include Melba toast, bread sticks, toasted pita chips, crostini, Wheat Thins, or Carr's Table Water Crackers.

- Softer bread choices could include party rye, small pita rounds, Middle Eastern flatbread, or Indian naan.

- Arrange the crisps and breads around a dish of the spread on a large platter, along with celery, carrot, and zucchini sticks for those who prefer their spread on crudités.

APPETIZERS

PESTO BRUSCHETTA

Crusty French or Italian bread is toasted with tomatoes, fresh pesto, and grated cheese

At its most basic, this simple snack or appetizer consists of grilled bread rubbed with garlic and topped with extra-virgin olive oil, salt, and pepper. The Tuscan term for bruschetta is *fettunta,* or "oiled slice."

In Italian restaurants in the United States, bruschetta is usually topped with fresh tomato, basil, and mozzarella or with a kind of Italian salsa made from chopped tomatoes, garlic, and basil. The following recipe is a variation that uses fresh pesto as the spread, topped with tomato and two cheeses and broiled to a toasty brown. *Yield: Approximately 20 slices*

Ingredients

1 fresh baguette or loaf of French or Italian bread

2 cups packed fresh basil leaves

$1/3$ cup pine nuts

3 medium garlic cloves, coarsely chopped

$1/2$ cup extra-virgin olive oil

$1/2$ cup freshly grated Parmesan or Romano cheese

Salt and freshly ground black pepper, to taste

6–8 Roma tomatoes

8 ounces shredded mozzarella cheese

Pesto Bruschetta

- Cut the bread into 1-inch slices and place on a baking sheet.

- Spread each slice with 1–2 teaspoons of pesto, depending on the size of the bread.

- Place a slice of tomato on each bread slice. For larger bread slices, use 2 slices or 1 slice of a larger tomato.

- Top each piece of bread with mozzarella and place under the broiler for approximately 1 minute, or until the cheese begins to brown.

Bruschetta Burgers: Combine 1½ pounds ground beef, 3 tablespoons Italian-seasoned bread crumbs, 2 teaspoons Worcestershire sauce, 2 tablespoons ketchup, ½ teaspoon seasoned salt, ¼ teaspoon ground pepper, and ½ teaspoon onion powder. Shape into four ½-inch thick patties and grill over direct heat, 4–5 minutes per side. Top with the pesto, tomato, and a slice of provolone cheese and serve on buns.

Spanish Bruschetta: For the Spanish version of bruschetta, *pa amb tomàquet,* grill thick slices of country bread, then rub with garlic and extra-virgin olive oil and rub half a tomato right onto the bread.

Choose the Tomatoes

- Look for firm, juicy tomatoes with bright, unblemished skin, deep color, and a little give when squeezed.

- When buying tomatoes, do the "nose test." A ripe tomato smells like a tomato; unripe tomatoes, on the other hand, have no aroma.

- The Roma, or Italian plum tomato, is the perfect size for baguette slices.

- With their meaty texture and large size, beefsteak tomatoes are a good choice for French or Italian bread slices.

Make the Pesto

- Pulse the basil and pine nuts several times in a food processor. Add the garlic and pulse a few times more.

- With the food processor running, slowly add the olive oil in a constant stream.

- Scrape down the sides of the food processor with a rubber spatula.

- Add the Parmesan or Romano cheese and pulse again until blended. Add salt and pepper to taste. Makes 1 cup.

APPETIZERS

CHEESY SPINACH SQUARES

Puff pastry bites filled with spinach and feta cheese melt in your mouth

This appetizer, called spanakopita, features a combination of spinach, feta cheese, and light, flaky filo dough. In Greek, phyllo means "leaf" or "sheet," which is what this pastry is: paper-thin sheets of raw unleavened flour dough used to make pies and pastries in Middle Eastern, Greek, and Turkish cuisines.

If you've ever had baklava, that heavenly Greco-Turkish dessert made of layers of filo drizzled with honey, melted butter, and nuts, you know how delicate filo dough is. It must be handled carefully, or else it can easily tear or crack. It's also an art to make—an ancient art which, fortunately, you don't need to master, as you can purchase perfectly good prepared filo sheets in any supermarket. *Yield: Approximately 20 squares*

Ingredients

8 scallions, white and green parts, chopped

2 teaspoon chopped garlic

1/4 cup finely chopped red bell pepper

4 tablespoons olive oil

2 pounds fresh spinach, rinsed and shredded

3 tablespoons chopped fresh dill

3 tablespoons chopped fresh parsley

8 ounces feta cheese, finely crumbled

4 large eggs, beaten

Salt and pepper, to taste

10 tablespoons (1 1/4 sticks) butter, melted

14 sheets frozen filo dough, thawed

Cheesy Spinach Squares

- Sauté the scallions, garlic, and red pepper in olive oil until softened.

- Stir in the spinach, dill, and parsley and cook until the liquid evaporates, about 10 minutes.

- In a large bowl, add the spinach mixture and feta cheese to the eggs and season with salt and pepper to taste.

- Prepare the filo. Spread the spinach mixture over half the filo sheets in an 11 x 8-inch baking pan. Top with remaining filo. Bake in a 325°F oven for 1 hour. Cut into squares and serve hot.

Spinach Moussaka: Omit the cheese and dill. Make a béchamel (see Chapter 9, Gnocchi with Spinach Bécha-mel). Spread half the spinach mixture over the first half of the filo layers, then cover with the béchamel sauce and 2 chopped hard-boiled eggs. Add the remaining spinach mixture and filo layers and bake at 350°F for 45 minutes.

Filo Tartlets: Brush 6 sheets of filo with melted butter and cut each sheet into 3-inch squares. Line each cup of a muffin tin with 2 squares, tucking them in until they frill around the edges. Bake at 350°F for 4–5 minutes, until crisp but not too brown. Fill each muffin cup with Cheesy Spinach Square mixture, return to the oven, and bake 2–3 minutes more.

Keep the Spinach Fresh

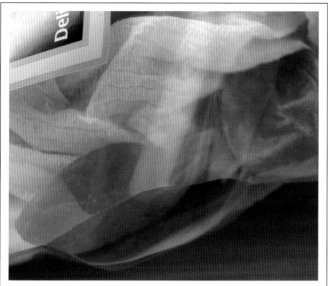

- While you can use frozen spinach for this dish, fresh is just as easy and is a better source of antioxidants.

- When buying fresh spinach in a bag, choose baby spinach.

- Shake the bag gently, open it, and remove any damaged leaves.

- Place a paper towel in the bag, seal loosely, and store in your refrigerator's crisper. The spinach should remain fresh for at least a week.

Prepare the Filo

- Thaw filo in original packaging in refrigerator for 24 hours.

- Generously brush the baking pan with melted butter. Line the pan with a sheet of filo, carefully pressing it into the sides and corners of the pan. Brush with butter. Repeat with 6 more sheets.

- On top of the spinach mixture, repeat the layering and buttering with the remaining 7 sheets.

- Trim away excess dough with kitchen scissors and tuck the filo edges into pan. Brush top with remaining butter and bake until crisp and golden brown.

APPETIZERS

ARTICHOKE AVOCADO CAESAR SALAD

Artichoke bottoms and avocado slices enhance a classic Caesar salad

There are several claims to Caesar salad fame, but the most likely one gives the credit to Italian restaurateur Caesar Cardini. On busy July 4, 1924, Cardini was short on supplies at his Tijuana restaurant. Grabbing what he had on hand, he threw together a salad, preparing it at the table to add a special flair. "Caesar's Salad" became a hit forevermore.

The traditional Caesar salad consists of romaine lettuce tossed with garlic, lemon juice, olive oil, egg, Worcestershire sauce, croutons, and Parmesan. Cardini originally served the dressed lettuce leaves intact, to be held by the stem and eaten whole. Here, artichoke hearts and avocado add a little *oomph* to this elegant, simple classic. *Yield: 6 servings*

Ingredients

1 head romaine lettuce

1/2 head butter lettuce

9 tablespoons extra-virgin olive oil

3 tablespoons balsamic vinegar

1 1/2 teaspoons minced garlic

1 teaspoon Worcestershire sauce

3 tablespoons fresh lemon juice

1 teaspoon ground mustard

1 egg, beaten

1/2 teaspoon salt

1/4 teaspoon lemon pepper

1/4 teaspoon dried thyme

1 2-ounce can anchovy fillets

1 14-ounce can artichoke bottoms, quartered

1/3 cup freshly grated or shredded Parmesan

1 cup homemade croutons

Freshly ground pepper, to taste

1 medium avocado, peeled, pitted, and thinly sliced

Artichoke Avocado Caesar Salad

- Clean lettuces thoroughly and wrap in paper towels to absorb moisture. Refrigerate until crisp, at least 1 hour.

- Make the dressing and croutons (see techniques). Chop the lettuces and toss together in a large mixing bowl with the artichokes.

- Spoon the dressing over the lettuce, enough to coat the lettuce lightly but not so much that it gets soggy. Refrigerate extra dressing.

- Add the grated cheese, croutons, and freshly ground pepper to taste. Toss, top with the avocado slices, and serve immediately.

Make the Dressing

- In a small mixing bowl, whisk together the olive oil, vinegar, garlic, Worcestershire sauce, lemon juice, mustard, egg, and seasonings.

- If you prefer a creamy Caesar dressing, omit the egg and substitute ⅓ cup of mayonnaise.

- Finely chop the anchovies and add to the dressing.

- Shake the dressing vigorously in a covered jar and refrigerate until ready to use.

Make the Croutons

- Cut a loaf of day-old French bread in half lengthwise and rub each half thoroughly with a crushed garlic clove.

- Cut the bread into small cubes and toss with ½ cup extra-virgin olive oil, 1 tablespoon dried basil, ½ teaspoon salt, and ¼ teaspoon coarsely ground pepper.

- Spread the bread cubes on a shallow baking pan or cookie sheet.

- Bake at 400°F for 5–10 minutes or until lightly brown and toasted.

SALADS

PEA & RADISH SPRING SALAD

Radishes, lemon, and mint partner with sugar snap and green peas in this spring medley

Peas have been around as long as cultures have had a mythology to spin around them. The earliest charred remains of peas were found in Egyptian tombs of the twelfth dynasty. Peas weren't always as appreciated as they are today: in Norse mythology, Thor disliked peas so much that he gave them to humans as a punishment and sent flying dragons to use them to fill up and foul all of the wells on earth. In the Middle Ages, peas were not enjoyed; they were eaten only during Lent or during times of famine.

Today, however, peas are a much admired vegetable, valued for their delicate flavor and crunchy sweetness, particularly in light salads like this one. *Yield: 4 servings*

Ingredients

2 cups sugar snap peas

1 cup frozen peas

1 tablespoon rice wine vinegar

1 tablespoon olive oil

1 teaspoon lemon zest

1 tablespoon fresh lemon juice

1/4 teaspoon salt

1 cup thinly sliced radishes

1 6-ounce can sliced water chestnuts

1 tablespoon chopped fresh mint

8 lettuce leaves

Freshly ground pepper, to taste

Pea and Radish Spring Salad

- Boil the sugar snap peas until crisp-tender, 2–3 minutes. Add the frozen peas during the last minute.

- Drain the peas and rinse with cold water until cool. Blot dry with paper towels

- Whisk together vinegar, oil, lemon zest, lemon juice, and salt. Add the peas, radishes, water chestnuts, and mint and toss well until coated.

- Line four salad plates with the lettuce leaves. Top with the salad and let your guests grind their own fresh pepper to taste.

Pea Pasta Salad: Combine 2 cups of cooked, cooled peas with ½ cup chopped scallions, 2 cups cooked corkscrew pasta, ½ cup mayonnaise, ½ cup plain yogurt, ½ teaspoon seasoned salt, ¼ teaspoon freshly ground pepper, 1 tablespoon freshly chopped parsley, and 3 strips of crisp bacon, crumbled. Chill for 2 hours and serve topped with shredded cheddar.

Cashew Pea Salad: Combine 1½ cups fresh shelled peas, 1 cup diced celery, 1 cup chopped water chestnuts, ¼ cup chopped scallions, and 1 cup cashews. Blend with ½ cup sour cream and ¾ cup blue cheese dressing. Season to taste with salt and pepper and serve chilled on lettuce leaves.

Select the Radishes

- While radishes are grown year-round, spring radishes are somewhat milder than their winter counterparts.

- The most common radish is the red globe, which adds a peppery flavor to salads. You can salt and wash it or steam it for 5–10 minutes to draw out the heat.

- The French breakfast spring radish has an elongated shape and a delicately sweet flavor.

- To keep radishes crisp, soak them in a bowl of ice water for 1–2 hours.

Cook the Sugar Snap Peas

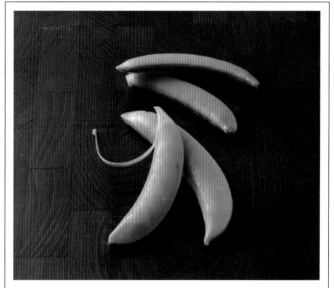

- You may need to "string" the snap peas—remove the membranous string running along the pod from base to tip—before cooking.

- String the peas by pulling the strings down from the tips. Cut off the stem ends and rinse the intact pods in a colander under cold water.

- The peas should be cooked barely covered in water, for no more than 3 minutes.

- Plunging the peas into ice water immediately after cooking preserves their crunch and bright color.

SALADS

ASPARAGUS POTATO SALAD
Unique textures and flavors enhance this beautifully presented dish

Asparagus is such an enticingly versatile vegetable that one wishes its growing season was all year round. While it might be permissible to use frozen asparagus in cooked dishes like stir-fries, it's always best fresh. And you'd never want to use anything but fresh asparagus in a salad.

This salad features roasted fresh asparagus teamed up with cooked new potatoes and drizzled with a sweet citrus dressing. It should be served slightly warm, meaning that it could also double as a side dish, or even a light luncheon entree when accompanied by a cup of soup and some hot, crusty bread. *Yield: 4 servings*

Ingredients

2 pounds fresh asparagus

Olive oil for drizzling

Salt and pepper

2 pounds new potatoes

6 tablespoons extra-virgin olive oil

1 tablespoon fresh lime juice

1 tablespoon fresh lemon juice

1/2 tablespoon balsamic vinegar

1 teaspoon Dijon mustard

1 tablespoon honey

1 teaspoon minced garlic

1/2 teaspoon herbes de Provence

2 tablespoons minced scallions

Fresh dill

Asparagus Potato Salad

- Place asparagus on a cookie sheet. Drizzle with olive oil and sprinkle with salt and pepper. Roast in a 400°F oven for 15 minutes.

- In a saucepan, cover potatoes with salted water, bring to a boil, and reduce to a simmer, cooking just until tender. Cool and slice.

- Make the vinaigrette and toss the cooled potatoes with the vinaigrette and scallions.

- Arrange asparagus on a platter in a spoke pattern. Mound potatoes in the center. Drizzle remaining dressing over the asparagus and garnish with fresh dill.

52

The standard recipe for vinaigrette is three parts oil to one part acid. However, this can vary according to taste. This recipe calls for half oil and half acid: The tangy lemon and lime cut the taste of the oil, and the honey modifies the acidity.

Asparagus Salade Niçoise: The typical salade niçoise, features steamed or blanched green beans. Substitute roasted asparagus and arrange it on a platter with the cooked new potatoes, sliced cherry tomatoes, grilled or seared salmon or tuna (canned may be substituted), anchovies, and sliced hard-boiled eggs. Drizzle with the citrus vinaigrette.

Select the Potatoes

- While new potatoes are preferred for their thin, delicately flavorful skin, other types of potatoes will also work. If using larger potatoes, cut them into quarters.

- Yukon Gold potatoes are noted for their sweet flavor and attractive yellow hue.

Round red potatoes have a texture and flavor similar to that of new potatoes. Choose smaller ones for this dish.

- For a truly colorful effect, try the more exotic but widely available Peruvian Purples.

Make the Vinaigrette

- You'll want to use extra-virgin olive oil for its light texture and flavor.

- An old-fashioned hand juicer is perfect for juicing limes and lemons.

- Combine the olive oil, citrus juices, balsamic vinegar, mustard, honey, garlic, and

herbes de Provence. Whisk until well blended and season to taste with salt and pepper.

- When tossing the dressing with the potatoes, use only enough to coat them. Leftover dressing is great on any salad.

TAILGATE THREE-BEAN SALAD

Cooked dried beans meld with green beans, corn, and other vegetables in a sweet hot chili sauce

Three-bean salad is about as American as the old red, white, and blue. It's a staple of Fourth of July, Memorial Day, and Labor Day picnics. You won't find a church potluck without one. And how could a tailgate party survive without three-bean salad?

Although you can use canned beans, this recipe calls for cooking your own dry beans because they're tastier and much more nutritious. Presoaking the dried beans allows them to absorb water, which helps dissolve those infamous gaseous starches that cause digestive discomfort. *Yield: 6–8 servings*

Ingredients

¹/₂ cup dry kidney beans

¹/₂ cup dry garbanzo beans

1 cup green beans, cooked

1 cup frozen corn kernels, cooked

2 slices bacon

1 medium onion, chopped

2 teaspoons minced garlic

1 tablespoon canola or corn oil

1 tablespoon flour

¹/₂ cup ketchup

1 cup chicken broth

1 tablespoon mustard

¹/₄ cup brown sugar

1 tablespoon chill powder

¹/₂ cup chopped celery

1 small green bell pepper, chopped

¹/₂ cup minced parsley

Salt and pepper, to taste

Tailgate Three-Bean Salad

- Cook dry beans. Combine cooked beans, green beans, and corn in large bowl.

- Brown bacon in a large skillet, drain it on paper towels, and crumble when dry.

- Lightly brown the onion and garlic in the bacon drippings and oil, mix in the flour, and add the bacon, ketchup, broth, mustard, sugar, and chili powder.

- Add celery and green pepper and cook for 15 minutes. Add minced parsley, salt and pepper to taste and toss with beans. Refrigerate for 1–2 hours.

Three-Bean Salad Italiano: Substitute cannellini beans for the kidney beans, olive oil for the canola oil, and canned diced tomatoes for the ketchup. Omit the mustard, brown sugar, and chili powder and replace with ½ teaspoon oregano, ½ teaspoon basil, ½ teaspoon onion powder, and 1 tablespoon honey.

Exotic Three-Bean Salad: Roast 1 teaspoon whole cumin in ¼ cup olive oil until fragrant, 30 seconds. Add 1½ cups cooked edamame; 1 15-ounce can each of black beans and black-eyed peas, drained; ½ cup chopped red onion; 2 cups thinly sliced celery; 2 tablespoons fresh lime juice; ½ cup chopped fresh cilantro; 1 teaspoon minced garlic; 1½ teaspoons seasoned salt; and ¼ teaspoon lemon pepper. Toss and serve.

Cook the Dry Beans

Add the Mustard

- Soak ½ cup each of dried kidney and garbanzo beans in 4 cups of water in a lidded container and refrigerate for 6–8 hours.

- Drain and rinse the beans and simmer in 3 cups of water for 45–60 minutes.

- Do not boil the beans or the skins will break.

- When the beans are tender, drain them and rinse with cold water.

- You can use one or more different kinds of mustard for this salad. Prepared yellow, or American, mustard is the mildest variety.

- Dijon mustard contains both white and Burgundy wine and is more pungent.

- Whole grain mustard contains whole seeds mixed with other ingredients.

- For a hotter kick, try English mustard; for a sweeter flavor, honey mustard.

GRILLED MEDITERRANEAN SALAD
Raw and grilled vegetables are tossed together with a lemon-herb Greek dressing and feta cheese

We're used to salads being cold dishes composed of fresh vegetables. But cooked vegetable salads are common in other countries. This Middle Eastern salad, for instance, combines grilled vegetables like eggplant, tomatoes, and zucchini with cucumber, lettuce, artichokes, and scallions in a salad that's both warm and cool.

While you can grill the vegetables on an outdoor grill, pan-grilling them on top of the stove is a quicker, less involved alternative. Although you won't get the more intense flavor and overall browning of charcoal or gas grilling, the vegetables will still be nicely seared without all the prep and cleanup. *Yield: 6 servings*

Ingredients

2 small Japanese eggplants, halved, or 1 small globe eggplant, cut into 1-inch round slices

2 medium zucchini, cut lengthwise into 1-inch slices

2 medium tomatoes, cut into 1-inch slices

Salt and coarsely ground pepper

3 tablespoons light olive oil, divided

3 tablespoons extra-virgin olive oil

1 tablespoon balsamic vinegar

1 tablespoon brown sugar

2 teaspoons fresh lemon juice

1 teaspoon chopped garlic

¼ teaspoon oregano

½ teaspoon fresh basil leaves, finely chopped

9 scallions, white and green parts, chopped

1 cucumber, sliced lengthwise and cubed

1 cup canned artichoke quarters

½ cup crumbled feta cheese

⅔ cup Kalamata olives

1 head romaine lettuce

Grilled Mediterranean Salad

- Toss eggplant, zucchini, and tomatoes with salt and pepper and just enough light olive oil to coat.

- Lightly coat a grill pan with remaining light olive oil. Grill vegetables until nicely browned. Cool.

- Whisk the extra-virgin olive oil with the vinegar, brown sugar, lemon juice, garlic, oregano, basil, and salt and pepper to taste.

- Cube the grilled vegetables and toss with the scallions, cucumber, artichokes, cheese, olives, and dressing. Serve on beds of romaine.

56

To season a cast-iron grill pan, coat it with vegetable oil and bake it, empty, for about an hour in a 350°F oven. When it's cooled, wipe out any excess grease and give it a quick, soapy rinse.

Grilled Vegetable Pockets: Lightly coat your grill pan with olive oil. Over medium-high heat, grill pita bread pockets until hot but still soft. If they're too crisp, they'll crack when you try to open them. Cut 1½ inches off the tops of the pockets. Carefully pull the pockets open and just as carefully stuff the pitas with grilled vegetable salad. Top with hummus, tahini, or plain yogurt.

Select the Eggplant

- The most common varieties of eggplant are the Western eggplant, also known as the globe and the Japanese or Asian eggplant.

- The little slices of the smaller Japanese eggplant are great for this dish, but the larger eggplant slices can be easily cubed.

- Choose firm, glossy, deep purple fruits without blemishes, which can sometimes be the start of rot.

- An eggplant should feel heavier than it looks. The more moisture inside the eggplant, the fresher it will be.

Using a Grill Pan

- Cast-iron grill pans are excellent for cooking at very high heat with little or no added fat.

- Cast-iron utensils must be seasoned (see Zoom). This retains the nonstick surface.

- Let the pan heat on high for a few minutes. When you can feel a lot of heat coming off it, it's ready.

- The vegetables will cook at different rates. Figure on 5 minutes per side for the zucchini, 4 minutes for the eggplant, and 2–3 minutes for the tomatoes.

ROASTED GREEN BEAN SALAD

The sweetness of goat cheese and sun-dried tomatoes perfectly complements crunchy caramelized green beans

Green beans are available year-round, with a peak season of May to October. Interchangeably referred to as "string beans" and "snap beans," green beans have no strings attached. Just break off the ends as you wash them and leave them whole, snap them in half, or cut into desired lengths. When roasting green beans, however, roast them whole and snap or cut

them later, depending on the dish you're making.

Goat cheese, or *chèvre,* which is French for "goat," comes in many forms, from soft and semifirm to hard aged. The goat cheese used here is the semifirm crumbled variety. The high concentration of medium-chain fatty acids in goat's milk gives goat cheese a tangy edge. *Yield: 4 servings*

Ingredients

1 pound fresh mature green beans

1 tablespoon olive oil

Salt and coarsely ground pepper

1 teaspoon extra-virgin olive oil

1 tablespoon fresh lemon juice

$^1/_2$ cup sun-dried tomatoes

$^1/_2$ cup pitted Kalamata olives

1 teaspoon chopped garlic

1 teaspoon minced fresh oregano leaves

1 teaspoon minced fresh mint leaves

$^1/_2$ cup crumbled goat cheese

Roasted Green Bean Salad

- Preheat oven to 450°F. Wash the beans and snap off the stem ends.

- Toss the beans with 1 tablespoon olive oil, salt, and pepper. Place them in a single layer on a foil-lined baking sheet.

- Roast the beans for 10 minutes, turn, and roast another 10 minutes.

- Combine the extra-virgin olive oil, lemon juice, tomatoes, olives, garlic, oregano and mint. Toss with the beans, add salt and pepper to taste, and top with goat cheese.

· · · · RECIPE VARIATION · · · ·

Roasted Green Beans with Shallots and Pecans:
Toss 1 pound fresh green beans with 1 chopped shallot, 2 teaspoons chopped garlic, 3 tablespoons olive oil, and salt and lemon pepper to taste. Roast at 425°F until the beans are golden brown. Remove from the oven, toss with 1 tablespoon fresh lemon juice and ⅓ cup chopped toasted pecans, and serve.

Roast the Beans

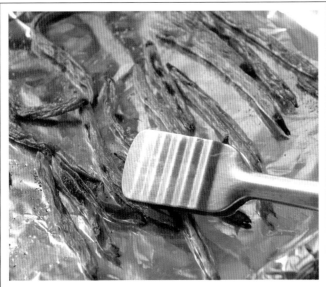

Chop the Herbs

- Use mature green beans for roasting. The dry oven heat turns the starch in the older beans to sugar, making them extra sweet.

- Lining the baking sheet with foil prevents burning on dark nonstick baking sheets and makes cleanup a snap.

- Using only a single tablespoon of oil encourages browning without making the beans slick and greasy.

- After the initial 10-minute roasting, remove the beans from the oven, redistribute them with tongs, and return them to the oven.

- Rinse the oregano and mint and carefully dry them with paper towels.

- If the leaves are on stems, strip them off with your fingers.

- Place the herbs in a small pile on a cutting board. Holding a knife with one hand, place your other hand on top of the knife near the tip, and raise the handle up and down rapidly, chopping with a rocking motion.

- Gadgets like stainless steel herb and nut choppers are inexpensive and cut chopping time to a minimum.

SALADS

BACON HOLLANDAISE ASPARAGUS

Roast or grill asparagus for a smoky flavor that adds to the vegetable's natural sweetness

The official signs of spring are tulips, lilacs, leaves on the trees, and . . . asparagus. In most areas, the asparagus growing season runs from March through June. The rules of thumb for buying asparagus are firm, crisp stalks; tightly closed tips; and moist, fresh ends. If asparagus is flexible or soft, if there's a questionable odor emanating from the tips,

or if the ends are dry or cracked, keep moving!

Roasted asparagus with bacon hollandaise is a great accompaniment to any meat, poultry, or fish. Poached salmon, roasted chicken, leg of lamb, pork chops, steak . . . what doesn't go well with asparagus and hollandaise? *Yield: 4 servings*

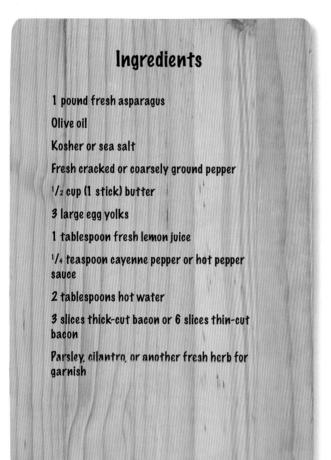

Ingredients

1 pound fresh asparagus

Olive oil

Kosher or sea salt

Fresh cracked or coarsely ground pepper

$1/2$ cup (1 stick) butter

3 large egg yolks

1 tablespoon fresh lemon juice

$1/4$ teaspoon cayenne pepper or hot pepper sauce

2 tablespoons hot water

3 slices thick-cut bacon or 6 slices thin-cut bacon

Parsley, cilantro, or another fresh herb for garnish

Bacon Hollandaise Asparagus

- Place the asparagus on a baking sheet. Drizzle with olive oil and sprinkle with salt and pepper.

- Roast in a 400°F oven for 15–20 minutes, until the asparagus is lightly browned and tender but not soft.

- Prepare the hollandaise sauce and bacon while the asparagus is roasting.

- Serve the asparagus topped with the hollandaise and garnished with fresh herbs.

• • • • RECIPE VARIATIONS • • • •

Grilled Asparagus with Balsamic Vinaigrette: Grilling and roasting are pretty much the same, except that a charcoal grill gives a smokier flavor. Prepare a dressing of 4 tablespoons balsamic vinegar, the juice of 1 lemon, ⅓ cup of olive oil, 1 tablespoon chopped garlic, 2 tablespoons chopped fresh cilantro, ¼ teaspoon pepper, and ½ teaspoon salt. Heat grill and prepare asparagus as you would for roasting. Grill asparagus 3–4 minutes per side and drizzle with dressing.

Roasted Asparagus and Prosciutto Roll-ups: For an easy , delicious appetizer roast your asparagus as directed. When it's cool, lightly coat each spear with mayonnaise or ranch dressing and wrap it in a paper-thin slice of prosciutto. Sprinkle with fresh shaved Parmesan.

Prepare the Asparagus

Make the Hollandaise

- Wash the asparagus and dry thoroughly. Cut off the ends at the first joint.

- A light coating of olive oil or butter gives the asparagus a crispy outer surface that seals in flavor.

- Arrange the spears on the cookie sheet in a single layer. Don't stack them, or you'll get steamed instead of roasted asparagus.

- The asparagus is done when it's fork-tender but still juicy and lightly browned but not burned.

- Heat the butter in a heavy saucepan until foamy but not browned.

- In a small bowl, whisk egg yolks with lemon juice, salt, and cayenne or hot sauce.

- Add the egg mixture to the butter in the saucepan. Add the hot water and beat over very low heat until slightly thickened. The hollandaise can stand over warm water for up to 30 minutes.

- Fry the bacon until crisp; drain and crumble into the hollandaise.

61

GREEN BEANS PAPRIKASH

Paprika in a sour cream sauce adds a Hungarian flair to modest green beans

French-cut green beans are simply regular green beans cut into thin strips and then cut at an acute angle. Unlike those frozen or canned beans that are cut at a 45-degree angle and sold as "French Style" or "French Cut," true French-cut beans are closer to julienned or shredded green beans.

"Paprikash" refers to the paprika sauce in which the beans are simmered. A traditional Eastern European dish, paprikash is usually made with chicken, onion, and green bell peppers. When made with beef, it becomes goulash, or gulyas. *Yield: 4 servings*

Ingredients

1 pound fresh green beans

$1/2$ cup sour cream

$1/2$ cup plain yogurt

1 tablespoon paprika

$1/2$ teaspoon seasoned salt

$1/4$ teaspoon pepper

2 teaspoons butter

3 slices cooked bacon, crumbled

1 14–16 ounce can fried onions

Green Beans Paprikash

- French cut the beans and add them to 1 inch of salted boiling water in a skillet. Cook 3 minutes and drain.

- Mix the sour cream, yogurt, paprika, seasoned salt, and pepper together in a small bowl.

- Return beans to skillet and add sauce mixture. Simmer for 15 minutes.

- Add butter and bacon and stir through. Top with fried onions.

• • • • RECIPE VARIATIONS • • • •

French-Cut Green Beans with Cashews and Ham: In a medium skillet, brown ½ cup chopped ham in 2 tablespoons butter. Add 1 teaspoon chopped garlic and brown, 20 seconds. Add 1 pound cooked French cut green beans, ½ cup cashew pieces, 1 tablespoon lemon juice, and salt and pepper to taste. Mix, warm through, and serve topped with 1 can fried onions.

Goulash: In a skillet mix 3 tablespoons canola oil, brown 1 pound seasoned and floured beef stew meat. Add 1 cup chopped onion, 2 teaspoons chopped garlic, ½ cup chopped red bell pepper, 1 pound French cut green beans, 3 cups beef broth, 2 tablespoons paprika, and salt and pepper to taste. Simmer 1½ hours. Stir in 1 cup of sour cream and heat through. Serve with egg noodles.

French Cut the Beans

- French-cut beans are made by cutting the beans in half lengthwise.

- Run the knife down the flat part between the seams of the bean.

- Wider beans can be cut into ⅛-inch-wide strips.

- You can also use an inexpensive handheld "Frencher," which pulls the bean through a triple-blade chamber, cutting it into four slices.

Select the Paprika

- Paprika comes from the dried pods of a variety of peppers, ranging from sweet red bell peppers to hot chiles.

- There are two basic varieties of paprika, sweet and hot. Paprikas labeled "mild" are sweet.

- For this type of dish, sweet paprika is preferable because of its bright, well-balanced, smoky flavor. Hot paprika can have a bitter edge.

- If you like a touch of heat, add ¼ teaspoon of cayenne pepper flakes.

ZUCCHINI BOATS PROVENÇAL

Hollowed-out zucchini "boats" carry a delectable meat and vegetable filling

Zucchini easily lends itself to an infinite number of dishes because it is so accommodating. Bland as can be, it never overwhelms and is delicious almost any way you cook it, whether steamed with a little butter, salt, and pepper, sautéed in olive oil and garlic, deep-fried and drizzled with lemon sauce, stir-fried with chicken, beef, or shrimp... there's really nothing you can't do to zucchini.

A truly tasty way to serve this congenial squash is in the form of little hollowed-out "boats" filled with a mixture of cheese, mushrooms, onion, sausage, and bread crumbs, a dish that's as picturesque as it is divine. *Yield: 4 servings*

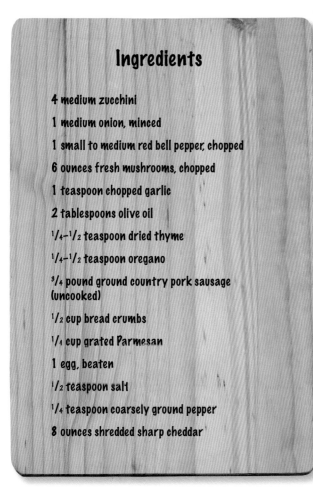

Ingredients

4 medium zucchini

1 medium onion, minced

1 small to medium red bell pepper, chopped

6 ounces fresh mushrooms, chopped

1 teaspoon chopped garlic

2 tablespoons olive oil

$1/4$–$1/2$ teaspoon dried thyme

$1/4$–$1/2$ teaspoon oregano

$3/4$ pound ground country pork sausage (uncooked)

$1/2$ cup bread crumbs

$1/4$ cup grated Parmesan

1 egg, beaten

$1/2$ teaspoon salt

$1/4$ teaspoon coarsely ground pepper

8 ounces shredded sharp cheddar

Zucchini Boats Provençal

- Parboil the washed stemmed zucchini 10–15 minutes. Remove from the water and cool.

- In a large skillet, sauté the chopped vegetables and garlic in the olive oil. Add the thyme and oregano.

- Halve and core zucchini.

Combine ground meat with chopped zucchini "innards," cooked vegetables, bread crumbs, Parmesan, egg, salt, and pepper.

- Fill the boats with the ground meat mixture. Top with the cheddar and bake 20–30 minutes at 375°F until brown and bubbly.

Prepare the Zucchini

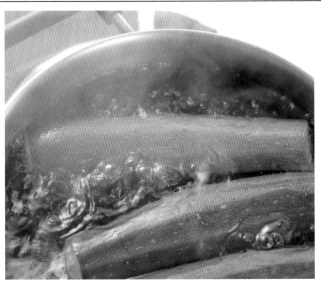

- Choose squash that's firm, heavy for its size, dark in color, and about 8 inches long for stuffing.

- Parboiling is boiling to partially cook food that will be finished cooking later.

- Place the washed whole zucchini in a pot of salted cold water.

- Bring to a boil and cook until tender but firm, about 10–15 minutes. Rinse the zucchini with cold water to "fix" the color and texture of the vegetable and allow to cool.

Make the Boats

- Slice the cooled zucchini in half lengthwise.

- Using a melon scoop or similar sharp instrument, hollow out the centers, leaving a little flesh. The zucchini should resemble a canoe.

- Chop up the removed zucchini flesh and add it to the ground meat mixture.

- Fill the boats with a generous helping of the mixture, pressing it down firmly.

RED CABBAGE WITH BACON & WINE

This traditional German side dish is sweet, spicy, and loaded with flavor

Cabbage is one of those vegetables you either love or hate. Part of that has to do with how it's cooked. If you grew up eating tasteless boiled cabbage or too-salty canned sauerkraut, you're not likely to be a cabbage fan. If, on the other hand, you ever tasted a *choucroute*, the French version of the Polish cabbage, sausage, and potato delicacy, or German red

cabbage with apples, onion, and bacon, cooked in a sweet, spiced wine sauce, your cabbage memories may be fond ones indeed.

German red cabbage, or *rotkohl*, is a wonderful fall and winter dish that goes beautifully with pork, beef, or veal and, of course, potatoes. *Yield: 8 servings*

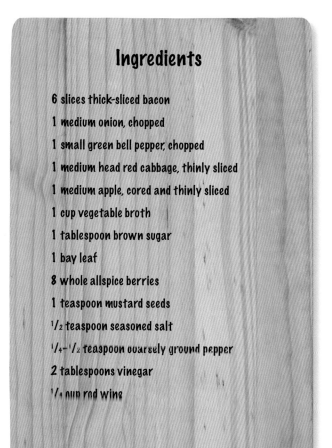

Ingredients

6 slices thick-sliced bacon

1 medium onion, chopped

1 small green bell pepper, chopped

1 medium head red cabbage, thinly sliced

1 medium apple, cored and thinly sliced

1 cup vegetable broth

1 tablespoon brown sugar

1 bay leaf

8 whole allspice berries

1 teaspoon mustard seeds

$^1/_2$ teaspoon seasoned salt

$^1/_4$–$^1/_2$ teaspoon coarsely ground pepper

2 tablespoons vinegar

$^1/_4$ cup red wine

Red Cabbage with Bacon and Wine

- Cut the bacon into small chunks and brown in a Dutch oven or other large pot with a tight-fitting lid.

- Add the onion and green pepper and sauté in the bacon drippings until slightly browned.

- Add the cabbage, apple, broth, sugar, and seasonings and mix well.

- Simmer for about 40 minutes. Stir in the vinegar and red wine just before the cabbage is done to give this dish its famous red color.

•••• RECIPE VARIATIONS ••••

Choucroute Rouge: A choucroute is a hearty Alsatian sauerkraut. Add the following to your red cabbage: halved boiled new potatoes, a 16-ounce can of prepared sauerkraut, and any kind of cooked meat, such as sausage, bratwurst, ham, hot dogs, or pork. Serve with the mustard.

Red Slaw: For a colorful coleslaw, combine 2 cups shredded red cabbage with 1 cup shredded carrots, ½ cup chopped red onion, ½ cup lightly cooked fresh or frozen corn (canned can be substituted), and ½ cup fresh or canned julienned beets. Toss in a mixture of 1 cup mayonnaise, ½ cup plain yogurt, ¼ cup ranch dressing, 1 tablespoon vinegar, 1 tablespoon sugar, and salt and pepper to taste.

Prepare the Cabbage

- While green cabbage works just as well in this dish, red cabbage is somewhat spicier and certainly more colorful.

- Wash the cabbage, removing any bad outer leaves.

- Slice cabbage in half lengthwise and cut a V-shaped notch around the white core with a sharp knife. Discard the core.

- Slice both pieces in half again to make four quarters. Thinly slice each quarter crosswise into ¼-inch-thick strips.

Cook the Bacon

- Applewood-smoked or other smoked bacon is a good choice for this dish.

- The thick bacon slices provide the fat and add flavor.

- Don't overcook the bacon. You want it browned but not crisp.

- You can substitute ham slices for the bacon, but make sure they're well-marbled with fat. Otherwise, brown the ham in 1 tablespoon vegetable or canola oil and add 1 tablespoon butter when sautéing the onion and green pepper.

SWEET & SOUR ROASTED BEETS

A tangy mixture of honey, orange marmalade, and sherry vinegar makes roasted beets sparkle

Beets have been a valued vegetable ever since the Assyrians saw them growing in the Hanging Gardens of Babylon in the ninth century B.C. The Romans and Greeks were familiar with white and black beets, and they used the leaves and roots for healing remedies until around the third century A.D., when the Romans finally figured out that beets were a food and

hailed their juice as an aphrodisiac.

Beets are high in vitamin C and potassium and low in calories, making them a good diet food. And roasted in a citrus honey sauce, they're as good as any dessert. *Yield: 6–8 servings*

Ingredients

3¹/₂ pounds assorted fresh medium beets, trimmed

¹/₃ cup honey

¹/₄ cup orange marmalade

¹/₄ cup sherry vinegar

2 tablespoons unsalted butter

2 tablespoons water

1 teaspoon minced fresh mint

¹/₄ teaspoon salt

¹/₈ teaspoon coarsely ground pepper

Sweet and Sour Roasted Beets

- Preheat oven to 425°F. Pre-cook the beets, drain, and cool. Peel off skins.

- Cut the beets into quarters and crosswise slices and place in a large bowl.

- In a small bowl, combine the honey, marmalade, vinegar, butter, water, mint, salt, and pepper. Pour over the beets and toss.

- Roast the beets until glazed and cooked through, about 15–20 minutes.

• • • • RECIPE VARIATIONS • • • •

Beet Salad: Roasted beets can be instantly transformed into a fabulous salad. Omit the honey sauce and lightly toss the cooked cubed beets with olive oil, salt, and pepper. Roast, cool, and toss with greens, a little feta or blue cheese, balsamic vinaigrette, and maple syrup. Top with toasted walnuts.

Unbeetable Potato Salad: In a large bowl, combine 2 cups diced roasted beets with 2 cups halved boiled new potatoes. In a smaller bowl, whisk together 1 tablespoon fresh dill, 1 teaspoon horseradish, 1 cup plain yogurt, ⅓ cup mayonnaise, ¼ cup blue cheese dressing, and salt and pepper to taste. Toss all ingredients. Serve warm or cold.

Precook the Beets

- When selecting fresh beets, buy small to medium globes with stems and leaves attached, firm, smooth skin, and no soft spots.

- Wash the beets whole, and trim to 1 inch from the stem to minimize bleeding.

- Pierce the beets with fork tines and place them in a microwave-safe dish. Add 3 cups of water.

- Seal the dish airtight with a double layer of plastic wrap and microwave on high 8–10 minutes, until beets are crisp-tender.

Roast the Beets

- While some recipes call for cubing and cutting the beets after roasting them, doing it ahead of time promotes faster, more thorough cooking.

- Lightly coat a large nonstick baking pan with vegetable oil.

- Transfer the coated beets to the pan and arrange in a single layer.

- Turn the beets occasionally during roasting to ensure even cooking.

CARROT & PARSNIP GRATIN

Homemade bread crumbs and two flavorful cheeses transform simple carrots and parsnips into a quick and easy masterpiece

A gratin is essentially a casserole. It gets its name from the French word meaning "crust," and its distinguishing feature is a bread crumb topping that bakes to a golden brown. *Au gratin* means "in gratin style," or topped with bread crumbs and butter. A gratin is usually baked in a traditional oval baking dish, whereas casseroles are generally baked in a simple glass baking dish. Because they may feature a cheesy cream sauce, gratins are sometimes confused with scalloped dishes. This recipe is really scalloped carrots and parsnips au gratin. *Yield: 6–8 servings*

Ingredients

³/₄ pound each carrots and parsnips, sliced into ¹/₂-inch rounds

1 small onion, finely chopped

6 tablespoons unsalted butter, divided

3 tablespoons flour

1¹/₂ cups whole milk

6 ounces grated Gruyère cheese

¹/₂ cup mascarpone cheese

¹/₂ teaspoon salt

¹/₂ teaspoon coarsely ground pepper, divided

2 teaspoons Dijon mustard

1¹/₂ cups day-old bread, cubed

2 tablespoons olive oil

2 teaspoons finely chopped garlic

¹/₂ teaspoon seasoned salt

1 tablespoon fresh parsley

Carrot and Parsnip Gratin

- Microwave sliced carrots, parsnips, and 3 tablespoons water until crisp-tender, 6–8 minutes.

- Sauté the onion in 1 tablespoon of butter until golden. Melt 3 more tablespoons butter and whisk in flour. Gradually whisk in the milk and bring to a low boil.

- Remove from heat and stir in the cheeses, regular salt, ¼ teaspoon pepper, and mustard.

- Layer the carrots and parsnips in a gratin dish and cover with sauce. Top with the bread crumbs and bake at 350°F until golden brown.

Prepare the Bread Crumbs

Bake the Gratin

- Cut the bread into ¼-inch cubes. Crusty French bread is standard, but 4 slices of toasted whole grain bread work as well.

- Heat 2 tablespoons of butter and the olive oil in a skillet. The mixture of the two prevents the butter from burning and the olive oil taste from overpowering the dish.

- Sauté garlic until golden but not browned.

- Add the bread, seasoned salt, parsley, and ¼ teaspoon pepper, and cook for 3–5 minutes.

- To bake a gratin, use a shallow, ovenproof pan. The classic gratin pan is a heavy-bottomed oval earthenware dish called a tian.

- Arrange the vegetables and cheese sauce in a single layer. The bread crumb topping should be spread evenly but not too thickly.

- A gratin is done when it is well-browned, crusty, and bubbling, with a delicious aroma.

- The gratin should sit 15 minutes before being served.

CREAMY THYME ASPARAGUS SOUP

Carrots give this soup a burst of sweetness, while fresh thyme adds an aromatic punch

Homemade soups are easy to prepare and incredibly delicious, nutritious, and economical. Once you start making them, you just may never be able to eat canned soup again. They're the perfect way to take advantage of low-priced in-season vegetables, and when paired with a salad, they can be a lunch or dinner entree. A cup of soup is a perfect appetizer or snack. A big pot of soup with fresh vegetables, meat, and noodles, barley, or rice serves the whole family for practically pennies.

While thyme is a key ingredient in this soup, time isn't. It can be prepared very quickly and will impress everybody. *Yield: 6–8 servings*

Ingredients

2 pounds fresh asparagus

1 medium yellow onion, chopped

2 teaspoons chopped or minced garlic

3 carrots, shredded

3 tablespoons butter

4 cups vegetable broth

2 cups chicken broth

1 teaspoon seasoned salt

$1/4$ teaspoon coarsely ground pepper

$1 1/2$ tablespoons fresh thyme, divided

1 tablespoon fresh lemon juice

$1/2$ cup heavy cream

Creamy Thyme Asparagus Soup

- Trim the ends off of the asparagus and cut the stalks into 1-inch pieces.

- Sauté the onion, garlic, and carrots in butter that's foamy but not brown. Add lightly cooked asparagus, both kinds of broth, salt, pepper, 1 tablespoon of the thyme, and lemon juice.

- Simmer the soup, then puree in a blender.

- Return the soup to the pot. If serving immediately, add the cream. If refrigerating and serving later, add the cream upon reheating.

- Garnish with asparagus tips and fresh thyme.

GREEN ● LIGHT

To prepare asparagus stalks without damaging them, place them flat on a cutting board and peel with a vegetable peeler from the tip toward the end. Always buy freshly picked stalks, but be careful: A fresh asparagus stalk breaks very easily and the juice will seep out.

• • • • RECIPE VARIATION • • • •

Cheesy Asparagus Soup: Make the asparagus thyme soup and add 2 cups grated sharp cheddar, or 1 cup cheddar and 1 cup grated Gruyére cheeses. Heat on medium just until the cheese is melted. Garnish with crumbled bacon.

Prepare the Vegetables

- Cut the tips off the asparagus 1½ inches from the top. If the tips are very thick, halve them.

- Microwave the asparagus with ¼ cup water for 5 minutes. Reserve ½ cup of the tips.

- Cut the carrots into 1-inch pieces and shred or chop them in a blender or mini food processor.

- Finely chop the onion by hand. If using a food processor, cut the onion into quarters and process for just a few seconds.

Puree the Soup

- Simmer the broth, vegetables, lemon juice, and seasonings for 15 minutes, so that all the flavors begin to combine.

- The steam from hot items can blow a blender lid off, so set your blender at a slow speed.

- Divide the soup into three batches.

- Puree each batch at a slow speed for approximately 15 seconds, with the blender lid slightly ajar to vent steam. Then seal the lid and increase the speed to "blend" or "liquefy" for another 10 seconds.

BEST BORSCHT EVER

Cabbage and beets are the basis of this hearty Russian staple

In Russia, borscht is called "the blood." This is not just because of its deep red color (the central ingredient being beets), but because it's the ultimate healing brew, a powerhouse blend of as many as ten different vegetables and meat or sausage that energizes, cleanses, and warms the blood on freezing winter days and nights.

It's said that every housewife in Russia has her own version of borscht, and "borscht wars" are common, each woman defending her family recipe. This one is mine, and I'm proud to say that when a native of Moscow tasted it, he declared it to be "just like home." *Yield: 10 servings*

Ingredients

1 small head cabbage, quartered and chopped
1 medium yellow onion, chopped
1 medium to large green bell pepper, chopped
3 tablespoons vegetable or canola oil, divided
1 16-ounce package turkey kielbasa
1 16-ounce can julienned beets with liquid
1 15-ounce can diced tomatoes with juice
6 cups chicken or vegetable broth (or 6 cups water and 6 teaspoons of bouillon powder)
3 medium to large carrots, grated
1 medium zucchini, diced
2 medium potatoes, cut into large cubes
2 teaspoons chopped garlic
2 tablespoons fresh parsley or 2 teaspoons dried parsley
2 bay leaves
1/2 cup chopped celery tops and leaves
2 tablespoons paprika
1 teaspoon seasoned salt
1/4–1/2 teaspoon coarsely ground pepper
Sour cream

Best Borscht Ever

- In a large soup pot, sauté the cabbage, onion, and green pepper in 2 tablespoons oil.

- Slice the kielbasa into 1-inch rounds and brown in 1 tablespoon oil. Add to cabbage mixture.

- Add the beets, tomatoes and 6 cups canned broth and bring to a boil.

- Add the rest of the ingredients (except the sour cream), stir well, and simmer covered for 45 minutes. Serve topped with sour cream.

Ukrainians claim borscht as their national dish. But they're the first to admit that there's no one borscht that represents their country. Instead, each region has its own borscht recipe, all distinguished by different names. There's Hetman borscht, Kiev borscht, Lviv borscht, Tarasha borscht . . . And then there's Ukranian Christmas borscht, a sweet spiced soup served over mushroom onion dumplings.

Creamy Polish Beet Borscht: For classic Polish *barszcz,* combine 4 cups beef or vegetable stock with 2 cups roasted, sliced beets, 1 tablespoon sugar, and salt and pepper to taste. Simmer 10 minutes, puree in a blender and return to pot. Whisk in ½ cup each heavy cream and sour cream. Heat through, and serve garnished with fresh dill.

Use Fresh or Canned Beets

Serve the Borscht

- Canned beets work for this recipe because the beet liquid adds to the stock.

- Using fresh beets is more of a production because they'll stain your fingers, counters, and cutting board. But some cooks feel it's worth the effort.

- If you prefer the fresh alternative, trim and wash 3 large beets well and cut into ½-inch round slices.

- Cut the slices into thin julienne strips and add to the soup.

- For an authentic Russian presentation, serve the borscht as a centerpiece in a soup tureen.

- The typical garnish for borscht is a dollop of sour cream topped with a sprig of fresh dill, parsley, or both.

- Spread slices of Russian rye bread or chunks of fresh-baked whole grain bread with butter and arrange on a plate.

- Accompany the bread and borscht with a platter of Swiss, Havarti, Gouda, or other flavorful cheeses.

CREAMY CARROT GINGER SOUP
Fresh ginger and brown sugar make this soup sweet and spicy

Carrots are inexpensive and available year-round, which means you can always have fresh carrot soup. And with its sweet richness, subtle blend of flavors, and numerous health benefits, you'll want to.

A key ingredient in this recipe is fresh ginger, which gives the soup a sharp kick. Yes, you can use ground ginger from your spice rack if you must. But the fresh grated stuff is so much tastier, not to mention so much more effective as a time-honored digestive aid, that you really should make every effort to get some. *Yield: 6–8 servings*

Ingredients

8 medium carrots, coarsely chopped (about 4 cups)

1 large sweet onion, coarsely chopped

1 large or 2 medium potatoes, cut into large cubes

1 tablespoon olive oil

1 tablespoon unsalted butter

6 cups chicken or vegetable broth

3 tablespoons minced fresh ginger

1/4 teaspoon nutmeg

1 teaspoon chopped garlic

1/2 teaspoon salt

1/2 teaspoon coarsely ground black pepper

1 tablespoon brown sugar

1/3 cup whipping cream

Fresh parsley

Crème fraiche

Creamy Carrot Ginger Soup

- In a large saucepan, cook the vegetables in the heated oil and butter until crisp tender, 5–10 minutes.

- Stir in the broth, ginger, nutmeg, garlic, salt, and pepper and bring to a boil. Cover and cook until vegetables are tender, about 20 minutes.

- Puree in batches in a blender. Return to saucepan and reheat until just simmering.

- Remove from heat and add the brown sugar and cream. Serve garnished with parsley and a drizzle of crème fraiche.

Grate the Ginger

Make the Crème Fraiche

- When buying fresh ginger root, look for thin, tan-colored skin with pinkish tips, and stay away from pieces that are soft or withering.

- Peel the ginger with a small, sharp paring knife.

- Grip a grater (Microplanes are excellent) with one hand and the fresh ginger root with the other, working over a cutting board.

- Draw the ginger in a rapid upward and downward motion along the Microplane or across the finest holes of the grater.

- Crème fraiche is a slightly fermented thickened cream with a tangy taste that's somewhere between whipping cream and sour cream.

- Crème fraiche is sometimes difficult and expensive to get, but you can easily make your own.

- Heat but do not boil a cup of whipping cream and mix in a tablespoon of butter-milk or yogurt.

- Allow the mixture to sit at room temperature for 12–24 hours. The crème fraiche can be refrigerated up to a week.

77

ROASTED TOMATO & BARLEY SOUP
Who knew good old tomato soup could taste like this?

If the only tomato soup you've ever eaten is Campbell's, get ready for a surprise. Roasted tomato soup with carrot, celery, and barley is a whole different experience.

While this recipe calls for canned tomatoes, you can of course use fresh. If doing so, try to get them at a farmers' or produce market, where the tomatoes should be at their peak, rather than at the supermarket, where they are often picked too early and not as flavorful. You'll want ripe tomatoes, which, if they're the best quality, should be bursting with sweetness. *Yield: 8 servings*

Ingredients

1 28-ounce can diced tomatoes, undrained

1 tablespoon olive oil

1 large carrot, chopped

1 tablespoon butter

1 large onion, chopped

1 teaspoon chopped garlic

4 cups chicken broth

1 cup diced celery

$1/2$ cup uncooked pearl barley

1 tablespoon chopped fresh basil

$1/2$–1 teaspoon kosher salt

$1/4$ teaspoon freshly ground pepper

2 tablespoons chopped fresh parsley

Roasted Tomato and Barley Soup

- Drain the tomatoes, reserving the juice. Drizzle them with olive oil and roast in a 425°F oven for 20 minutes.

- Sauté the carrot in the butter over medium heat for 5 minutes. Add the onion and garlic and cook 1 minute more.

- Put the vegetables in a 3-quart saucepan with the reserved tomato juice, broth, celery, barley, basil, salt, and pepper and bring to a boil.

- Simmer for 35 minutes, or until barley is tender. Stir in the parsley.

Roasted Tomato and Eggplant Bisque: Roast the diced tomatoes with 4 cups of peeled diced eggplant and 2 sliced garlic cloves. Puree the vegetables in a blender or food processor with 1 cup vegetable broth and ½ cup crumbled feta cheese. Pour into a 3-quart saucepan, add 3 more cups broth, bring to a boil, and reduce heat to low. Stir in 2 tablespoons light cream and 1 tablespoon chopped fresh basil. Season with salt and pepper and serve topped with crumbled feta.

Cream of Tomato Soup: Brown 1 cup yellow onions and 2 teaspoons chopped garlic. Add the roasted tomatoes and juice, broth, basil, 1 teaspoon thyme, salt and pepper. Simmer 35 minutes, blend, and return to pot. Add 1–2 cups heavy cream and heat just to simmering.

Prepare the Barley

- Pearl barley is the most common form of barley and it comes in both regular and quick-cooking forms. Use the regular for this recipe.

- Unlike legumes such as beans, pearl barley requires no soaking.

- Sort through the barley and remove any stones or particles that might have slipped through the packaging process.

- Rinse the barley thoroughly, using a strainer.

Choose the Chicken Broth

- Canned chicken broth is perfectly acceptable for this recipe. An organic choice will have less sodium and no preservatives.

- Chicken bouillon can be used, but it's much higher in sodium so taste the soup before adding more salt.

- The concentrated soup base Better Than Bouillon has ⅓ less salt but a much richer flavor than ordinary bouillon.

- Vegetarians can substitute canned or packaged vegetable broth for the chicken broth.

KICKED-UP MUSHROOM LEEK SOUP
Madeira wine adds rich color and flavor to mushroom soup

I once saw a standup routine where the comedian did a hilarious monologue on vegetables that included the irresistible line, "Take a leek . . ." Well, go ahead. Take a leek, or two, or three, chop them up, add some mushrooms, garlic, broth, and Madeira, season the whole thing, and you've got a delicious soup that took you about 20 minutes to whip up.

Members of the onion family, leeks have an ever so slightly

sweet taste that could be described as a cross between mild onion and cucumber. Their subtle grace goes well with mushrooms, making this soup light and delicately flavored.
Yield: 8 servings

Ingredients

1 ounce dried shiitake, morel, or cèpes mushrooms

¹/₂ cup Madeira wine

1 tablespoon sherry

6 cups canned vegetable broth, divided

4 tablespoons (¹/₂ stick) butter

3 leeks, white parts only, chopped

1 teaspoon chopped garlic

2 tablespoons flour

1 8-ounce package sliced white mushrooms

¹/₂ teaspoon salt

¹/₄ teaspoon coarsely ground black pepper

Fresh parsley

Kicked-up Mushroom Leek Soup

- Heat dried mushrooms, Madeira, sherry, and 1 cup of broth in a saucepan until boiling. Remove from heat and let cool 30 minutes.

- Melt the butter in a 4-quart saucepan. Add the leeks and cook until crisp-tender. Add the garlic and cook for 1 minute. Stir in the flour.

- Stir in rehydrated mushroom liquid, remaining 5 cups of broth, white mushrooms, and salt and pepper, and simmer for 30 minutes.

- Puree the soup in the blender in batches until smooth, then reheat for 5 minutes. Serve in bowls garnished with parsley.

• • • • RECIPE VARIATION • • • •

Mushroom Leek Soup with Other Vegetables:
Almost any vegetable marries well with mushrooms. To the leeks, you may add 2 cups of the following: cooked baby spinach, finely chopped zucchini, cooked broccoli florets, artichoke hearts, or shredded carrots, to name a few possibilities.

Select the Mushrooms

- Shiitake mushrooms have an intense, meaty flavor that goes well with soups and heavy sauces.

- The rich, "heady" taste of cèpes, or dried porcini mushrooms, makes them perfect for soups.

- The morel mushroom is prized for its delicate balance of earthy, nutty, and smoky flavors.

- The blander white mushrooms or brown cremini mushrooms are used more as a main ingredient than for flavoring.

Prepare the Leeks

- Leeks have a crunchy texture when cooked and a heartier flavor than scallions.

- The part of the leek that is underground remains tender and white, while the part exposed to sunlight becomes tough and fibrous.

- To wash leeks, cut them lengthwise and rinse them in the sink under running water until all dirt is removed from the layers.

- Discard the green parts of the leeks. Slice the remaining white parts into strips and coarsely chop them.

81

CURRIED BUTTERNUT SQUASH SOUP

In Asia, squash and curry go together like a horse and surrey

In Australia, butternut squash is considered a pumpkin. That makes sense, as its sweet, nutty taste is indeed pumpkiny. Its yellow skin is much lighter than a pumpkin's, but it has an orange, fleshy pulp that becomes sweeter and richer as it ripens.

No wonder butternut squash makes a delicious soup. And it's even better when made the Thai way, with coconut milk,

fresh ginger, and red curry garnished with fragrant fresh cilantro. This soup can be served as an accompaniment to a Thai or Indian meal, or it's good enough to serve by itself. *Yield: 6–8 servings*

Ingredients

1–2 tablespoons canola oil

1 tablespoon red curry powder

1 butternut squash (about 2¹/₂ pounds) peeled, seeded, and cubed

1 large sweet onion, cut into eighths

1 teaspoon Thai red chili paste

3 cups chicken broth

1 15-ounce can cream of coconut

1 tablespoon chopped fresh ginger

1 teaspoon turmeric

¹/₂ teaspoon salt

¹/₄ teaspoon coarsely ground black pepper

¹/₄ teaspoon crushed red pepper flakes

1 tablespoon brown sugar

3 tablespoons chopped fresh cilantro

Curried Butternut Squash Soup

- Stir the oil and curry powder together in a large bowl. Add the squash and onion and toss to coat.

- Roast the vegetables in a pan at 425°F for 25 minutes, turning over once.

- In a large saucepan, combine the roasted vegetables

with the chili paste. Add the broth, the cream of coconut, and all the other ingredients except the cilantro. Bring to a boil, then cook on low for 20 minutes.

- Puree soup in a blender in batches, return to saucepan, and heat through. Garnish with fresh cilantro.

82

Pumpkin Spiced Squash Soup: Omit the curry powder, chili paste, turmeric, and cilantro. Add a cinnamon stick to the soup as it's cooking, along with ½ teaspoon nutmeg and ¼ teaspoon ground cloves. Discard the cinnamon stick before pureeing. Serve garnished with mascarpone cheese and chopped fresh parsley.

Butternut Cream Cheese Soup: In a large saucepan, sauté 1 chopped onion in butter until tender. Add squash, broth, salt, pepper and red pepper flakes, and ½ teaspoon dried marjoram. Cook 20 minutes. Puree with 8 ounces chive cream cheese until smooth, return to saucepan and heat through.

Prepare the Squash

- Using a sharp kitchen knife, cut 1 inch from the top and bottom of the squash and discard.

- Slice the squash lengthwise and peel away the thick skin with a sturdy serrated peeler until you reach the deeper orange flesh.

- Scoop out the seeds and membrane with a spoon, a melon baller, or a round metal cookie cutter that matches the curves.

- Cut squash into 2-inch cubes (1 good-sized squash should yield about 6 cups).

Choose the Curry Powder

- Curry powder is actually a mixture of many spices known as garam masala.

- You can buy garam masala, as well as products marked "curry powder."

- Curry powders range from yellow to reddish orange in color and mild to hot in flavor.

- Indian or Thai red curry powder has a bright, pungent, slightly hot edge that is perfect for this dish.

CUCUMBER & PORK PITAS
Cucumber is the foundation of the famous Greek yogurt sauce tzatziki

Gyros (pronounced *heeros*) are traditional Greek sandwiches made with marinated meat, usually lamb, that's slow-roasted on a rotating vertical spit in front of a multiple-level charcoal brazier and stuffed in pita pockets with onion, cucumber sauce, and tomato.

The cucumber sauce, or tzatziki, is delicious on meats and also as a salad dressing. It's fresh and cool, with a minty zing. We recommend using creamy Greek yogurt if you can get it. *Yield: 4 servings*

Ingredients

1 pound pork tenderloin, cut into strips

$\frac{1}{4}$ cup plus 2 teaspoons fresh lemon juice, divided

4 tablespoons olive oil, divided

1 teaspoon Dijon mustard

2 teaspoons minced garlic, divided

1 teaspoon dried oregano

1 teaspoon seasoned salt, divided

$\frac{1}{2}$ teaspoon coarsely ground pepper, divided

1 cup plain yogurt

$\frac{1}{2}$ cup ranch dressing

2 tablespoons mayonnaise

1 cup peeled and finely diced cucumber

1 teaspoon chopped fresh mint

4 pita breads, regular or whole wheat

1 cup chopped lettuce

1 cup chopped fresh tomatoes

$\frac{1}{2}$ cup chopped scallions

Cucumber and Pork Pitas

- Toss pork in a mixture of $\frac{1}{4}$ cup lemon juice, 2 tablespoons olive oil, mustard, 1 teaspoon garlic, oregano, $\frac{1}{2}$ teaspoon salt, and $\frac{1}{4}$ teaspoon pepper. Marinate pork for 3–4 hours.

- Combine yogurt, ranch dressing, mayonnaise, 2 teaspoons lemon juice,

- cucumber, mint, and remaining garlic, salt, and pepper. Refrigerate.

- Remove pork from marinade and stir-fry in remaining olive oil for 3–4 minutes.

- Fill each pita with the pork, tzatziki, lettuce, tomatoes, and scallions.

Chicken Flatbread Gyros: Substitute chicken for the pork. Grill Middle Eastern flatbread on a grill pan until heated through but not stiff. Line one end of the flatbread with the cooked chicken and top with tzatziki, chopped tomato, sliced red onion, and lettuce. Roll up without folding the ends and serve in wax paper or napkin cones.

Asian Pork Pitas: Marinate the pork in a mixture of ⅓ cup soy sauce, ¼ cup teriyaki sauce, ½ cup water, 2 teaspoons cornstarch, 2 teaspoons chopped garlic, 2 teaspoons chopped ginger, 2 chopped scallions, 1 tablespoon brown sugar, salt, and pepper. Stir fry with vegetables of your choice.

Make the Tzatziki

- You can use regular, nonfat, or Greek yogurt for this sauce. Greek yogurt is especially creamy and is also low in fat.

- Peel the cucumber with a vegetable peeler. Cut in half crosswise. Slice the halves lengthwise and then into strips. Finely dice.

- Wash and dry the mint. Finely chop the leaves on a cutting board.

- Refrigerating the tzatziki for several hours allows the flavors to blend. Serve tzatziki chilled or at room temperature.

Assemble the Pitas

- Slice 1 inch off the tops off the pitas so that you have an open pocket.

- Since store-bought pita tends to be dry, heat each pita in the microwave for 30 seconds to soften.

- When cool enough to handle, pull the pitas open.

- The bread is thin and delicate and tears easily, so go slowly and carefully.

- Place ¼ of the pork strips in each pita and layer with tzatziki, lettuce, and tomato. Top with the scallions.

SANDWICHES & PIZZA

PORTOBELLO CIABATTAS
Thick portobello mushrooms make a great substitute for meat

Portobellos are flat-topped mushrooms that can grow up to a whopping 6 inches in diameter. That's what you want for this recipe. Portobellos are hearty and satisfying, with a deep, earthy flavor. They become chewy as they cook, releasing less liquid than button mushrooms.

Roasted to tasty perfection, combined with tangy blue cheese dressing, and served on crusty, crunchy ciabatta bread, portobellos make an outstanding sandwich that you don't have to be vegetarian to enjoy. *Yield: 4 servings*

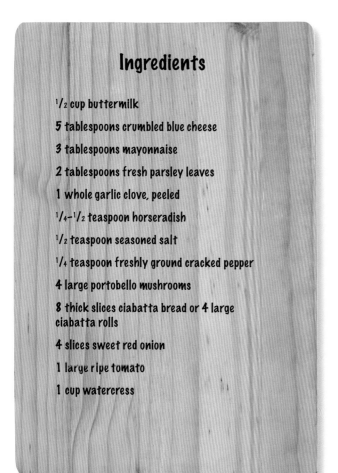

Ingredients

$1/2$ cup buttermilk

5 tablespoons crumbled blue cheese

3 tablespoons mayonnaise

2 tablespoons fresh parsley leaves

1 whole garlic clove, peeled

$1/4$–$1/2$ teaspoon horseradish

$1/2$ teaspoon seasoned salt

$1/4$ teaspoon freshly ground cracked pepper

4 large portobello mushrooms

8 thick slices ciabatta bread or 4 large ciabatta rolls

4 slices sweet red onion

1 large ripe tomato

1 cup watercress

Portobello Ciabattas

- Blend the buttermilk, cheese, mayonnaise, parsley, garlic, horseradish, salt, and pepper until smooth. Set aside in a bowl.

- Roast mushrooms at 475°F, 10 minutes on each side.

- Remove the mushrooms from the oven and place the bread on the rack. Toast briefly, 1–2 minutes.

- Spread the blue cheese dressing on 4 bread slices and place the mushrooms on top of the dressing. Layer with the onion and tomato slices and top with the watercress and remaining bread.

Grilled Portobellos: Clean the mushrooms and marinate for ½ hour in a mixture of melted butter, chopped garlic, chopped parsley, dried oregano, dried basil, salt, and pepper. Place them stem side down on a medium-hot grill and cook 3 minutes. Turn and cook 3–4 minutes.

Seared Portobellos in Wine: Season 4 large cleaned and stemmed portobello mushrooms with salt, pepper, and herbes de Provence. Brown the mushrooms in olive oil until tender, approximately 3 minutes per side. Add 1 tablespoon each port wine and balsamic vinegar and cook 2–3 minutes. Garnished with fresh parsley.

Roast the Portobellos

Make the Dressing

- When buying portobello mushrooms, look for smooth, firm caps without wet, slimy patches.

- Rinse the mushrooms and rub dry with paper towels, removing any dirt. Trim and slice the caps ½ inch thick.

- Lightly brush both sides of the mushroom slices with extra-virgin olive oil and arrange in a single layer on two lightly oiled baking sheets.

- Place the baking sheets next to each other in the oven. The mushrooms should be tender when pierced with a fork.

- "Blue cheese" refers to cheeses made from cow's, sheep's, or goat's milk to which penicillium cultures have been added, resulting in an odiferous product veined with blue or blue-green mold.

- Roquefort, Gorgonzola, Danish Blue, and Stilton are some common blue cheeses that you can use for this dressing.

- For extra flavor, add a little lemon juice or Worcestershire sauce.

- Whisk all ingredients in a bowl until smooth or shake in a bottle until blended.

VEGETABLE PO'BOYS
Who says this Louisiana fried favorite can't be healthy?

A po'boy is a Louisiana submarine sandwich that generally consists of meat or seafood, usually fried, served on baguette-like Louisiana French bread. Half po'boys, called "Shortys," are 6 inches, and full po'boys are about a foot long.

Nobody knows for sure how the term "po' boy" originated. Some say it was born during a 1920s strike against a New Orleans streetcar company, when restaurants served free sandwiches to the unemployed workers, or "poor boys." Others claim it came from a New Orleans sandwich shop that threw in a free sandwich with a nickel beer. One thing's for certain: You won't feel poor eating this lip-smacking vegetarian version of the classic sandwich. *Yield: 4 servings*

Ingredients

3 Japanese eggplants

3 medium zucchini

1 red bell pepper

1 large red onion

Seasoned salt and pepper

2 tablespoons olive oil

6 ounces sliced mushrooms

¼ cup roasted garlic

¼ cup mayonnaise

¼ teaspoon salt

⅓ teaspoon black pepper

4 6-inch po'boy loaves, cut in half horizontally

2 large tomatoes, sliced

8 slices fontina cheese

Vegetable Po'boys

- Wash, dry, slice, and dice the eggplant, zucchini, bell pepper and onion. Lightly toss with seasoned salt and pepper.

- Heat the olive oil in a large skillet and sauté the eggplant, zucchini, onion, pepper and mushrooms until tender.

- Combine the roasted garlic, mayonnaise, ¼ teaspoon salt, and ⅓ teaspoons pepper in a blender and puree.

- Spread both halves of the po'boy loaves with roasted garlic spread. Layer bottoms with vegetables, tomato, and cheese slices and top with loaf tops.

Louisiana French bread, or po'boy loaves, are different from standard American submarine rolls: They have a crisp crust with a soft, airy center. Although any New Orleans native will insist that they're the only bread you can use to make po'boys, regular French or Italian bread makes a good substitute if you can't find traditional po'boy loaves.

Oyster and Vegetable Po'boys: Stir 1 quart of fresh shelled oysters into 3 beaten eggs. In a large zip-top bag, combine 3 cups cornmeal, ¼ cup flour, 1½ teaspoons salt, 1 teaspoon Cajun seasoning, and 1 teaspoon black pepper. Toss oysters in the bag until coated and fry them in 350°F oil until golden brown. Top vegetable po'boys with fried oysters.

Roast the Garlic

Cook the Vegetables

- Cut the top (pointed end) off a head of garlic.

- Place the unpeeled head of garlic on a large piece of foil.

- A clay garlic roaster is a nice accessory to have, but the garlic will generally roast faster in foil.

- Drizzle olive oil over the garlic, wrap well in the foil, and bake in a 375°F oven until soft, about 40 minutes.

- When cutting the eggplant and zucchini, slice them in half crosswise and again lengthwise. Then slice into strips and cut into 1-inch cubes.

- The red onion has a snappy sweetness, but a sweet yellow or Vidalia onion is fine, too.

- Sauté the eggplant and zucchini first, turning them until browned. Then add the onion and mushrooms and sauté 1–2 minutes.

- You'll probably need to add more olive oil during the sautéing process, as the eggplant absorbs oil very quickly.

BROCCOLI CARROT POTATO BURRITOS
Unexpected vegetables make a delicious filling for burritos

Most people think of burritos as flour tortillas filled with beans, rice, ground or shredded beef or chicken, lettuce, tomato, and salsa. In reality, however, burritos are open to any combination of fillings, and in certain parts of Mexico, they are filled with fresh vegetables like carrots, broccoli, corn, and potatoes. You can experiment with different vegetables to create a healthy, delicious burrito your family will love.

Topped with cheese and enchilada sauce and baked until brown and bubbly, these vegetable burritos are so tasty that nobody will ever miss the meat. *Yield: 8 medium or 6 large burritos*

Ingredients

1 pound fresh broccoli florets

3 medium carrots, cut into 1/4-inch slices

3 medium potatoes, cubed

1 medium green bell pepper, chopped

1 medium sweet onion, chopped

2 teaspoons chopped garlic

1 tablespoon canola oil

8 10-inch or 6 12-inch flour tortillas

1 can refried or black beans

1/3 cup chopped fresh cilantro

Bottled salsa verde

1 28-ounce can enchilada sauce, such as Old El Paso

8 ounces shredded sharp cheddar or Pepper Jack cheese

3 scallions, green and white parts, chopped

Broccoli Carrot Potato Burritos

- Microwave the broccoli, carrots, and potatoes in 1/4 cup of water on high until crisp-tender, about 7 minutes.

- Sauté the green pepper, onion, and garlic in the oil and add the other vegetables.

- Fill each tortilla with a mixture of beans, vegetables, cilantro, and salsa verde.

- Place the burritos in a thin layer of enchilada sauce in a 13 x 9-inch baking dish. Top with more sauce and cheese. Bake at 350°F for 25 minutes. Garnish with the scallions.

Homemade Enchilada Sauce: Simply add 1 tablespoon butter, 2 tablespoons flour, and 2 tablespoons chili powder to the sautéed green pepper, onion, and garlic, making a paste. Whisk in 2 cups vegetable or chicken broth, ½ teaspoon seasoned salt, 1 teaspoon Tabasco, and 1 teaspoon whole cumin. Bring to a boil, reduce heat, and simmer 20–30 minutes, or until smooth, adding a little water if the sauce becomes too thick.

Vegetable Tostadas: In a heavy skillet, lightly fry 8 corn tacos in a thin layer of oil until browned but still soft. Place a layer of the beans on each taco, followed by a layer of the vegetables and a few spoonfuls of enchilada sauce. Top with lettuce, chopped tomatoes, shredded cheese, avocado slices, salsa, and sour cream.

Select the Cheese

- Sharp cheddar is rich and tangy with a tiny bit of a bite.

- Queso Chihuahua is a pale yellow semisoft cheese that ranges from mild to a cheddar-like sharpness.

- Monterey Jack is a mild white cheese that is closer to traditional Mexican queso blanco.

- With its blend of Monterey Jack and spicy jalapeño peppers, Pepper Jack cheese is a perfect topping for these burritos.

Assemble the Burritos

- Heat the tortillas on high in a cast-iron or nonstick skillet until they just begin to brown, about 10–15 seconds per side. No oil is necessary.

- Make sure the tortillas are hot but not crisp. Otherwise they'll break.

- Use enough beans and vegetables to fill the center of the burrito, but not so much filling that it squeezes out the sides.

- Fold over the left and right sides of the tortilla about an inch, and roll up the burrito.

SANDWICHES & PIZZA

VEGETABLE BACON CAESAR WRAPS
Here's a snazzy health-conscious version of a BLT

There's a widespread misconception that bacon is high in fat and therefore bad for you. While the preservatives in most bacon aren't exactly great, the fat is not a problem if you fry the bacon until crisp and drain it well. This means that BLTs are actually among the healthiest sandwiches around. They're low in calories—crisp, drained bacon only has around 50 calories per slice; the lettuce and tomato are freebies; bread's

maybe 70 calories a slice; and if you don't slather it on, the mayo won't wreck your diet.

These wraps have the added value of carrots and green pepper, with an herbed cheese spread, Caesar dressing, and a little Parmesan. How healthy can you get? *Yield: 4 servings*

Ingredients

¹/₂ cup Philadelphia or a store brand garlic herb cheese spread

¹/₄ teaspoon coarsely ground pepper

4 Flatout breads or other wraps

1 ¹/₄ cups julienned fresh carrots

1 ¹/₄ cups chopped fresh tomatoes

³/₄ cup chopped red bell pepper

4 bacon strips

4 romaine lettuce leaves

4 tablespoons shredded Parmesan

Bottled Caesar dressing

Vegetable Bacon Caesar Wraps

- Combine the cheese spread and ground pepper and spread 2 tablespoons of the mixture on each wrap.

- Toss the carrots, tomatoes, and red pepper together and divide into 4 portions.

- Cook the bacon until crisp. Drain on paper towels.

- Place one lettuce leaf and one bacon strip on the cheese spread on each wrap. Sprinkle with the vegetables and Parmesan, drizzle with the Caesar dressing, and roll up tightly, securing with a toothpick.

Choose the Wrap Bread

- Flatout bread is a nutritious, low-calorie, low-carb wrap that's heavier than a tortilla but lighter than flatbread.

- Italian or Mediterranean seasoned Flatout bread is perfect for these wraps.

- A large flour tortilla also makes a good wrap. Sun-dried tomato, pesto, or spinach tortillas add even more flavor.

- Lebanese flatbread is delicious but is thicker and not as easy to roll up. If choosing this bread, serve the wrap in a wax paper or paper towel cone.

Julienne the Carrots

- With a sharp knife, cut a clean, peeled carrot in half crosswise.

- Slice four sides of the halves to create rectangles.

- Cut the rectangles lengthwise into approximately ⅛-inch slices.

- Stack the ⅛-inch slices and, again, cut lengthwise into approximately ⅛-inch matchsticks.

SANDWICHES & PIZZA

93

VEGGIE MEDLEY PESTO PIZZA
This pizza is a veritable vegetable feast

Once upon a time, pizza, like ice cream, came in three flavors: cheese, pepperoni, and sausage. Today, in our designer food age, there probably isn't a form of pizza that hasn't been invented. Barbecued chicken, pineapple and ham, shrimp and Alfredo sauce, curried catfish, turkey and cranberry sauce . . . the toppings are endless, if sometimes weird.

Pesto is the important ingredient in this mile-high vegetable pizza. You can buy bottled pesto, which usually tastes quite good, but homemade pesto is very simple to prepare and nothing really beats its pungent freshness. *Yield: One 12-inch pizza*

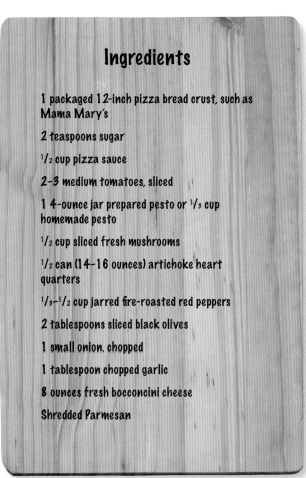

Ingredients

1 packaged 12-inch pizza bread crust, such as Mama Mary's

2 teaspoons sugar

1/2 cup pizza sauce

2–3 medium tomatoes, sliced

1 4-ounce jar prepared pesto or 1/3 cup homemade pesto

1/2 cup sliced fresh mushrooms

1/2 can (14–16 ounces) artichoke heart quarters

1/3–1/2 cup jarred fire-roasted red peppers

2 tablespoons sliced black olives

1 small onion, chopped

1 tablespoon chopped garlic

8 ounces fresh bocconcini cheese

Shredded Parmesan

Veggie Medley Pesto Pizza

- Place the pizza crust on a round pizza pan lightly coated with olive oil.

- Mix the sugar into the pizza sauce and spread a layer of sauce on the crust. Layer the tomato slices on top, followed by 2 tablespoons of pesto.

- Top with remaining vegetables interspersed with bocconcini balls. Dot with pesto and top with Parmesan.

- Bake at 450°F for 20–25 minutes, or until cheese is bubbling.

• • • • RECIPE VARIATION • • • •

White Vegetable and Clam Pesto Pizza: Sauté the mushrooms, onion, garlic, and 2 cups chopped clams in 2 tablespoons each olive oil and butter. Spread on a thin pizza crust with a little more olive oil to cover the crust. Top with spoonfuls of ricotta cheese and sprinkle with shredded mozzarella and fresh chopped basil. Bake at 400°F for 15 minutes.

Choose the Crust

- Most supermarkets carry pizza bread crusts in their bread or deli sections.

- Look for a heavier crust, as this pizza is heavy with ingredients.

- You can also use prepared pizza dough like Pillsbury.

- Avoid the Boboli bread crusts as they tend to be very high in salt and somewhat rubbery in texture.

Assemble the Pizza

- Use a soup spoon to dot the pesto over the tomato and other ingredients.

- Scatter the mushrooms, artichokes, red pepper strips, and olives over the tomatoes. Dot, but don't overload, the pizza with bocconcini balls.

- Finish by scattering the Parmesan over the pizza and top with the onion and garlic, so that they brown during baking.

- The finished pizza should be mounded high with ingredients.

PEA & MUSHROOM TORTELLINI
Stuffed tortellini packs this dish with an extra cheesy punch

Tortellini, that ring-shaped pasta stuffed with cheese, meat, or a combination thereof, has an enchanting origin. It seems that during a road trip, the infamous Lucrezia Borgia stopped at an inn in the little town of Castelfranco Emilia. Entranced by her beauty, the innkeeper peeped into her room through the keyhole. But in the dim candlelight, all he could see was her navel. Nonetheless, this vision was all he needed to spark

his imagination, and he created tortellini that night, in homage to Lucrezia's belly button.

Tortellini tossed with fresh mushrooms and peas in a light cheese sauce is a winning main course or side dish. *Yield: 4 servings*

Ingredients

1½ pounds cheese tortellini, fresh or frozen

2 tablespoons butter

2 tablespoons olive oil

2 shallots, finely chopped

6 ounces fresh mushrooms, sliced

1¼ cups fresh spring peas

1 teaspoon grated lemon zest

Salt and freshly ground pepper

1 tablespoon chopped fresh basil

Shredded Parmesan

Pea and Mushroom Tortellini

- Cook the tortellini about 2 minutes less than the package directions suggest. Drain, reserving ½ cup of the cooking water.

- Cook the shallots and mushrooms in butter and olive oil until soft, 2–3 minutes.

- Add the peas, tortellini, lemon zest, ½ teaspoon salt, ¼ teaspoon pepper, basil, and reserved pasta water. Cook over medium-low heat until the peas are tender, about 3 minutes.

- Season with salt and pepper to taste, top with shredded Parmesan, and serve in individual pasta bowls.

• • • • RECIPE VARIATION • • • •

Tuna Pasta with Tortellini and Peas: Combine 4 cups of cooked tortellini with 1 cup lightly cooked spring peas, ½ cup sliced cherry tomatoes, ⅓ cup sliced black olives, 1 6-ounce can albacore tuna (drained), and 1 cup quartered artichoke bottoms. Season with salt and pepper and toss with any dressing of your choice.

Shell the Peas

Choose the Tortellini

- Wash the pea pods thoroughly to remove any dirt and grit. You can also soak them in water for 15 minutes to soften them.

- Look at the pods, which have two seams: one indented, one ridged.

- Tear the stem backwards and pull it down toward the indented side, removing the string and essentially "unzipping" the pod.

- You'll want two bowls on hand—one for the peas and one for the discarded pods.

- Tortellini comes in a wide variety of flavors to suit different tastes and dishes.

- Three-cheese tortellini contains a blend of ricotta, Romano, and Parmesan cheeses.

- Spinach and cheese, sun-dried tomato, or herb chicken tortellini are some other good choices for this dish.

- The boiled tortellini should be just slightly underdone, as it will finish cooking in the skillet.

PASTA DISHES

97

BROCCOLI MUSHROOM ALFREDO
Fresh vegetables and spinach pasta lighten up rich Alfredo sauce

Fettuccine Alfredo was named for Alfredo di Lelio, a restaurateur who became a favorite of American tourists in Rome when, in 1914, he created a pasta dish with fresh Parmesan cheese and a triple dose of butter and prepared it at the table in, according to one witness, "a performance worthy of grand opera."

While the original Alfredo consisted simply of butter and

cheese, "Alfredo" has become a ubiquitous term that covers everything from a rich white sauce to additions of vegetables, chicken, and seafood. Crisp broccoli and tender mushrooms are just a few of the many vegetables you can use to make this delicious but calorie-laden dish a little more nutritious. *Yield: 4 servings*

Ingredients

1 pound spinach fettuccine

1 6-ounce package sliced white or brown mushrooms

1 small yellow onion, finely chopped

2 teaspoons chopped garlic

1 tablespoon olive oil

3 tablespoons butter, divided

2 tablespoons flour

2 cups half and half

6 ounces shredded or grated fresh Parmesan

1 teaspoon kosher salt

$1/4 - 1/3$ teaspoons freshly ground pepper

$1 1/2$ cups broccoli florets

1 tablespoon chopped fresh basil

Chopped fresh parsley

Broccoli Mushroom Alfredo

- Prepare the fettuccine according to package directions, adding a little oil to the boiling water to prevent the pasta from sticking and stirring often. Drain.

- In a large skillet, sauté the mushrooms, onion, and garlic in the oil and 1 tablespoon of butter until slightly brown.

- Make the Alfredo sauce (see technique).

- Add the broccoli, pasta, and basil to the skillet and toss with the sauce. Serve in bowls garnished with fresh parsley and a little Parmesan.

Spinach pasta is simply basic pasta dough (made with flour, eggs, water, and a little olive oil) to which cooked, drained, and chopped spinach has been added. You can buy fresh spinach pasta in the refrigerated areas of larger supermarkets and specialty stores. Dried spinach pasta can be found in the regular pasta aisle. Or it's quite easy to make your own.

• • • • RECIPE VARIATION • • • •

Fettuccine Alfredo alla Spinaci: Cook plain or spinach fettuccine to al dente firmness. Sauté only the garlic, omitting the onion and mushrooms. Toss the cooked pasta in the skillet with the Alfredo sauce and 1 cup of cooked chopped spinach in place of the broccoli. Serve garnished with chopped fresh basil and a dollop of ricotta cheese.

Floret the Broccoli

Make the Alfredo Sauce

- Always buy broccoli with deep green heads and lighter green stalks. Heads that are yellowing are not fresh.

- Cut the stalk off the head with a sharp knife, high enough so that large bouquets fall away as you cut.

- Take each bouquet and cut it in half.

- Gather the two halves and cut them into quarters. Repeat for bouquet, and remove from heat.

- Heat 2 tablespoons of butter in a 1-quart saucepan over medium-low heat until just melted.

- Whisk in the 2 tablespoons of flour until it forms a paste, or roux.

- Whisk in the half and half and continue whisking until the sauce begins to thicken. Do not leave it or it will scorch.

- When the sauce is just bubbling, blend in the Parmesan, salt, and pepper.

VEGETABLE NOODLE KUGEL
This traditional sweet Jewish dish gets a veggie makeover

A kugel is an Eastern European Jewish dish whose name roughly translates to "pudding." We would think of a kugel more as a casserole. It generally consists of noodles to which either sweet or savory ingredients are added, held together with beaten egg, bread crumbs, or matzo meal and cottage cheese and sour cream.

Sweet kugels are desserts, usually featuring a fruit with sugar and raisins. The best-known savory kugel is potato kugel, but you can make a kugel with all sorts of vegetables. Sweet or savory, kugels are easy to love. *Yield: 8 servings*

Ingredients

1 small onion, minced

1 8-ounce package sliced mushrooms

1 tablespoon butter

1 teaspoon chopped shallots

1 pound fresh spinach, washed and dried

1 cup grated carrots

1/3 cup chicken or vegetable broth

2 large eggs, lightly beaten

1 cup ricotta cheese

1/2 cup sour cream

1/4 cup plain yogurt

1/2 cup shredded cheddar

1 teaspoon paprika

1 tablespoon fresh parsley or 2 teaspoons dried parsley

1 teaspoon fresh chives or 1/2 teaspoon dried chives

1/4 teaspoon coarsely ground pepper

4 cups cooked egg noodles

Vegetable Noodle Kugel

- In a medium skillet, sauté the onion and mushrooms in melted butter until soft, 2–3 minutes. Add the shallots and brown quickly.

- Over medium-low heat, add the spinach, carrots, and broth and simmer.

- In a large bowl, combine the eggs, ricotta, sour cream, yogurt, cheddar, and seasonings. Mix in the vegetables and noodles.

- Pour the mixture into a lightly greased 9-inch baking dish and bake at 375°F until golden brown, about 45 minutes.

Potato kugel is a tradition in Eastern European Jewish cuisine. Moist on the inside, crisp on the outside, a potato kugel is like baked/mashed/fried potatoes all rolled into one. The classic potato kugel combines grated potatoes with a mixture of beaten eggs, chopped onions, oil, flour or matzoh meal, and salt and pepper. It's baked until golden brown and served with sour cream and pride.

• • • • RECIPE VARIATION • • • •

No-Noodle Vegetable Kugel: Cut 2 small zucchini, 2 carrots, 2 potatoes, and 1 small yellow onion into chunks and coarsely grate them in a food processor. Combine with 2 teaspoons chopped garlic, 1 tablespoon chopped parsley, 3 beaten eggs, ⅓ cup flour or matzoh meal, 4 tablespoons vegetable oil, and seasoned salt and pepper to taste. Bake as below.

Cook the Vegetables

- You can use any mushrooms for this dish, but white button, cremini, or small portobellos come conveniently pre-sliced.

- While they seem like a hybrid of garlic and onions, shallots are really a separate member of the onion family. Buy them firm, avoiding any with green shoots.

- If shallots are hard to find, you can substitute 1 teaspoon of chopped garlic.

- You want to cook the spinach lightly, just until wilted, and the carrots until slightly tender, about 5 minutes.

Bake the Kugel

- Because of their excellent heat distribution and retention, French clay baking dishes are always good to have on hand.

- An oval or rectangular clay baking dish makes a nice presentation at the table.

- A glass baking dish or quart casserole dish isn't quite as impressive but will do the job.

- Check the kugel about 30 minutes into baking to make sure it isn't getting too dry.

SPINACH LASAGNA

This delicious lasagna with water chestnuts can be made with or without meat

Lasagna is basically a layered noodle pie—sort of the Italian version of kugel. Although the word "lasagna" originally referred to a cooking pot, it came to describe both a type of flat sheet noodle and the dish made from those noodles.

Lasagna varies by region in Italy and beyond. Lasagna alla Bolognese is made with Parmigiano-Reggiano cheese and a combination of Bolognese and béchamel sauces. There are artichoke-spinach, spicy chipotle, and seafood lasagnas. The water chestnuts in this vegetarian lasagna give it a unique crunchy texture. *Yield: 10 servings*

Ingredients

- 1 1/2 pounds lasagna noodles
- 1 large onion, chopped
- 1 8-ounce package sliced fresh mushrooms
- 2 teaspoons chopped garlic
- 2 tablespoons olive oil
- 1 6-ounce can tomato paste
- 1 cup dry red wine
- 1 15-ounce can chicken or vegetable broth
- 1 16-ounce jar prepared marinara sauce
- 1 15-ounce can diced tomatoes
- 1 tablespoon chopped fresh basil or 1 teaspoon dried basil
- 1/2 teaspoon dried oregano
- 1 large or 2 small bay leaves
- 1/2 teaspoon seasoned salt
- 1/4–1/2 teaspoon coarsely ground pepper
- 1 tablespoon sugar
- 24 ounces ricotta cheese
- 2 medium eggs, beaten
- 2 pounds fresh spinach or 20 ounces frozen spinach, cooked
- 1 8-ounce can sliced water chestnuts
- 16 ounces shredded mozzarella cheese
- 1/2 cup grated Parmesan

Spinach Lasagna

- Cook the lasagna noodles according to package directions. Drain.

- In a large skillet, sauté the onion, mushrooms, and garlic in the oil.

- Add the tomato paste, wine, broth, marinara, diced tomatoes, seasonings, and sugar and simmer sauce 20 minutes. Remove the bay leaves.

- Mix ricotta with egg. Layer sauce, noodles, ricotta mixture, spinach, water chestnuts, and mozzarella, and then add more sauce. Top with the Parmesan and bake 40 minutes at 350°F.

While this recipe incorporates the trusty old-fashioned method of cooking the lasagna noodles first, you can also make a no-boil lasagna. Assemble it as directed, only with uncooked instead of cooked noodles. Cover tightly with aluminum foil and bake for 45 minutes. The steam created by the sauce and other ingredients cooks the noodles. After 45 minutes, remove the foil and continue baking another 15 minutes, or until the cheese is browned.

· · · · RECIPE VARIATION · · · ·

White Spinach Lasagna with Clams: Replace the marinara with a béchamel sauce (see "Gnocchi with Spinach Béchamel", next recipe) or just use 2 16-ounce jars of bottled Alfredo sauce. Sauté the mushrooms and onion and use them in the layers with the spinach, water chestnuts, cheeses, and 2 6-ounce cans of baby clams.

Make the Sauce

- Sauté the onion and mushrooms together until soft, adding the garlic last. If you like a buttery flavor, use 1 tablespoon butter and 1 tablespoon olive oil.

- Stir in the tomato paste, gradually adding the wine to thin it out.

- Prepared marinara sauce with mushroom, garlic, or herbs add even more flavor.

- If you prefer to substitute chopped fresh tomatoes for the canned, you may want to add extra liquid. The sauce should be smooth but not runny.

Assemble the Lasagna

- Spread a couple of ladlefuls of sauce in a thin, even layer on the bottom of a deep-dish pan large enough for two layers of lasagna.

- Make a layer of lasagna noodles on top of the sauce, crisscrossing if necessary to cover the bottom of the pan.

- Spoon ricotta cheese mixture across noodles in dollops an inch apart.

- Layer half the spinach and water chestnuts on top of the ricotta, followed by half the mozzarella and more sauce. Repeat with a light layer of Parmesan on top.

PASTA DISHES

GNOCCHI WITH SPINACH BÉCHAMEL

Potatoes and semolina flour form the basis for these bite-size Italian dumplings

Gnocchi is a potato pasta in Italy and a potato dumpling everywhere else. Gnocchi are softer and more absorbent than the flour-based pastas we're familiar with, and, as Diana Shaw observes in her excellent cookbook *Almost Vegetarian*, "The sensation of eating good gnocchi is unique; each one sops up sauce, then releases it as you chew."

This recipe covers fresh, chewy gnocchi with a blanket of creamy spinach béchamel sauce delicately flavored with nutmeg. *Yield: 4 servings*

Ingredients

3 large russet potatoes (about 1 1/2 pounds), baked and skinned

1 large egg, beaten

1 1/2 cups semolina flour

2 cups whole milk (low-fat or nonfat is okay, too)

1 tablespoon unsalted butter

2 tablespoons all-purpose flour

1 pound fresh or 10 ounces frozen spinach, cooked

1/4 teaspoon ground nutmeg

1/2 teaspoon salt

1/4 teaspoon freshly ground pepper

1/2 cup shredded Pecorino-Romano cheese

Gnocchi with Spinach Béchamel

- Mash the potatoes with the egg, adding the semolina flour 1/2 cup at a time.

- Make the gnocchi (see technique).

- Scald the milk in a heavy saucepan. Melt the butter in a separate saucepan and whisk in the all-purpose flour until it forms a roux.

- Whisk in the hot milk and bring to a gentle simmer, whisking until the sauce thickens. Add the spinach and stir in the seasonings and cheese. Serve at once in individual bowls over the gnocchi.

Gnocchi in Butter and Herb Sauce: Sauté 1 medium chopped onion in butter and olive oil until golden. Add 2 teaspoons chopped garlic and brown, 20 seconds. Add the gnocchi and toss with ½ stick melted butter, 1 tablespoon olive oil, ¼ cup fresh chopped parsley, 1 tablespoon fresh basil and salt and pepper to taste. Top with Parmesan.

Gnocchi with Chestnut Béchamel: Prepare the béchamel sauce, omitting the spinach and cheese and adding 1 cup of chopped preserved chestnuts, 1 cup chopped sautéed mushrooms, 1 tablespoon Madeira wine, and 2 teaspoons brown sugar. Toss with the gnocchi and serve garnished with chopped pecans.

Make the Gnocchi

- Mash the potatoes and egg with a potato masher or the back of a wooden spoon.

- Stop adding flour once the dough is smooth and firm enough to hold its shape.

- Dust your hands and a flat work surface with flour and

tear off ⅓ of the dough. Roll it into a rope about ½-inch thick and cut into 1-inch pieces.

- Add the gnocchi to salted boiling water and boil until they rise to the surface, about 2 minutes. Drain thoroughly in a colander.

Scald the Milk

- Scalding means heating milk slowly over medium-low heat to just below the boiling point.

- Place the milk in a heavy saucepan, preferably enamel.

- Turn the heat to medium-low and keep your eye on the pan, as milk comes to a boil quickly.

- When the level of the milk starts to rise, indicating that it's about to break into a boil, remove the pan from the heat.

PASTA DISHES

CREAMY VEGGIE PASTA SALAD

Buttermilk dressing replaces the standard vinaigrette in this healthy, hearty pasta salad

Pasta salad is a great way to get your vegetables and your pasta fix all at the same time. Keep the ratio of vegetables to pasta at two to one and you've got a satisfying salad, side dish, or entree that won't pack on either pounds or guilt.

Pasta salad with Italian dressing or vinaigrette is a familiar sight at salad bars across the land. But this pasta salad sings

a new note with a dressing of sour cream, mayonnaise, and buttermilk, enhanced with crumbled feta cheese. *Yield: 8–10 servings*

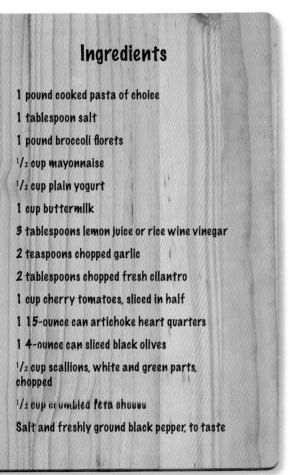

Ingredients

1 pound cooked pasta of choice

1 tablespoon salt

1 pound broccoli florets

$1/2$ cup mayonnaise

$1/2$ cup plain yogurt

1 cup buttermilk

3 tablespoons lemon juice or rice wine vinegar

2 teaspoons chopped garlic

2 tablespoons chopped fresh cilantro

1 cup cherry tomatoes, sliced in half

1 15-ounce can artichoke heart quarters

1 4-ounce can sliced black olives

$1/2$ cup scallions, white and green parts, chopped

$1/2$ cup crumbled feta cheese

Salt and freshly ground black pepper, to taste

Creamy Veggie Pasta Salad

- Cook the pasta in boiling salted water to al dente firmness. Rinse with cold water and drain.

- Microwave the broccoli with ¼ cup water 4–5 minutes.

- In a small mixing bowl, whisk the mayonnaise,

yogurt, buttermilk, lemon juice, garlic, and cilantro until smooth.

- In a large salad bowl, toss the cooled pasta with the vegetables and feta and enough dressing to coat but not overwhelm. Add salt and pepper to taste.

Curried Pasta Salad with Crabmeat and Peas: In a large salad bowl, combine 3 cups cooked pasta with 1 cup cooked peas, 1 cup chopped crabmeat, 1 teaspoon curry powder, 2 teaspoons lemon juice, ½ cup plain yogurt, ⅓ cup mayonnaise, 1 teaspoon tarragon, and salt and lemon pepper to taste. Toss well.

Cordon Bleu Pasta Salad: To the Creamy Veggie Pasta Salad, add ½ cup cubed cooked chicken, ½ cup cubed ham, and 1 cup cubed Swiss cheese. Serve on beds of mixed greens.

Select the Pasta

Make the Dressing

- There are many bite-size pastas that work well in this dish.

- Pasta is often named for its shape. Farfalle, or "bowtie" pasta, is Italian for "butterflies." The twisted fusilli means "corkscrew." Pointed tubular penne translates as "quills."

- Other smaller pastas include torchietti ("little torches"), and ziti, which resemble thin little hoses.

- There are also the stuffed pastas like mezzalune ("half moons") or tortellini ("little hats").

- Contrary to its name, buttermilk is not made with butter and is very low in fat.

- You can substitute nonfat yogurt for the sour cream without losing any flavor.

- If you like, substitute 1 tablespoon each chopped

fresh chives and parsley for the cilantro.

- You can either whisk all the ingredients in a bowl for 1 minute, shake them in a jar for the same amount of time, or put them in a blender and blend until smooth.

VEGETABLE FRIED RICE
This veggie-loaded Asian favorite is a one-bowl meal

Fried rice can—and should—be so much more than what we've been conditioned to expect from American Chinese restaurants. You know, that stuff with the frozen peas and carrots and little bits of egg and meat. First of all, it should never be really fried; instead, cooked rice should be added to a little oil and lightly sautéed until heated through. And second, you can load fried rice with so many fresh vegetables

that it becomes a meal in itself: I make fried rice with everything from chopped zucchini, fresh mushrooms, fresh bean sprouts, celery, carrots, onions, and water chestnuts to scallops, clams, shrimp, crab, lobster . . . the sky's the limit. *Yield: 6 servings*

Ingredients

2 large stalks celery, chopped

1 medium green bell pepper, chopped

1 small to medium zucchini, chopped

6 ounces sliced fresh mushrooms

4 tablespoons oil (for stir-frying) or as needed, divided

1 teaspoon chopped garlic

2 large eggs, lightly beaten

4 cups cold cooked rice

1 teaspoon seasoned salt

1/2 teaspoon coarsely ground pepper

1 8-ounce can sliced water chestnuts

1 cup canned bean sprouts

4 scallions, white and green parts, chopped

Soy sauce

Vegetable Fried Rice

- Fry the celery, green pepper, zucchini, and mushrooms in 2 tablespoons oil in a wok or large frying pan until crisp-tender, about 5 minutes.

- Add the garlic and brown for 30 seconds. Push all the vegetables to the sides of the wok.

- Scramble the eggs in the center of the wok and push aside with the vegetables.

- Add the remaining oil and stir-fry the rice. Mix in the vegetables and egg and stir in the salt, pepper, water chestnuts, bean sprouts, and scallions. Sprinkle with soy sauce to taste.

···· GREEN ● LIGHT ····

While fried rice is a great way to use leftover rice, another way to make it is to scramble the eggs and set them aside. Sauté the onion, garlic, zucchini, green pepper, and celery; add a little more oil and quickly brown 1 cup of uncooked rice. Then add 2 cups of chicken broth and cook the rice until the liquid is absorbed. Finally, fluff the rice and add the rest of the vegetables and the scrambled egg.

···· RECIPE VARIATION ····

Pineapple Fried Rice: To the Vegetable Fried Rice, add 1 chopped, sautéed red or green chile, 3 tablespoons chicken broth, 2 teaspoons red curry powder, 2 teaspoons brown sugar, ½ cup roasted, unsalted cashews, and 1 cup pineapple tidbits. Serve garnished with fresh cilantro.

Chop the Celery, Pepper, and Zucchini

- These tougher vegetables should be chopped into pieces small enough to fry quickly.

- With a sharp knife, cut the tips and thick ends off the celery and remove any leaves. Cut the stalks in half crosswise, and then into lengthwise strips. Dice.

- Slice the top off the green pepper and run the knife around the inside of the pepper, removing the membrane and seeds. Cut the pepper in half, and the halves into strips. Dice.

- Cut the zucchini as you did the celery, making julienne-type strips and dicing them.

Fry the Rice

- Long-grain rice is best for this dish.

- The cooked rice should be firm but not sticky. Day-old rice works well.

- Fry the rice in the hot oil until it browns, breaking it up with chopsticks or a wooden spoon.

- A large wok affords room for the other ingredients to be moved up and along the sides of the utensil while the rice is frying.

RICE & GRAIN DISHES

SPANISH RICE WITH GREEN BEANS
Green beans are a nice surprise in traditional Spanish rice

One of the more common cooking questions is what's the difference between Spanish rice and Mexican rice? Well, although there are numerous variations of both, Spanish rice is made with tomatoes or tomato paste and may use seasonings like oregano and basil, while Mexican rice is usually made with tomatoes, saffron, chili powder, and cilantro.

This Spanish rice has a hint of Mexico with the green chiles, but the addition of fresh cooked green beans and bacon gives it its own unique identity. *Yield: 4 servings*

Ingredients

4 slices thick-cut bacon

1 small sweet onion, chopped

1 small red bell pepper, chopped

1 teaspoon chopped garlic

1 1/2 cups uncooked white rice

1 15-ounce can diced tomatoes

3 cups chicken broth

1 small can diced mild green chiles

1/2 pound cooked fresh green beans

1/2 teaspoon dried oregano

1/2 teaspoon dried basil

1/2 teaspoon seasoned salt

1/4 teaspoon coarsely ground pepper

8–10 drops Tabasco

Spanish Rice with Green Beans

- In a large skillet, cook the bacon until crisp. Drain and crumble.

- Brown the onion, red pepper, and garlic in the bacon drippings.

- Add the uncooked rice and stir until golden brown, adding a little olive oil if the pan is too dry.

- Add the tomatoes, broth, chiles, green beans, seasonings, and Tabasco. Stir to blend, then cover and simmer on low heat for about 20 minutes, until rice is tender. Top with crumbled bacon.

To remove starch from the uncooked rice so it won't stick, place it in a fine-mesh strainer and rinse under cold running water for approximately 1½ minutes. Vigorously shake the rice to remove any excess water. This step ensures that the cooked rice will be dry and fluffy.

· · · · RECIPE VARIATION · · · ·

Mexican Rice: Omit the oregano and basil and substitute 1 tablespoon chili powder, 1 teaspoon turmeric, and ½ cup chopped fresh cilantro. Since saffron is somewhat difficult to obtain and can be expensive, it's optional, but if you can find and afford it, use a little for special flavor. If you like a spicier rice, chop and sauté 2 medium jalapeño peppers. Serve with lime wedges.

Cook the Beans

Try Brown Rice

- Wash the green beans and trim the ends, or buy a bag of already trimmed beans.

- If the beans are more than 3 inches long, snap them in half.

- Cover the beans with water and bring to a boil, blanching them for 4 minutes.

- Drain the beans in a colander and pour cold water over them to stop the cooking. When added to the rice, they should be bright green and crisp.

- Brown rice is white rice that has not had its brown bran covering removed, making it a whole grain.

- Brown rice has three times the fiber of white rice and many more nutrients.

- If using brown rice, brown it in the butter as you

would the white rice, add all the ingredients as listed, and simmer 30 minutes. Remove it from the heat and let the rice sit in the pot another ten minutes.

- The cooked rice should be slightly chewy, not mushy.

RICE & GRAIN DISHES

RISOTTO WITH SUMMER SQUASH

This creamy Italian rice dish is the perfect way to get your vegetables

While pasta is the lifeblood of southern Italy, rice is the pasta of the north. That's where risotto originated. You've probably heard of risotto Milanese, which came from Lombardy's Milan, seat of classic risotto. The region's ideal conditions for growing rice produce several varieties, including ordinario, semifino, fino, and superfino. The last is what you want for risotto, and Arborio rice is among the best.

Risotto can be mixed with meat or fresh vegetables to create a creamy, cheesy dish that sends your taste buds into orbit. *Yield: 4–6 servings*

Ingredients

2 medium summer squash, diced

1 tablespoon olive oil

1 small onion, chopped

2 medium fresh tomatoes, diced

1 teaspoon chopped garlic

1 tablespoon fresh parsley

1 tablespoon chopped fresh basil or ¹/₂ teaspoon dried basil

¹/₄ teaspoon dried oregano

¹/₄ teaspoon coarsely ground pepper

¹/₂ teaspoon salt

2 tablespoons white wine

1 cup Arborio rice

3 cups canned chicken or vegetable broth, warmed

1 tablespoon yogurt cheese or cream

Grated Parmesan or Romano cheese

Risotto with Summer Squash

- In a large skillet over medium-high heat, sauté the squash in the oil until tender-crisp, 4–5 minutes. Add the onion and cook until golden brown, 1–2 minutes.

- Stir in the tomatoes with their juice and add the seasonings and wine.

- Add the rice and stir, about 3 minutes. Add the hot broth in batches, stirring each time until it's been absorbed and the rice is plump.

- Add the yogurt cheese or cream and stir well to blend. Top with grated cheese.

GREEN ● LIGHT

Risotto can range from very creamy to almost crunchy, and you can prepare it to your taste by slowly cooking it and periodically adding small amounts of liquid, tasting until you've got the texture you prefer.

• • • • RECIPE VARIATION • • • •

Risotto Milanese: Omit tomatoes, squash, and garlic. Brown 2 chopped medium onions and 1 chopped fennel bulb in 3 tablespoons olive oil until golden. Add 3 tablespoons more olive oil and stir in rice and ½ cup wine. Reduce liquid by ¾ and slowly ladle in 4 cups of broth. When rice is creamy, add yogurt cheese, and seasonings. Top with grated Parmesan.

Make the Risotto

- Slow and steady cooking is the key to risotto.

- Arborio rice is generally used because its short, plump kernels are high in starch and able to absorb quite a bit of liquid without becoming mushy.

- The rice is almost done when the kernels are still separate but starting to bind and the broth pools on the surface.

- The risotto is done when all the liquid has been absorbed and the mixture looks like creamy rice pudding.

Make the Yogurt Cheese

- Yogurt cheese is an easy and tasty nonfat substitute for cream or cream cheese.

- Line a strainer or fine colander with a coffee filter and prop it up so that it will drain into a bowl.

- Pour 1 cup of nonfat yogurt into the filter and allow it to drain in the refrigerator for 6 hours or overnight.

- Scoop the cheese out of the filter. The yogurt cheese will keep in the refrigerator for up to 3 days.

113

RICE & GRAIN DISHES

TOMATO CARROT RICE PILAF

Here's a vegetable pilaf that's bursting with flavor

Pilaf or pilau, pilav or pulao, depending on the country it comes from, is a traditional rice dish popular in Central Asia and the Middle East. India, Armenia, Iran, Turkey, Saudi Arabia, Afghanistan, and Uzbekistan all have a version of pilaf, made with or without meat. In Italy, busy chefs often use the pilaf method in precooking to cut down on prep time for risotto.

In a pilaf, the rice grains stay separate, resulting in rice that's fluffy and loose. This tomato carrot pilaf combines rice and orzo pasta, somewhat like Rice-A-Roni. Serve it as a side dish with meat or chicken, or all by itself as a light entree. *Yield: 4 servings*

Ingredients

- 1 tablespoon butter
- 1 tablespoon olive oil
- 1/2 cup uncooked long-grain rice
- 1/2 cup uncooked orzo pasta
- 1 teaspoon chopped garlic
- 1 small onion, chopped
- 1 cup grated carrots
- 1 celery stalk with leaves, finely chopped
- 2 fresh tomatoes, chopped, with juice, or 1 15-ounce can diced tomatoes
- 2 cups chicken broth
- 2 tablespoon fresh chopped parsley
- 1/2-1 teaspoon seasoned salt
- 1/4 teaspoon coarsely ground pepper
- 1/3 cup toasted pecans

Tomato Carrot Rice Pilaf

- Melt butter and oil in a large skillet over medium heat.

- Sauté rice, orzo, garlic, onion, carrots, and celery, stirring until rice is lightly browned.

- Add the tomatoes, chicken broth, parsley, salt, and pepper. Bring to a boil, then reduce heat to low, cover skillet, and allow to simmer for 15 minutes.

- Remove from heat and let stand 10 minutes. Just before serving, add the toasted pecans.

As when making risotto, rinse the rice under running water before cooking to remove excess starch. Always use raw long-grain rice, which has the best absorptive capacity for this dish. When adding the rice to the skillet, coat each grain with some of the oil in the pan. This key step keeps each grain separate.

···· RECIPE VARIATION ····

Pilaf-stuffed Acorn Squash: Remove the pulp from 4 baked acorn squash halves, leaving a little in the shells, and mash with butter, 1 teaspoon fennel seeds, and 1 teaspoon cumin seeds. In a large bowl, combine the squash pulp with the pilaf and fill the squash shells with the mixture. Add salt and pepper to taste and top with toasted pecans.

Using Orzo

Toast the Pecans

- Orzo is a pasta shaped like grains of rice. It's often referred to as "Italian rice," although its name actually means "barley."

- If you're familiar with Rice-A-Roni, which is a combination of rice and vermicelli pasta, you have the basic idea of this pilaf.

- Although pastas have decidedly different cooking times than rice, in a pilaf, the orzo and rice are cooked together.

- Orzo adds nice, chewy body to rice, resulting in a hearty, filling dish.

- Make sure you buy coarsely chopped pecans for this dish, not finely chopped or pecan chips.

- Heat a nonstick pan over high heat and then immediately turn the heat down to medium. This process extracts enough oil from the nuts to keep them from sticking or scorching.

- Stir the nuts frequently, or toss them around in the skillet.

- As soon as you sniff the toastiness, get the pan off the heat. Otherwise nuts can go from finished to burned very quickly.

RICE & GRAIN DISHES

SHIITAKE & WILD RICE CASSEROLE
Smoky, meaty shiitake mushrooms star in this hearty casserole

Technically, wild rice is not a rice but a grass, and it comes from a reed-like aquatic plant. It is quite expensive because it's difficult to cultivate. Fortunately, however, wild rice has such a strong flavor that you can combine it half-and-half with less expensive white or brown rice, which is the preferred method of cooking it.

Cooked wild rice is rich, nutty, and slightly smoky to the taste, with a delightfully toothsome texture, making it a perfect partner for chewy, smoky shiitake mushrooms. *Yield: 6 servings*

Ingredients

10 ounces fresh shiitake mushrooms, sliced, or 2 ounces dried

$1/2$ cup (1 stick) butter

$1/4$ cup flour

2 15-ounce cans chicken or vegetable broth

$1^1/2$ cups light cream

1 cup raw wild rice

1 cup long grain rice

1 small can sliced olives

1 small can pimientos

4 scallions, white and green parts, chopped

$1/4$ cup slivered blanched almonds

2 tablespoons chopped fresh parsley

1 tablespoon chopped fresh chives

1 teaspoon celery salt

$1/4$ teaspoon lemon pepper

Shiitake and Wild Rice Casserole

- Cook the mushrooms in the butter until tender but not brown.

- Stir in flour and chicken broth gradually until mixture is smooth.

- Add the cream and stir until thick. Remove from heat.

- Add the two rices, olives, pimientos, scallions, almonds, and seasonings. Turn into a lightly buttered casserole dish and bake at 350°F, uncovered, for 35–45 minutes.

Wild rice comes in three grades. Giant or long-grain is the top quality and highest priced. Fancy or medium-grain is not as long as the giant. Select or short-grain is the least expensive grade and the best choice for casseroles and combinations with other types of rice.

Wild Rice Stuffing: Before baking the casserole, add ½ cup chopped water chestnuts; 1 teaspoon dried sage; 2 tablespoons butter; and 2 cups cubed toasted whole grain bread. Substitute ½ cup chopped pecans for the almonds. Add 2 beaten eggs and mix well. Bake at 375°F for 30 minutes, or until browned.

Cook the Wild Rice

- Because of its tougher texture, more liquid is needed to cook wild rice than to cook brown or white rice.

- Wash the rice until it's clean. Drain it, put it in a sauce-pan, and pour in 3 cups boiling water.

- Let the rice stand for 20 minutes and remove. Transfer to the casserole.

- When fully cooked, the wild rice grains should pop open.

About Shiitakes

- Unlike many other mushrooms, shiitakes absorb rather than release liquid when cooked. As a result, when sautéed, they become plump and chewy.

- Store fresh shiitakes in a paper bag. In a plastic bag, they'll become slimy and unusable.

- If you buy dried shiitakes, figure 2 ounces for 10 ounces fresh. Reconstitute them by rinsing in cold water and soaking in hot water for 20 minutes.

- The soaking liquid makes a flavorful addition to sauces and casseroles.

TABBOULEH

This Middle Eastern vegetable and grain dish is tangy and refreshing

Tabbouleh is a Levantine Arab dish made of bulgur, cracked wheat kernels that have been steamed and dried, to which lemon juice, olive oil, fresh mint, tomato, and scallions are added. Generally served as a salad or appetizer, tabbouleh is traditionally eaten with a lettuce or grape leaf in the Middle East, although the preferred method of consumption here is

as a dip for pita bread. This recipe adds carrots and cucumber to basic tabbouleh, but such a simple dish is open to any combination of raw vegetables. *Yield: 6 servings*

Ingredients

1 cup chopped flat-leaf parsley, stems discarded

2 tablespoons chopped fresh mint

1 small onion, finely chopped

4 scallions, chopped

1 1/4 cups water

1/2 cup bulgur, medium grind

4 tablespoons extra-virgin olive oil

6 tablespoons lemon juice

1 teaspoon minced garlic

1 teaspoon seasoned salt

1/2 teaspoon freshly ground black pepper

8 medium tomatoes, diced

1 medium cucumber, peeled and diced

3/4 cup grated carrots

1 16-ounce jar grape leaves

Tabbouleh

- The parsley, mint, onion, and scallion should be very finely chopped.

- Bring water to a boil, pour in bulgur, stir, cover, and turn off heat.

- Let stand 20 to 25 minutes or until most of the liquid is absorbed and bulgur is fluffy and tender. Pour off any remaining liquid.

- In a small mixing bowl, whisk together the olive oil, lemon juice, garlic, salt, and pepper. Toss the dressing with the vegetables, parsley, mint, onion, scallion and bulgur and serve on beds of grape leaves.

If you want to be a tabbouleh purist, flat-leaf parsley is important. In the words of famed Lebanese chef Kamal Mouzawak, there are two "unchangeable rules" of tabbouleh. "Only flat-leaf parsley is used, and only bulgur wheat, no other cereal. Tabbouleh and couscous do not go together—they are complete strangers."

• • • • RECIPE VARIATION • • • •

Tabbouleh 1-2-3-4: Here are four variations on the tabbouleh theme. 1. Add diced raw zucchini, quartered artichoke hearts or bottoms, or fresh baby spinach. 2. Add rinsed and drained canned chickpeas and lentils. 3. Serve tabbouleh in pita pockets with diced grilled chicken breast or lamb. 4. Add ¼ cup lime juice, 2 cups fresh sorrel leaves, and 1 diced avocado.

About Bulgur

- Bulgur is wheat that has been parboiled, dried, and cracked.

- Bulgur comes in a variety of grinds, from fine to extra coarse. Medium grind is best for tabbouleh.

- Bulgur cooks very quickly and does not require lengthy periods of vigorous boiling like other grain products.

- The cooked bulgur should be tender and chewy.

Prepare the Grape Leaves

- Grape leaves are an edible Mediterranean staple used in a variety of dishes.

- You can find grape leaves in the international sections of most larger supermarkets.

- When using grape leaves from a jar, make sure to wash off the brine, which can leave a bitter taste.

- If you can procure fresh grape leaves, rinse them well under cold water, remove the stems without cutting into the leaf, and blanch by placing them in a pan of boiling water for 3–5 minutes.

MEXICAN SCALLOPED POTATOES

Green chiles and salsa con queso add spicy flair to scalloped potatoes

Scalloped potatoes have nothing to do with scallops, as in seafood. Scalloping, or escalloping, is the process of layering thin slices of potatoes or other vegetables in a casserole and baking them in a cream sauce. Scalloped potatoes are thought to have originated in England, as the Old English word "collops" meant to slice meat thinly.

What makes scalloped potatoes so delicious is the way they absorb the sauce as they bake, becoming tender on the inside as they crisp on the outside. They are the perfect accompaniment to any meat, poultry, or fish. *Yield: 6–8 servings*

Ingredients

2 tablespoons butter or margarine

1 medium onion, finely chopped

1 red bell pepper, finely chopped

2 tablespoons flour

2 cups whole milk

1 15.5-ounce jar salsa con queso

1 8-ounce package shredded sharp cheddar, divided

2 teaspoons paprika

1 teaspoon seasoned salt

$1/4$ teaspoon coarsely ground pepper

6–8 drops Tabasco or hot sauce

5 large potatoes

1 small can diced mild green chiles

Mexican Scalloped Potatoes

- Melt butter in a medium saucepan over medium-high heat. Sauté onion and red pepper until soft. Add flour and stir.

- Slowly whisk in the milk. Add 1 cup of the salsa con queso, ½ cup of cheese, the seasonings, and the Tabasco, stirring until the sauce is smooth.

- Layer half the potatoes, chiles, and sauce in a lightly buttered 9 x 13-inch baking dish or shallow casserole. Repeat.

- Top with remaining cheese and bake uncovered at 350°F for 45–55 minutes.

···················· RED ● LIGHT ····················

Use a shallow casserole dish. If the dish is too deep and the potatoes are stacked too high, you'll end up with overcooked potatoes on top and underdone potatoes inside. A 13 x 9 x 2-inch baking dish or a French clay baking dish works very well.

···· ● ● ● ● **RECIPE VARIATION** ● ● ● ● ····

Scalloped Potatoes Lorraine: Omit the cheddar, queso, red peppers, and chiles. Add to the white sauce 1 cup each grated Swiss and Gruyère cheese, 2 teaspoons ground mustard, and salt and pepper. Sprinkle crumbled cooked bacon, fresh chopped parsley, and thin slices of onion on top of each layer of potatoes and sauce. Top with grated Parmesan and bake.

Prepare the Potatoes

- Because of their low starch content, red skinned or white round potatoes are best for scalloped dishes.

- Wash and pat dry the potatoes. It's not necessary to peel them.

- Scallop potatoes by slicing them width-wise to create very thin circles, about ¼-inch thick.

- You can also slice the potatoes in a food processor using the 6 millimeter or 8 millimeter blade.

Make the Sauce

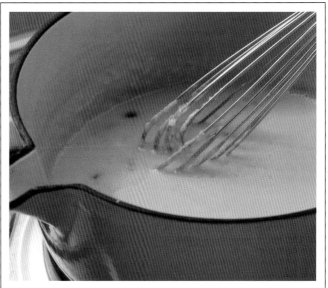

- Salsa con queso, similar to cheese fondue, consists of a blend of cheeses, cream, and chile peppers melted into a smooth, creamy sauce.

- Combining ready-made salsa con queso with milk and cheese gives this sauce richer flavor and texture.

- After cooking the onion and pepper, you may want to add a little more butter or margarine before stirring in the flour.

- If the sauce is too thick after adding the cheese, add more milk until it's the right consistency.

BROCCOLI MASHED POTATO BAKE
This is a combination green vegetable and potato dish

I once knew a guy who just couldn't seem to get mashed potatoes right. They were always watery and tasteless. Needless to say, he had trouble getting people to come to dinner.

Mashed potatoes are like people. They can be plain or alluring, boring or exciting. They can make you never want to see them again, or they can become one of your favorite friends. This recipe is one you'll want to visit on a regular basis. It's

creamy and garlicky, and it packs broccoli, potatoes, and cheese into a one-two punch of flavor and nutrition. *Yield: 6 servings*

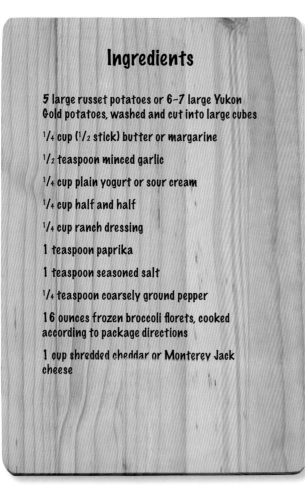

Ingredients

5 large russet potatoes or 6–7 large Yukon Gold potatoes, washed and cut into large cubes

¼ cup (½ stick) butter or margarine

½ teaspoon minced garlic

¼ cup plain yogurt or sour cream

¼ cup half and half

¼ cup ranch dressing

1 teaspoon paprika

1 teaspoon seasoned salt

¼ teaspoon coarsely ground pepper

16 ounces frozen broccoli florets, cooked according to package directions

1 cup shredded cheddar or Monterey Jack cheese

Broccoli Mashed Potato Bake

- Cover the potatoes with water in a medium saucepan. Add ½ teaspoon salt and bring to a boil.

- Reduce heat to low and simmer 5–10 minutes. Drain in a colander.

- In a large mixing bowl, whip potatoes with the butter, garlic, yogurt, half and half, dressing, and seasonings.

- Stir in the broccoli and cheese and transfer to a casserole dish. Bake at 350°F for 15 minutes. Then bake 10 minutes more at 450°F until golden brown.

Extra moisture can wreak havoc with mashed potatoes, so get the cooked potatoes as dry as possible before mashing them. Drain them completely. Then return them to the pot over low heat, gently stirring, to dry any residual moisture before mashing or ricing.

· · · · RECIPE VARIATION · · · ·

Broccoli Potato Breakfast Cakes: Make the mashed potatoes as directed, adding just enough yogurt or sour cream, half and half, and ranch dressing, to keep them firm and make into patties. Brush the patties with beaten egg, dip them in bread crumbs, and fry them in a skillet in 1 inch of hot oil until golden brown, 1–2 minutes per side. Drain on paper towels.

Make the Potatoes

- The boiled potatoes should be tender but not crumbly, so check them after 5 minutes by piercing them with a fork.

- Add the butter to the hot potatoes first and mash with a potato masher.

- Add the cream, yogurt, dressing, and seasonings and beat with a strong spoon until smooth.

- For really fluffy potatoes, try an electric mixer, which whips air into the potatoes, giving them more volume. Just make sure you add the broccoli and cheese after mixing!

Bake the Dish

- A lightly greased 2-quart casserole dish or 9 x 13 x 2-inch glass or clay baking dish works well for this dish.

- You can also make the dish a day ahead and refrigerate overnight.

- To ensure a golden brown crust, bake at 350°F for 15 minutes. Then bake 10 minutes more at 450°F.

- The finished dish should be slightly crisp on the outside and fluffy but not dry on the inside.

SHERRIED VEGETABLE POTATO SKINS
There's a bit of a stroganoff twist to these scrumptious stuffed skins

Everybody loves a good old-fashioned potato skin loaded with cheddar, bacon, and sour cream. But most people don't know how versatile skins can be. You can fill them with everything from cheese and vegetables to seafood, chicken, turkey, steak, pork, and hot dogs. How about pepperoni pizza skins or Philly cheesesteak skins? Ever tried Greek falafel skins? Or breakfast skins with scrambled eggs and hash? Yes, potato skins definitely spark a cook's creativity.

These flavorful, filling vegetable-stuffed skins can do triple duty as appetizers, side dishes, or entrees. *Yield: 4 servings*

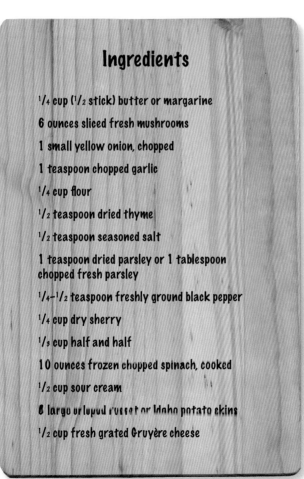

Ingredients

1/4 cup (1/2 stick) butter or margarine

6 ounces sliced fresh mushrooms

1 small yellow onion, chopped

1 teaspoon chopped garlic

1/4 cup flour

1/2 teaspoon dried thyme

1/2 teaspoon seasoned salt

1 teaspoon dried parsley or 1 tablespoon chopped fresh parsley

1/4–1/2 teaspoon freshly ground black pepper

1/4 cup dry sherry

1/3 cup half and half

10 ounces frozen chopped spinach, cooked

1/2 cup sour cream

8 large or loped russet or Idaho potato skins

1/2 cup fresh grated Gruyère cheese

Sherried Vegetable Potato Skins

- In a large skillet, melt the butter and sauté the mushrooms and onion until soft. Add the garlic and brown.

- Blend in the flour and seasonings. Turn heat down to very low and stir in the sherry and half and half.

- When thickened, remove the sauce from the heat and stir in the spinach and sour cream.

- Mound the filling high into the potato skins. Top with the Gruyère and broil about five minutes until the cheese begins to brown.

GREEN LIGHT

Use russet or Idaho potatoes because they are large enough and strong enough to hold the fillings. Their skins are thick and flavorful and become even better when crisped or fried. Look for heavy, full-size potatoes with smooth, firm surfaces and no green skins. If the potatoes have begun to sprout, check them for firmness. If they're still reasonably fresh, remove the sprouts with a knife or apple corer.

RECIPE VARIATION

Cauliflower and Broccoli Skins with Swiss Cheese: Replace spinach and mushrooms with 1½ cups steamed broccoli and cauliflower and 1 diced large tomato. Cook 3 slices of chopped bacon with onions, omitting butter. Make sauce with grated Swiss cheese. Add vegetables and seasonings and fill the skins, topping with bread crumbs and grated Parmesan.

Prepare the Potato Skins

- Scrub the potatoes under cold water and pat dry. Rub the skin with margarine or butter.

- Prick the potatoes several times with a fork.

- Bake at 400°F for 45 minutes to 1 hour or more, depending on the size of the spud. If the potatoes feel soft when gently squeezed with a pot holder, they're done.

- When cool, slice the potatoes through the center with a serrated knife and scoop out the innards, leaving a little behind so that the skins don't tear.

Crisp the Skins

- Place the skins on a baking sheet and coat them with melted butter.

- Bake the skins at 400°F for 10 minutes, or broil until crispy. If broiling, watch them closely—you don't want them to burn.

- For extra crispy skins, broil them until they start to sizzle and brown.

- For lightly crisped skins, bake or broil them until they're hot and the edges just begin to crisp.

COCONUTTY SWEET POTATOES
These extra-sweet potatoes could double as a dessert

We think of sweet potatoes as richer, more caloric cousins of the humble potato. But did you know that sweet potatoes actually contain less sugar and starch than regular potatoes and are recommended for diabetic diets? Of course, once you start adding the cream and syrup and butter—and oh yes, marshmallows for the kiddies—well, you've sort of negated the nutritive pluses of sweet potatoes. But dang,

they just taste so good that way!

For coconutty sweet potatoes, you'll need coconut milk, easily found in the Asian or Mexican food sections of the supermarket. *Yield: 6–8 servings*

Ingredients

3 large sweet potatoes

2 tablespoons butter

1 cup canned coconut milk

1/4 cup maple syrup

2 tablespoons brown sugar

1 tablespoon minced fresh ginger

1/4 teaspoon cinnamon

1/4 teaspoon cloves

1/4 teaspoon nutmeg

1/2 teaspoon salt

Toasted coconut and toasted pecans

Coconutty Sweet Potatoes

- Wash and pat dry the sweet potatoes, and pierce several times with a fork.

- Microwave on high 10–15 minutes or bake at 425°F for 1 hour, or until tender all the way to the center. When cool, peel off and discard skins.

- Transfer to a large bowl and mash with the butter. Add the coconut milk, maple syrup, brown sugar, ginger, spices, and salt and beat until fluffy.

- Top with toasted coconut and pecans.

• • • • RECIPE VARIATIONS • • • •

Coconutty Sweet Potato Pancakes: Combine 1 cup white flour, 1 cup whole wheat flour, 1 tablespoon baking powder, and ⅓ teaspoon salt. In another bowl, whisk 3 eggs, 1½ cups milk, ½ cup melted butter, ¼ cup honey, and ½ cup coconutty sweet potatoes. Beat well and thoroughly fold the wet ingredients into the dry. Drop batter by spoonfuls onto a lightly greased skillet and fry until golden brown on each side.

Coconutty Sweet Potato Pudding: Whisk together ⅓ cup dry nonfat milk powder, 1 cup skim milk, and 1 large beaten egg. Beat in 1½ cups of coconutty sweet potatoes. Pour into a lightly greased baking dish and bake at 375°F until springy, about 1 hour. Serve warm or cooled, topped with ice cream or whipped cream.

Choose the Sweet Potatoes

- When buying sweet potatoes, look for ones that are firm, without cracks, bruises, wrinkles, or soft spots.

- Store sweet potatoes loose, not in a bag, in a cool, dry, well-ventilated place away from heat sources.

- Sweet potatoes with light yellow skins are not particularly sweet and have a crumbly texture when cooked.

- For this dish, choose the darker-skinned variety, which have bright orange, sweet flesh and a moist texture.

Toast the Coconut

- You can use any type of dried coconut—shredded, flakes, chips, or shavings— as well as raw shredded coconut.

- Preheat the oven to 350°F and arrange the coconut in a single layer on a cookie sheet.

- Bake 10–15 minutes, or until golden brown, stirring and checking frequently to prevent burning.

- Remove from the oven and cool before using.

127

ROASTED TERIYAKI SWEET POTATOES
Teriyaki sauce gives sweet potatoes fabulous flavor

Sweet potatoes are popular in Asian cooking, particularly in Japanese and Thai recipes. If you've ever ordered vegetable tempura in a Japanese restaurant, you know how good slices of sweet potato, fried in fluffy tempura batter and served with a light, sweet soy or teriyaki-based sauce can be. And sweet potatoes add texture and flavor to Thai curries.

These teriyaki sweet potatoes are roasted in the oven until crisp on the outside and tender on the inside, with a delicious teriyaki glaze that aids in the browning. *Yield: 6 servings*

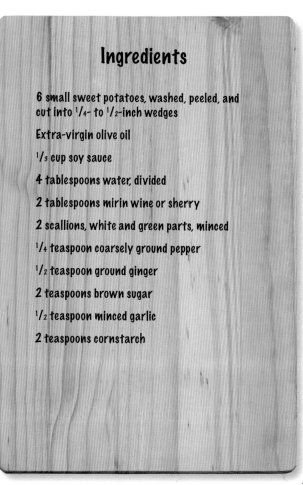

Ingredients

6 small sweet potatoes, washed, peeled, and cut into $1/4$- to $1/2$-inch wedges

Extra-virgin olive oil

$1/3$ cup soy sauce

4 tablespoons water, divided

2 tablespoons mirin wine or sherry

2 scallions, white and green parts, minced

$1/4$ teaspoon coarsely ground pepper

$1/2$ teaspoon ground ginger

2 teaspoons brown sugar

$1/2$ teaspoon minced garlic

2 teaspoons cornstarch

Roasted Teriyaki Sweet Potatoes

- Place the potato wedges in a large bowl and drizzle olive oil over them, tossing to coat.

- In a small saucepan, whisk together the rest of the ingredients, except the cornstarch and 2 table-spoons water. Bring to a low boil.

- Mix the cornstarch and water and add to the sauce, stirring until thick. Remove from heat.

- Brush the potatoes with the sauce and roast them at 450°F for 15–20 minutes.

•••• RECIPE VARIATIONS ••••

Garlic Sweet Potatoes: Toss the potato wedges with peanut oil, salt, and pepper. Roast them at 450° for 15 minutes. Then coat them with ⅓ cup melted butter and 2 teaspoons minced garlic and roast another 10–15 minutes until the potatoes are slightly crisp.

Sweet Potato Tropical Fruit Salad: Coat the potato wedges with a mixture of ¼ cup each orange and pineapple juice, ¼ cup maple syrup, and 1 tablespoon freshly grated ginger. Roast as directed, cool, and combine with 1 cup sliced bananas, ½ cup shredded coconut, ½ cup chopped mango, and 1 cup vanilla yogurt. Serve chilled.

Roast the Sweet Potatoes

- Because of their density, sweet potatoes require a higher roasting temperature than most other vegetables.

- Arrange the potatoes in a single layer in a lightly greased shallow roasting pan or baking dish.

- Place the pan on a rack in the lower third of the oven. Turn the potatoes once during roasting, drizzling with more sauce if they look dry.

- The finished potatoes should be brown and crisp and the sauce caramelized.

Make the Teriyaki Sauce

- Teriyaki is a combination of two Japanese words: *teri,* which means "luster," and *yaki,* meaning "to grill or broil."

- Japanese mirin is a sweet golden wine that gives teriyaki sauce its sheen. If you can't find it, substitute sherry—wine, that is, not cooking sherry.

- You can use low-sodium soy sauce without affecting the recipe.

- If you like, substitute 2 teaspoons fresh grated ginger for the ground ginger.

BRANDY YAMS MOUSSELINE
This super rich delicacy is a southern Thanksgiving tradition

A mousseline is a strained puree that is dominated by one particular ingredient. Mousselines can be made from vegetables, fish, meat, or dessert ingredients like chocolate or fruit. They're very smooth in texture and are usually served as either a course in a larger meal, an accompaniment to an entree, or a dessert. The word "mousseline" in French refers to fine, sheer muslin cloth, which may have been originally used to strain the sauce.

Down in French-influenced Louisiana, everybody saves room at the holiday table for rich, creamy yams mousseline, spiked with a touch of brandy. *Yield: 8–10 servings*

Ingredients

6 yams (about 3 pounds), halved crosswise

$^1/_4$ cup ($^1/_2$ stick) butter, melted, divided

1 teaspoon ground nutmeg

$^1/_2$ teaspoon ground cloves

$^1/_2$ teaspoon ground allspice

$^1/_2$ teaspoon salt

2 eggs, beaten

$^1/_2$ cup heavy whipping cream

$^1/_4$ cup maple syrup

$^1/_3$ cup brown sugar

$^1/_3$ cup orange juice

2 tablespoons brandy

Toasted pecans

Brandy Yams Mousseline

- Cook the yams in a large pot of boiling water on medium heat until fork-tender, 20–30 minutes.

- Drain yams, let cool, and slip off the skins.

- Whip up yams with 2 tablespoons of the melted butter and the spices, salt, eggs, cream, maple syrup, sugar, orange juice, and brandy.

- Bake yams, brushed with the remaining melted butter, in a buttered 2-quart baking dish, uncovered, at 350°F for 30–35 minutes. Serve topped with toasted pecans.

• • • • RECIPE VARIATIONS • • • •

Cranberry-Ginger Yams Mousseline: In a medium saucepan, melt ½ cup butter. Add ¾ cup light brown sugar, 2 cups fresh or frozen cranberries, and ⅓ cup chopped candied ginger. Cook over medium heat, stirring constantly, until cranberries pop and sugar dissolves. Pour over the yams mousseline in the casserole and bake.

Yams in Apricot Sauce: Microwave 2 peeled yams cut into ½-inch slices with ¼ cup water 15 minutes. In a saucepan, cook until thickened: 1 cup chopped canned apricots, ⅓ cup apricot jam, 3 tablespoons butter, ½ cup brown sugar, and 2 tablespoons maple syrup. Bake yams and sauce in greased baking dish at 350° for 45 minutes.

About Yams

- While yams are often used interchangeably with sweet potatoes, the true yam is the tuber of a tropical vine and is not even distantly related to the sweet potato.

- Yams have more natural sugar and a higher moisture content than sweet potatoes.

- The yam tuber's brown-black skin resembles the bark of a tree, and the flesh can be off-white, purple, or red, depending on the variety.

- Select yams as you would sweet potatoes, looking for unblemished, unwrinkled, tight skins and firm flesh.

Make the Mousseline

- Because you want the potatoes light and fluffy before adding the other ingredients, we recommend an electric hand mixer or food processor for mashing.

- For a more intense citrus flavor, reduce the orange juice to ¼ cup and add 1 tablespoon each minced orange and lemon peel.

- The beaten eggs give the mousseline a soufflé consistency.

- You can make the mousseline ahead and refrigerate for 2 days, or freeze it for up to 3 months.

CASSEROLE OF SPRING VEGETABLES

Called "Jardinière d'Avril" in French, this dish indeed seems to have sprung out of an April garden

With winter making way for warm weather, sunshine, and new growth, spring vegetables are just begging to be gathered up and enjoyed. Tender, sweet new carrots, peas, turnips, and spring onions add the flavor of the new season to any dish, and when combined with fresh herbs and a little vegetable stock, make a bright, fresh vegetable offering all on their own.

This "cassoulet," or casserole of spring vegetables, is cooked on the stove in the French style, not baked as we generally do with casseroles. It's quick and simple and it makes a delectable vegetarian entree. *Yield: 4 servings*

Ingredients

20 large spring onions

1 small lettuce

10 ounces small new carrots

10 ounces new turnips

1 tablespoon olive oil

3 tablespoons butter

2 cups baby new potatoes

1 tablespoon fresh thyme or 1 teaspoon dried thyme

2 sprigs fresh rosemary or 1 teaspoon dried rosemary

1 tablespoon fresh parsley

2 teaspoons sugar

Salt and freshly ground pepper

1 cup vegetable stock/broth

1 pound shelled peas

Casserole of Spring Vegetables

- Peel the onions, wash and quarter the lettuce, and dice the carrots and turnips.

- Heat the oil in a heavy-bottomed saucepan and add the butter. When melted, add the onions and carrots and cook for 10 minutes. Add the lettuce and cook for 3 minutes.

- Add the turnips, potatoes, herbs, sugar, salt, pepper and stock. Cover and cook on low heat for 30 minutes. Add the peas during the last 15 minutes of cooking.

- The vegetables should be crisp-tender, not soft or mushy.

132

• • • • RECIPE VARIATIONS • • • •

Lettuce with Mushrooms and Rice: Sauté one chopped head of lettuce with 1 chopped onion, 2 teaspoons minced garlic, and 6 ounces sliced mushrooms in butter and olive oil. Add 1 cup diced tomatoes with juice, 2 cups cooked rice, 1 teaspoon thyme, 1 teaspoon parsley, and salt and pepper to taste. Cook 10 minutes. Serve in soup dishes topped with croutons.

Escarole with Bacon: Cook and drain 5 slices bacon. Slice 1 pound escarole leaves into ribbons and sauté, with 2 teaspoons chopped garlic and 1 chopped onion, in the bacon drippings with a little butter and olive oil. Add chopped bacon, 2 cups vegetable broth, and salt and pepper to taste. Simmer 20 minutes.

Choose the Right Saucepan

- This dish requires a solid, good-sized saucepan with a tight-fitting lid that circulates heat and moisture evenly.

- A French cassoulet is a sturdy, deep dish, with rounded corners and a tight-fitting lid.

- Another choice is a Moroccan tagine, a heavy clay pot with a flat, circular base and a conical or domed-shaped cover.

- A tagine creates a great table centerpiece. When the cover is removed, the dish is served from the base.

Prepare the Turnips

- Tender young new turnips are planted in early spring and harvested in early summer or midsummer.

- The smaller, younger turnips are sweet and delicate. They should be heavy for their size, with firmly attached roots, bright leaves, and unblemished skin.

- Baby turnips do not have to be peeled; just wash and slice off the root end.

- Browning the young turnips in butter before adding them to the dish creates a rich, delicious flavor.

RED PEPPER EGGPLANT PARMESAN
Roasted red peppers lend extra flavor to this Italian favorite

Parmigiana di melanzane is a classic southern Italian dish made by slicing eggplant thinly and frying it in olive oil. The method of preparation depends on the cook: the eggplant slices may be simply seasoned and fried, dipped in egg and bread crumbs before frying, floured first and then fried, or just baked or grilled. The slices are then layered successively in a baking dish with marinara sauce, mozzarella, and Parmesan.

The traditional dish calls for sliced hard-boiled eggs as well.

This eggplant Parmesan features roasted red bell peppers, which add a nice sweetness. *Yield: 8–12 servings*

Ingredients

1 medium yellow onion, chopped

6 ounces sliced fresh mushrooms

$1/2$ cup plus 2 tablespoons olive oil, divided

2 teaspoons minced garlic

1 6-ounce can tomato paste

1 cup water

1 cup chicken stock

1 cup red wine

1 28-ounce cans diced tomatoes

1 tablespoon sugar

2 tablespoons fresh parsley or 2 teaspoons dried parsley

1 tablespoon fresh basil or 1 teaspoon dried basil

1 tablespoon fresh oregano or 1 teaspoon

dried oregano

2 bay leaves

$1/2$ teaspoon onion powder

1 teaspoon seasoned salt

$1/2$ teaspoon pepper

2 medium globe eggplants, cut crosswise into $1/2$-inch slices

Salt, as needed

3 cups Italian-seasoned bread crumbs

3 eggs, beaten with 2 tablespoons milk

2 medium red bell peppers, roasted and sliced

$1 1/2$ cups shredded mozzarella

$1 1/2$ cups shredded or grated Parmesan

Red Pepper Eggplant Parmesan

- Sauté onions and mushrooms in 2 tablespoons olive oil until browned. Add garlic and brown for 20 seconds. Stir in tomato paste, water, chicken stock, wine, tomatoes, sugar, and seasonings. Simmer 20 minutes

- Prepare the eggplant (see technique). Sauté breaded

eggplant slices in the $1/2$ cup of olive oil in batches until browned. Drain.

- Arrange layers of sauce, eggplant, peppers, and mozzarella in a greased baking dish, ending with sauce and Parmesan. Bake at 350°F for 30–40 minutes, until brown and bubbling.

• • • • RECIPE VARIATIONS • • • •

Eggplant Parmesan Lasagna: Prepare the sauce for eggplant Parmesan and fry the eggplant slices. In a deep baking dish, layer the sauce, lasagna noodles, fried eggplant slices, roasted pepper slices, and ricotta and mozzarella, ending with a layer of noodles covered with sauce, mozzarella, and Parmesan. Bake at 350°F for 45 minutes.

Eggplant Parmesan Casserole: In a large casserole dish, combine the fried eggplant slices with 1½ cups of the marinara sauce, ¾ cup sliced water chestnuts, 1 cup quartered artichoke hearts, 1 cup chopped roasted red peppers, 1 small can sliced black olives, and ½ cup each mozzarella and sharp cheddar cheese. Top with shredded Parmesan and bake at 350° 30–40 minutes.

Prepare the Eggplant

- Generously sprinkle the eggplant slices with salt and let sit on a baking sheet for 1 hour.

- Rinse eggplant well under cold running water and blot dry with paper towels.

- Place ⅓ of bread crumbs on wax paper. Dip eggplant in egg mixture and dredge on each side with crumbs, adding more crumbs if they get too sticky.

- Fry eggplant slices in ½ inch of hot oil, turning once, until golden brown, about 3 minutes per batch. Using tongs, remove slices and drain on paper towels.

Roast the Peppers

- Place clean whole fresh peppers on a baking dish.

- Broil under medium heat, turning frequently, as necessary, until the entire pepper skin has turned black and blistery.

- Remove from oven and place peppers in an airtight container, such as a bowl with a lid or a plastic or paper bag.

- Let the peppers rest in the container for 10–15 minutes to build up steam that will loosen the skin. Remove from container and peel off the skin.

MUSHROOM STROGANOFF

You don't need beef to make a delectable stroganoff

Would you believe that the classic Russian dish beef stroganoff was made popular in the United States by . . . the Chinese? After the fall of Imperial Russia in 1917, Russians living in China introduced beef stroganoff to the hotels and restaurants there, and Russian and Chinese immigrants later brought it to the United States, where it found an eternally enthusiastic audience.

The signature ingredients of beef stroganoff are lightly floured strips of beef, onion, sour cream, wine, and mushrooms. But believe it or not, if you omit the beef, it's every bit as good. *Yield: 4 servings*

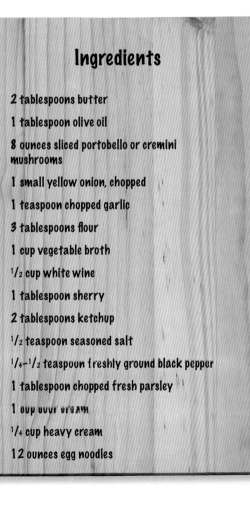

Ingredients

2 tablespoons butter

1 tablespoon olive oil

8 ounces sliced portobello or cremini mushrooms

1 small yellow onion, chopped

1 teaspoon chopped garlic

3 tablespoons flour

1 cup vegetable broth

$1/2$ cup white wine

1 tablespoon sherry

2 tablespoons ketchup

$1/2$ teaspoon seasoned salt

$1/4$–$1/2$ teaspoon freshly ground black pepper

1 tablespoon chopped fresh parsley

1 cup sour cream

$1/4$ cup heavy cream

12 ounces egg noodles

Mushroom Stroganoff

- In a large skillet, melt the butter and oil and sauté the mushrooms and onion until soft. Add the garlic and cook 1 minute.

- Add the flour to make a roux. Stir in the broth, wine, sherry, ketchup, salt, pepper, and parsley and cook over medium-high heat.

- When mixture is smooth and bubbling, reduce heat to a simmer and stir in sour cream and heavy cream. Remove from heat.

- Serve over cooked egg noodles.

• • • • RECIPE VARIATION • • • •

Mushroom Noodles Romanoff: Sauté 6 ounces sliced mushrooms and 2 teaspoons chopped garlic in 4 tablespoons butter. Add 2 cups light cream, ½ cup sour cream, 1 cup grated sharp cheddar, ¼ cup chopped parsley, 1 teaspoon seasoned salt, and ½ teaspoon black pepper. Heat through and serve over egg noodles.

Select the Wine

- When choosing wine to add to a dish, pick one similar to one you would drink with the dish.

- As stroganoff goes well with a dry white wine, Chardonnay, Pinot Gris, Pinot Blanc, and Sauvignon Blanc are all good choices.

- You needn't spend more than $8 for an acceptable wine.

- Use a dry sherry and avoid cooking sherry, which is a low-quality sherry with added salt.

Cook the Noodles

- Wide egg noodles are excellent for stroganoff.

- To be tender, but not mushy, the noodles should never cook more than 6 minutes.

- Fill a large, deep pot with about 3 quarts of water

for 12 ounces of noodles, adding 1 teaspoon salt to cut the blandness of the noodles.

- Drain the pasta in a large colander, but don't rinse it. That removes the starch that helps hold the sauce.

COCONUT VEGETABLE CURRY
This Thai dish is exotically seasoned and super nutritious

In Thailand, the word *kaeng*, or "curry," refers not to the curry spice per se, but to the process of mixing various kinds of vegetables with liquid like water or coconut milk. Thai kaeng can be spicy or mild, vegetarian or non-vegetarian, and it can take the form of soup, stew, a curry dish, or even dessert.

This coconut vegetable curry is essentially a vegetable stew. Containing everything from green beans and zucchini to carrots, sweet potato, and red bell pepper, it's as colorful as it is flavorful. *Yield: 6 servings*

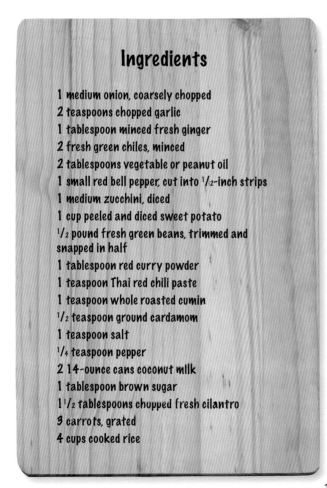

Ingredients

1 medium onion, coarsely chopped
2 teaspoons chopped garlic
1 tablespoon minced fresh ginger
2 fresh green chiles, minced
2 tablespoons vegetable or peanut oil
1 small red bell pepper, cut into ¹/₂-inch strips
1 medium zucchini, diced
1 cup peeled and diced sweet potato
¹/₂ pound fresh green beans, trimmed and snapped in half
1 tablespoon red curry powder
1 teaspoon Thai red chili paste
1 teaspoon whole roasted cumin
¹/₂ teaspoon ground cardamom
1 teaspoon salt
¹/₄ teaspoon pepper
2 14-ounce cans coconut milk
1 tablespoon brown sugar
1¹/₂ tablespoons chopped fresh cilantro
9 carrots, grated
4 cups cooked rice

Coconut Vegetable Curry

- In a food processor, pulse the onion, garlic, ginger, and chiles until almost smooth.

- In a large skillet, saute red pepper, zucchini, sweet potato, and green beans on medium-high in heated oil, 5 minutes.

- Add the onion mixture, curry powder, chili paste, cumin, cardamom, salt, and pepper and cook 5 minutes.

- Add the coconut milk, sugar, cilantro, and carrots and simmer 20 minutes, or until vegetables are tender. Serve over cooked rice.

• • • • RECIPE VARIATIONS • • • •

Vegetables with Tofu and Spinach: Stir-fry 6 ounces fresh mushrooms along with the celery, zucchini, and red bell pepper. Stir in the onion-garlic-chile mixture and seasonings, red chili paste, coconut milk, sugar, cilantro, and 2 teaspoons soy sauce and bring to a boil. Reduce heat immediately and add 4 ounces canned baby corn, cut in half, and 8 ounces baby spinach leaves, stirring until spinach has wilted. Serve topped with 8 ounces of tofu cubes, browned until crisp.

Some Non-Veggie Additions: While coconut vegetable curry is a complete meal in itself, the non-vegetarian version is simple to create. Just add 1–2 cups of one of the following: cooked shrimp, crab, chicken, pork or lamb; seared bay scallops; or fried or steamed fish.

Select the Coconut Milk

- You can find canned coconut milk in the international or specialty sections of most large supermarkets.

- Quality coconut milk will have a layer of coconut cream on top and the thinner milk on the bottom, so stir the contents well.

- Either regular or light coconut milk can be used in this dish. You can also use canned coconut cream, combining it with light coconut milk.

- Never leave coconut milk at room temperature, as it quickly spoils.

Cook the Rice

- Fragrant long-grain basmati and jasmine rice are two varietals frequently used in Thai and Chinese dishes.

- The standard ratio of water to rice is 1½ cups of water to 1 cup of rice.

- Place the rice and water in the saucepan together, add 1 teaspoon of butter and ½ teaspoon salt, and bring to a gentle boil. Turn down the heat immediately to very low, cover, and simmer 15–20 minutes.

- The finished rice should be fluffy and not sticky or dry.

TOMATILLO ENCHILADA PIE

Green salsa and cream are the secret ingredients in this tortilla casserole

Although a relative of the tomato, the tomatillo has a very tart taste, not at all like that of tomatoes. It's that tartness that makes it the desired ingredient in many Mexican sauces.

The tomatillo has a papery outer husk and is used when it is still green. You can buy tomatillos in large grocery stores as well as at your nearest Mexican markets. Select unblemished

fruit that completely fills the papery outside skin. Avoid tomatillos that are turning yellow, as they're past their prime.

This recipe calls for a salsa verde made with fresh tomatillos—never canned! *Yield: 8–10 servings*

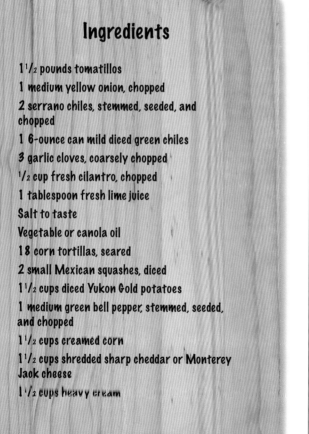

Ingredients

1 ¹/₂ pounds tomatillos

1 medium yellow onion, chopped

2 serrano chiles, stemmed, seeded, and chopped

1 6-ounce can mild diced green chiles

3 garlic cloves, coarsely chopped

¹/₂ cup fresh cilantro, chopped

1 tablespoon fresh lime juice

Salt to taste

Vegetable or canola oil

18 corn tortillas, seared

2 small Mexican squashes, diced

1 ¹/₂ cups diced Yukon Gold potatoes

1 medium green bell pepper, stemmed, seeded, and chopped

1 ¹/₂ cups creamed corn

1 ¹/₂ cups shredded sharp cheddar or Monterey Jack cheese

1 ¹/₂ cups heavy cream

Tomatillo Enchilada Pie

- Make the salsa verde (see technique). Then in a lightly oiled large skillet, quickly sear the tortillas, 10–15 seconds on each side until hot but not crisp.

- Sauté the squash and potato over medium heat until brown and crisp-tender. Add the green pepper and sauté

3 minutes more.

- In a 13 x 9 x 2-inch baking dish, make two layers of salsa, tortillas, vegetables, creamed corn, and cheese, ending with tortillas and cheese. Pour cream over top and bake at 350° for about 35 minutes, until brown and bubbly.

140

Roasted Tomatillo Guacamole: Toss 6 husked tomatillos with a little oil, salt and pepper and roast with 2 serrano chiles at 450° 10–15 minutes. Cool and finely chop. Cut 2 ripe avocados into chunks and mash with the tomatillos, chiles, 1 teaspoon chopped garlic, 3 chopped scallions, 2 tablespoons chopped cilantro, ½ teaspoon lemon pepper, ½ teaspoon salt, and 2 tablespoons fresh lime juice.

Tomatillo Ranch Dressing: Puree until smooth: 3 husked, quartered tomatillos, ½ cup cilantro, and 2 pickled jalapeno peppers. Combine 1 cup light sour cream, 6 oz. plain yogurt, ½ cup mayonnaise, and 1 cup ranch dressing. Whisk in the tomatillo puree.

Make the Salsa Verde

- Remove and discard the papery husks from the tomatillos and rinse the tomatillos well.

- Place the tomatillos in a saucepan, cover with water, and bring to a boil. Simmer for 5 minutes and remove with a slotted spoon. Cool.

- In a blender or food processor, combine the tomatillos, onions, serranos, canned chilies, garlic, cilantro, and lime juice and pulse until all ingredients are chopped well.

- Season to taste with salt. Makes 3 cups.

Assemble the Pie

- Place 6 tortillas in a thin layer of the salsa on the bottom of the baking dish.

- Cover the tortillas with ½ of the sautéed vegetables, creamed corn, cheese, and ⅔ cup salsa.

- Repeat with 6 more tortillas, the rest of the vegetables and creamed corn, and ⅔ cup more salsa. Top with the remaining tortillas and cheese.

- Distribute the cream evenly over the top and jostle the dish until it permeates all the layers.

VEGETABLE TOFU LO MEIN
Tossed soba noodles turn chow mein into lo mein

OK. What's the difference between chow mein and lo mein? The obvious answer is the type of noodles used. Chow mein noodles are crisp, while lo mein noodles are soft. The real difference, however, lies in how the noodles are prepared. In Chinese, *mein* or *mian* means "noodles." *Chao mian* means "fried noodles," and *lo mian* means "tossed noodles."

Soba noodles tossed with stir-fried vegetables and crisp

tofu make a delicious meatless lo mein that takes only minutes to prepare. *Yield: 4 servings*

Ingredients

2 teaspoons minced garlic

6 scallions chopped

2 teaspoons finely grated fresh ginger

2 tablespoons canola oil or peanut oil, divided

1 cup sliced white or brown mushrooms

1 cup grated carrots

1 1/2 cups shredded cabbage

1 large stalk celery with leaves, chopped

6 ounces firm tofu, cubed

3 tablespoons soy sauce

2 tablespoons oyster sauce

2 tablespoons hoisin sauce

2 teaspoons sesame oil

1/4 teaspoon crushed red pepper flakes

3 tablespoons water

16-ounces cooked soba noodles

1/2 cup roasted cashew nuts

1 teaspoon hot sauce

Vegetable Tofu Lo Mein

- In a wok over medium-high heat, sauté the garlic, scallion whites, and ginger in 1 tablespoon canola or peanut oil for 1 minute. Add the mushrooms, carrots, cabbage, and celery and sauté 3–4 minutes.

- Push the vegetables to the sides of the wok and stir-fry the tofu in 1 tablespoon oil until nicely browned.

- In a small bowl, combine the various sauces, sesame oil, red pepper flakes and water.

- Add the noodles, cashews, and hot sauce to the vegetables and tofu. Toss well.

· · · · RECIPE VARIATION · · · ·

Spicy Vegetable and Peanut Noodle Salad: Whisk together ½ cup honey Dijon mustard, ⅓ cup vegetable broth, ⅓ cup peanut butter, 2 tablespoons teriyaki sauce, and 2 tablespoons hot pepper sauce. Toss with 1 cup thinly sliced cucumber, 1 cup snow peas, 1 cup shredded cabbage, 3 chopped scallions, 1 teaspoon minced ginger, and 2 cups cooked lo mein noodles.

Prepare the Tofu

- Tofu, or soybean curd, comes in a number of textures, ranging from extra firm to soft. Choose firm for this dish.

- Firm tofu usually comes in a brick and can be found in the produce section of most supermarkets.

- Cut the desired amount of tofu into 1-inch cubes and drain on paper towels for about 15 minutes, changing towels as needed.

- A wok is the best utensil for stir-frying tofu because tofu needs uniform heat to brown.

Cook the Soba Noodles

- Soba noodles (also known as udon noodles) are made from a combination of wheat and buckwheat flour. You can also purchase 100 percent buckwheat soba noodles.

- Soba noodles have a thick, chewy texture and are much more nutritious than white flour pastas.

- Loosen precooked noodles by soaking them in a bowl of hot water for 2–3 minutes. Then drain and set aside.

- If using packaged dry noodles, cook 7–9 minutes in boiling salted water.

SPINACH & LEEK FRITTATA
This classic egg dish makes a beautiful presentation

In the strictest sense, the difference between frittatas and omelets boils down to a matter of folding in a filling rather than mixing it in. Omelets traditionally have the egg mixture cooked and folded around a filling. A frittata is a kind of open-faced Italian omelet that can contain cheese, vegetables, meat, seafood, or whatever sounds good. All the ingredients are fully mixed with the eggs first. And unlike an omelet, which is prepared in a pan, a frittata is finished under a broiler, which puffs it up and browns it.

For larger groups, consider frittatas instead of omelets. They can be made ahead of time and served at room temperature.
Yield: 4 servings

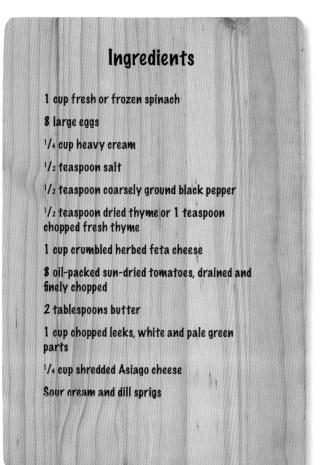

Ingredients

1 cup fresh or frozen spinach

8 large eggs

$1/4$ cup heavy cream

$1/2$ teaspoon salt

$1/2$ teaspoon coarsely ground black pepper

$1/2$ teaspoon dried thyme or 1 teaspoon chopped fresh thyme

1 cup crumbled herbed feta cheese

8 oil-packed sun-dried tomatoes, drained and finely chopped

2 tablespoons butter

1 cup chopped leeks, white and pale green parts

$1/4$ cup shredded Asiago cheese

Sour cream and dill sprigs

Spinach and Leek Frittata

- Preheat the broiler. Cook the spinach and squeeze out all excess moisture.

- Whisk the eggs, cream, salt, pepper, and thyme and stir in the feta and tomatoes.

- Melt the butter in a heavy broiler-proof 10-inch non-stick skillet over medium heat and sauté the leeks for 4 minutes. Add the spinach.

- Add the egg mixture to the skillet and cook until eggs start to firm and sides and bottom begin to brown. Top with the Asiago cheese and broil until cheese turns golden. Serve with sour cream and garnish with dill.

Except for maybe wars, famines, and taxes, there's nothing worse than a hard, dry, overcooked frittata. To avoid this fate, keep a close eye on the eggs in the skillet, making sure they are not quite set when you transfer them to the broiler. During the broiling, keep a close watch for the cheese to turn golden. Remove the frittata immediately as soon as it puffs up.

Spinach and Potato Frittata: Instead of leeks, substitute 6 thinly sliced small red potatoes, sautéed over medium heat and cooked about 10 minutes until tender/firm. Prepare as for spinach and leek frittata, and top with sharp shredded cheddar in place of the Asiago before broiling.

Cook the Eggs

Broil the Frittata

- On medium-low heat, gently fold the vegetables into the eggs with a spatula.

- As the mixture sets, run the spatula around the edge of the skillet, lifting the egg mixture.

- With a fork, gently push the egg mixture from side to side, allowing it to seep to the bottom of the pan. This will ensure that the eggs cook thoroughly.

- Continue cooking until the frittata is almost set.

- Place the skillet 5–6 inches from the heat and broil for 3–5 minutes.

- Never leave the broiler unattended—things happen fast at 500°F.

- The frittata is done when the center is set and the dish has puffed up like a soufflé.

- Serve in wedges garnished with a dollop of sour cream and fresh dill sprigs.

VEGETABLES & EGGS

MIXED VEGETABLE SOUFFLÉ
An elegant and light vegetable soufflé is amazingly easy to prepare

Soufflés are one of those intimidating affairs that frighten away inexperienced cooks. In French, soufflé means "breath," and that can be all it takes to blow one down. Who hasn't heard the horror stories of the fallen soufflé, wrecked by a slamming door or some other loud noise just as the guests arrive? While it's true that soufflés must be served immediately, it isn't all that hard to make a successful one. And all is

not lost if you fail; as one cartoon observed, a fallen soufflé makes a fine beret.

This vegetable soufflé features zucchini, cauliflower, carrots, and onion in a savory mustard and herb mixture. The classic soufflé should be puffed up and lightly browned when it arrives at the table. *Yield: 6 servings*

Ingredients

1 medium zucchini, finely diced

3 medium carrots, grated

4 tablespoons ($^1/_2$ stick) butter

$^1/_2$ cup minced onion

4 tablespoons flour

1 $^1/_2$ cups hot milk

5 large egg yolks

$^1/_2$ cup cooked cauliflower florets

$^1/_2$ cup mayonnaise

$^1/_2$ teaspoon celery salt

1 teaspoon Dijon mustard

1 teaspoon fresh dill

$^1/_2$ teaspoon dried tarragon

$^1/_2$ cup grated Emmental cheese

5 large egg whites, beaten to stiff peaks

Mixed Vegetable Soufflé

- In a medium saucepan over medium-high heat, sauté the zucchini and carrots in the butter until soft, about 8 minutes. Add the onion and sauté another 2 minutes. Stir in the flour and drizzle in the hot milk, stirring constantly until thickened. Remove from heat.

- Beat egg yolks with 1 tablespoon of white sauce and beat entire yolk mixture back into sauce. Stir in cauliflower, mayonnaise, seasonings, and cheese. Fold egg whites into mixture with a firm rubber spatula, transfer to a buttered soufflé dish, and bake for 40 minutes at 350°F.

Chicken and Corn Soufflé: Follow the Vegetable Soufflé recipe, substituting 2 cups diced cooked chicken and 1 cup cooked corn for the carrots, zucchini, and cauliflower, 1 cup cream-style corn for the mayonnaise, and sharp grated cheddar for the Emmental. You can, if you wish, also add 1 tablespoon chopped pimiento and ½ cup chopped green pepper.

VEGETABLES & EGGS

Separate the Eggs

- Set out two bowls. Crack the egg gently on a flat surface.

- Gently pry the egg halves apart with your thumbs.

- Let the yolk settle in the lower half of the eggshell while the whites run off the

sides of the egg into one bowl.

- Gently coddle the yolk back and forth between the shell halves until all the whites have dripped into the bowl. Carefully place the yolk in the other bowl.

Beat the Egg Whites

- Make sure the egg whites are completely free of any yolk and that no grease is on the bowl or beater.

- Using an electric mixer, start beating the egg whites slowly, increasing the speed until the mixer is on high.

- Beat until the whites are stiff but not dry.

- You can tell how stiff the whites are by the peaks that form. If the whites are too soft, the peaks will bow over. Stiff peaks stand up by themselves.

BROCCOLI & BACON QUICHE

This quiche is great for breakfast, lunch, brunch, or even a light dinner

"Quiche" has that elegant ring to it. We think of it as an entree at a sophisticated ladies' tea or luncheon or an item on one of those upscale cafe brunch menus. Yet what is a quiche but eggs, milk, cheese, flour, and a few other ingredients, whisked together and baked in a pie shell?

If you can make an omelet or a frittata, you can make a quiche. And once you learn the basics of quiche making, you'll want to experiment with all sorts of ingredients and eat quiche whenever, wherever. *Yield: 6–8 servings*

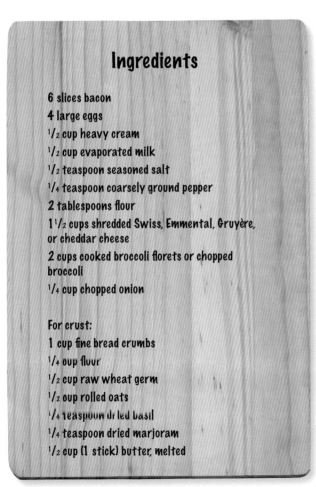

Ingredients

6 slices bacon

4 large eggs

$1/2$ cup heavy cream

$1/2$ cup evaporated milk

$1/2$ teaspoon seasoned salt

$1/4$ teaspoon coarsely ground pepper

2 tablespoons flour

$1 1/2$ cups shredded Swiss, Emmental, Gruyère, or cheddar cheese

2 cups cooked broccoli florets or chopped broccoli

$1/4$ cup chopped onion

For crust:

1 cup fine bread crumbs

$1/4$ cup flour

$1/2$ cup raw wheat germ

$1/2$ cup rolled oats

$1/4$ teaspoon dried basil

$1/4$ teaspoon dried marjoram

$1/2$ cup (1 stick) butter, melted

Broccoli and Bacon Quiche

- Make the pie shell (see technique).

- Fry the bacon until crisp. Drain and crumble.

- Whisk the eggs with the cream, evaporated milk, salt, pepper, and flour. Add the cheese.

- Sprinkle the bacon in the bottom of the pie shell, layer the broccoli and onion on top of the bacon, and pour the cream mixture over all. Bake at 375°F for 30–40 minutes, or until center is firm.

Broccoli and Bacon Breakfast Burritos: Reduce cheese to ½ cup and set aside with the onion. Prepare the ingredients as for the quiche, omitting the flour, onion and cheese. In a large skillet, sauté the onion until soft in 1 tablespoon oil. Add the egg mixture and scramble. Fill heated flour tortillas with the scrambled eggs topped with cheese and salsa.

Spinach Crust: Melt 3 tablespoons butter and add ¾ pound finely chopped fresh spinach. Cook quickly over fairly high heat, until wilted. Remove from heat and cool. Combine the spinach, ¾ cup flour, ¾ cup wheat germ, ¼ teaspoon salt, and ¼ teaspoon nutmeg. Mix well and pat into a buttered 9-inch pan. Bake at 375°F for 15 minutes.

Select the Cheese

- You can use virtually any cheese for quiche, so it all depends on what sort of flavor you want.

- The two most famous original Swiss cheeses are Emmental, which has a nutty, buttery flavor, and Gruyère, which is slightly sweeter.

- American Swiss cheese has a much shorter aging process than the original Swiss cheeses, making it softer and milder.

- If you prefer cheddar cheese, use a high–quality sharp variety, like English or Vermont cheddar.

Make the Crust

- Mix together the dry ingredients, combining thoroughly.

- Drizzle in the melted butter and toss with a fork until the mixture is moistened throughout.

- Using your fingers, press mixture into the bottom and up the sides of a buttered 9-inch glass pie plate.

- Bake in the center of a 400°F oven until the crust begins to brown, about 10 minutes.

VEGETABLES & EGGS

149

ASPARAGUS TIMBALES

This savory vegetable egg custard makes an excellent appetizer or side dish

A timbale, or savory egg custard, is basically a crustless quiche. Like quiches, omelets, and frittatas, timbales can be made with virtually any ingredients and lend themselves well to a variety of vegetables and cheeses. They differ from other egg dishes in that they usually use bread crumbs for body. The word "timbale" also refers to the type of dish in which the dish is made—a timbale mold.

Timbales are usually baked in individual ramekins in a pan of hot water, which steams the custard and makes it easy to unmold. With an attractive garnish, timbales make adorable little appetizers, first courses, or side dishes. *Yield: 6 servings*

Ingredients

1 cup fine bread crumbs, divided

$\frac{1}{2}$ cup minced onions

1 tablespoon butter

$\frac{3}{4}$ teaspoon white pepper

$\frac{1}{4}$ teaspoon seasoned salt

$\frac{1}{4}$ teaspoon nutmeg

$\frac{1}{8}$ teaspoons cayenne pepper

5 large eggs

1$\frac{1}{2}$ cups light cream, warmed

1$\frac{1}{2}$ pounds fresh asparagus, steamed and cut into $\frac{1}{2}$-inch pieces

$\frac{1}{2}$ cup grated Swiss cheese

Asparagus Timbales

- Generously sprinkle the interiors of six buttered individual ramekins with $\frac{1}{2}$ cup of the bread crumbs.

- Cook the onions in butter until translucent and transfer to a mixing bowl. Mix in the seasonings and remaining bread crumbs.

- Beat the eggs into the bread crumb mixture and slowly stir in the cream and cheese. Fold in the asparagus.

- Fill the ramekins with the custard and bake in a pan of hot water at 350°F for 30–35 minutes. Cool and unmold onto a platter.

Crab and Mushroom Timbales: Omit the onions and sauté instead 6 ounces sliced fresh mushrooms, 2 tablespoons minced shallots, and 2 teaspoons minced garlic in 2 tablespoons butter. When mixing the eggs and cream, add ¼ cup cognac. Omit the asparagus and nutmeg and add instead 1 pound fresh or imitation crabmeat and 1 tablespoon chopped fresh parsley.

Other Timbale Suggestions: Get creative with your timbales. Warm goat cheese and spinach timbales, timbales with mushrooms and shredded carrots, timbales with caramelized onion and tomato, or timbales with salmon, blue cheese and leeks are just a few possibilities.

VEGETABLES & EGGS

Choose the Mold

- The word "timbale" comes from the Arabic word for a tall drum that tapers to the bottom—the basic shape of traditional timbale molds.

- Timbale molds are usually stainless steel, aluminum, or silver. They also come in nonstick varieties.

- Ramekins are small, cylindrical dishes used for baking individual soufflés or custards. They are usually made of porcelain or Pyrex.

- You can also use heavy aluminum baba cups.

Bake the Timbales

- Place hot water in a 13 x 9 x 2-inch baking pan so that it comes halfway up the sides of the timbale dishes.

- Check the timbales after 30 minutes to make sure they aren't overdone.

- The timbales are set when a knife inserted into the center comes out clean.

- Cool the timbales to room temperature. Run a knife around the edges to loosen them and invert them onto a serving plate.

BAKED EGGS WITH ARTICHOKES
Vegetables and eggs, baked together, create a brunch sensation

Baking eggs has an effect similar to poaching them. The whites set and the yolks are soft but not runny. Eggs are delicious when baked atop a mixture of fresh sautéed vegetables and served with hash browns or on top of toasted croissant halves.

Shirred eggs are eggs baked in individual dishes or ramekins, with a little cream, seasonings, and cheese or other toppings. The French call these delightful portions *oeufs en cocotte,* or "eggs in cups." *Yield: 4 servings*

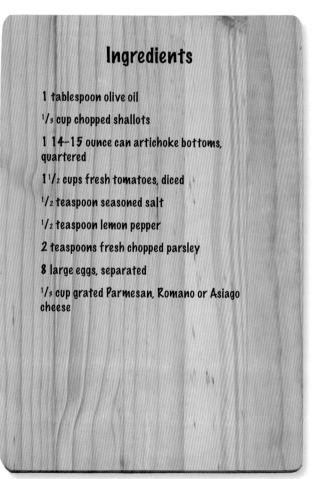

Ingredients

1 tablespoon olive oil

$1/3$ cup chopped shallots

1 14–15 ounce can artichoke bottoms, quartered

$1^1/2$ cups fresh tomatoes, diced

$1/2$ teaspoon seasoned salt

$1/2$ teaspoon lemon pepper

2 teaspoons fresh chopped parsley

8 large eggs, separated

$1/3$ cup grated Parmesan, Romano or Asiago cheese

Baked Eggs with Artichokes

- In a medium skillet, heat the oil and sauté the shallots and artichokes over medium-high heat.

- Add the tomatoes, salt, pepper, and parsley and simmer 3 minutes. Transfer to a 2-quart baking dish and cool 10 minutes.

- Beat the egg whites until foamy and pour them over the artichoke mixture. Place the whole yolks over the top, sprinkle with the cheese, and bake at 400°F until the whites are set, approximately 15 20 minutes.

152

Eggs Baked in Green Peppers: Cut 3 green peppers in half lengthwise, remove ribs and seeds, and blanch in boiling water for 10 minutes. Remove from water, drain, and dry, and half fill them with buttered Italian-seasoned bread crumbs. Break an egg into each pepper half, season with salt and pepper, sprinkle with grated Romano cheese, and bake at 350°F for 15 minutes.

Eggs Benedict with Artichokes and Tomatoes: Toast 8 English muffin halves. Make the artichoke-tomato-shallot sauté as directed. Poach the eggs. Top each muffin half with the vegetable mixture, an egg, and hollandaise sauce (see "Bacon Hollandaise Asparagus," page 61). Sprinkle with paprika and serve.

Prepare the Artichokes

Bake the Eggs

- The artichoke bottom is the fleshy base section of the artichoke.

- Like artichoke hearts, artichoke bottoms are tender and flavorful. They are preferable to canned hearts in this recipe because they are firmer and meatier.

- You can use either bottoms canned in water or marinated in a jar; the marinated artichokes will lend the dish an Italian flavor. Make sure to drain the artichokes beforehand.

- The sautéed artichokes should be nicely browned and tender.

- Baked eggs are easy but a little tricky, as you have to be careful not to overcook them.

- Eggs can be baked whole, but separating them and folding the beaten egg whites into the vegetables reduces the chance that the egg whites will become hard and rubbery.

- You want the yolks to be soft and velvety and the whites just set.

- While the dish is baking, check it after 10 minutes. If it's not done, continue baking and check it again at 5-minute intervals.

CABBAGE & CHICKEN EGG FOO YOUNG
This Chinese omelet is served like pancakes

Omelets were around centuries before the French coined the term in the 1500s. The ancient Chinese and Persians, for instance, developed various versions of egg pancakes filled with vegetables and meat. Egg foo young originated in Shanghai and was an elaborate dish made with beaten egg whites and minced ham. The northern Chinese used chicken in place of the ham. Today, egg foo young can

incorporate whatever you want to put into it.

While we're used to eating egg foo young for dinner in Chinese restaurants, it's actually a perfect dish for breakfast or brunch. *Yield: 4 servings*

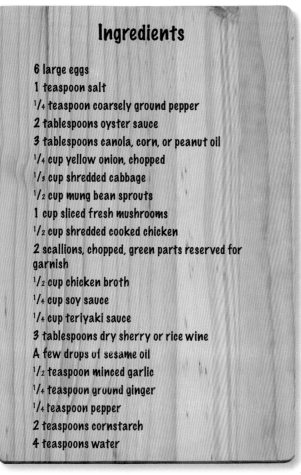

Ingredients

6 large eggs
1 teaspoon salt
¼ teaspoon coarsely ground pepper
2 tablespoons oyster sauce
3 tablespoons canola, corn, or peanut oil
¼ cup yellow onion, chopped
⅓ cup shredded cabbage
½ cup mung bean sprouts
1 cup sliced fresh mushrooms
½ cup shredded cooked chicken
2 scallions, chopped, green parts reserved for garnish
½ cup chicken broth
¼ cup soy sauce
¼ cup teriyaki sauce
3 tablespoons dry sherry or rice wine
A few drops of sesame oil
½ teaspoon minced garlic
¼ teaspoon ground ginger
¼ teaspoon pepper
2 teaspoons cornstarch
4 teaspoons water

Cabbage and Chicken Egg Foo Young

- Lightly beat the eggs with the salt, pepper, and oyster sauce.

- Heat the oil in a wok or nonstick skillet and add onion, cabbage, bean sprouts, and mushrooms. Stir-fry 2 minutes and remove from the pan. Cool 10 minutes.

- Combine the chicken and vegetables with the egg mixture and scallions before making the pancakes.

- Deep-fry or pan-fry the pancakes; deep-frying gives the egg foo young a light, airy texture. Serve with egg foo young sauce.

VEGETABLES & EGGS

Make the Sauce

- In a small saucepan, bring the chicken broth to a boil, then turn down to simmer. Whisk in the soy sauce, teriyaki sauce, sherry or rice wine, sesame oil, garlic, ginger, and pepper.

- In a cup, dissolve the cornstarch in the water.

- Turn up the heat slightly and add the cornstarch mixture to the sauce, stirring quickly to thicken.

- Keep the sauce warm over low heat while preparing the egg foo young.

Fry the Pancakes

- For deep-frying, heat 2 cups of oil to 350°F. Ladle in ¼ of the egg mixture.

- The pancake will float; as it sets, ladle in the rest of the mixture by fourths.

- Brown the pancakes on each side, then remove

each one with two spatulas, pressing lightly to squeeze out any excess oil.

- If pan-frying, heat 2 tablespoons oil and ladle in the egg mixture to form a pancake. Cook until golden brown; flip and brown on the other side.

THAI ASPARAGUS & SCALLOPS

Delicate asparagus and succulent scallops bring out the best in each other

Seafood is a staple of Thailand, where the warm tropical seas and the channels between the paddy fields bring an abundance of fish and shellfish. From the roadside food stands of a coastal town to the street markets of Bangkok, broiled fish with ginger, shrimp with coconut and cilantro, and fresh scallops with hot pepper and lime are common sights.

In Asian cuisine, asparagus and seafood are stir-fry best buddies. Paired with scallops, which cook very quickly, and tossed with lime juice, scallions, garlic, ginger, and hot chiles, asparagus acquires a racy persona. *Yield: 4 servings*

Ingredients

1 pound fresh asparagus

1 tablespoon butter

1 tablespoon vegetable oil

2 teaspoons chopped garlic

4 scallions, chopped

1 teaspoon grated fresh ginger

1 pound bay scallops

$1/2$ teaspoon salt

Finely grated zest and juice of 1 lime

1 small red chile, finely chopped

1 tablespoon Thai chili paste

Lime wedges

Thai Asparagus and Scallops

- Trim the tough ends off the asparagus and cut it into 1-inch pieces.

- Heat the butter and oil in a skillet or wok. Stir-fry the garlic, scallions, and ginger for 1 minute. Do not brown.

- Add the asparagus and scallops and continue stir-frying 4–5 minutes on high heat. Stir in the salt, lime zest, lime juice, chile, and chili paste.

- Serve garnished with lime wedges and freshly cooked jasmine or basmati rice.

Prepare the Scallops

- If using frozen bay scallops, defrost them in the refrigerator as directed or place them in a colander and run cold water over them for 3–5 minutes. Make sure to pat them dry.

- Buy fresh scallops, shelled and trim them with a sharp knife to remove any black intestine.

- Scallops should never be overcooked, or they will become rubbery.

- The finished scallops should have a slightly browned crust and a medium-rare center.

Choose the Chiles

- The distinctive Cal/Mex serrano chile is the most popular choice in hot green chiles.

- The Thai chile is thinner than the serrano and light green to green-orange in color. When it's hot, it's hot, so be cautious.

- The larger Hungarian wax chile gets a 1–3 ("entry-level hot") rating on the Scoville hotness scale.

- The dark green or red jalapeño gets a mid-range rating. But the Jamaican hot pepper gets a 9. Translation: "The weak have fallen by the wayside."

VEGETABLES & SEAFOOD

157

GREEN BEANS WITH SALMON
Fresh pico de gallo adds pizzazz to grilled green beans and salmon fillets

What's the difference between salsa and pico de gallo? Well, technically, salsa means "sauce" and the ingredients are cooked, or rather roasted, for a smoky spicy flavor. Pico de gallo is a fresh salsa and can vary depending on the seasons and what you have on hand. The term pico de gallo is Spanish for "rooster's beak," and is thought to refer to the beaklike shape and red color of the chiles used in its preparation.

In this quick, healthy, and incredibly tasty meal, both the green beans and the salmon are cooked on the grill for only a few minutes and topped with fresh pico de gallo. *Yield: 4 servings*

Ingredients

2 tablespoons olive oil

³/₄ teaspoon salt, plus more to taste

¹/₂ teaspoon coarsely ground pepper, plus more to taste

1¹/₂ teaspoons sugar, divided

2 tablespoons fresh lemon juice

1 pound green beans

4 6- to 8-ounce salmon fillets

2 cups diced fresh Roma tomatoes

¹/₂ cup chopped fresh cilantro

2 teaspoons minced garlic

1 6-ounce can chopped mild chiles

2 tablespoons fresh lime juice

4 scallions, chopped

Green Beans with Salmon

- Combine the olive oil, salt, pepper, ¾ teaspoon sugar, and lemon juice.

- Toss the green beans in half the mixture. Rub the salmon on both sides with the remaining mixture.

- Combine the tomatoes, cilantro, garlic, chiles, lime juice, ¾ teaspoon sugar, and scallions. Add salt and pepper to taste.

- Grill the salmon on medium-high for 5 minutes per side and the green beans 5 minutes total, turning them often. Serve topped with the salsa.

GREEN ● LIGHT

For the best salsa, use fresh, not canned tomatoes. Roma tomatoes are an excellent choice, as they are thicker and meatier and contain less water. And there are no hard and fast rules for salsa ingredients. Try adding some chopped cucumber, radish, or zucchini.

• • • • RECIPE VARIATION • • • •

Grilled Green Beans in Vinaigrette: Combine 2 teaspoons minced garlic, 2 tablespoons white balsamic vinegar, 1 tablespoon lemon juice, and 1 tablespoon maple syrup. Whisk in 4 tablespoons extra-virgin olive oil. Blend well and season with salt and lemon pepper. Serve drizzled on grilled green beans, garnished with lemon slices.

Grill the Beans

- Snap off the tips and stems of the beans and remove any strings. Wash and dry them.

- After coating the beans with the olive oil mixture, place them over a medium flame on a gas grill or in the middle of a medium-hot charcoal grill.

- To keep the beans from falling into the grill, position them lengthwise across the grate.

- Use a spatula instead of tongs to roll the beans back and forth.

Chop the Salsa Vegetables

- Dice the tomatoes into ½-inch cubes.

- Chop the root ends off the scallions and remove the thin skin. Cut the onions about midway along their length and chop, discarding the dry tops.

- Use both the leaves and stems of the cilantro. Chop everything finely.

- For a hotter salsa, add a chopped jalapeño pepper.

VEGETABLES & SEAFOOD

159

SHRIMP WITH SPRING LETTUCES

Lettuce and grilled shrimp in a tangy dressing make a perfect luncheon entree

In the salad department, shrimp usually turns up as shrimp cocktail or in a mayonnaise dressing. This light yet satisfying salad features shrimp brushed with a bottled vinaigrette, threaded onto skewers, grilled until tender and juicy, and served with a medley of crisp lettuces in a buttermilk blue cheese dressing.

When grilling shrimp, you don't want them too small. Otherwise they'll be done in a fraction of a second and overdone before you have time to rescue them. If buying frozen shrimp, look for bags that say 16–20 count per pound. Prawns or large fantail shrimp are great for grilling, but very expensive. *Yield: 6 servings*

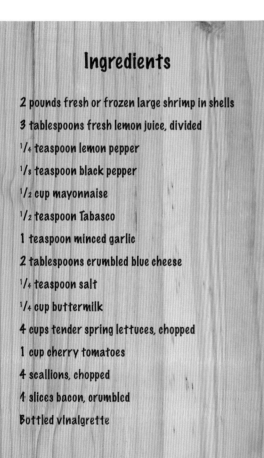

Ingredients

2 pounds fresh or frozen large shrimp in shells

3 tablespoons fresh lemon juice, divided

$1/4$ teaspoon lemon pepper

$1/8$ teaspoon black pepper

$1/2$ cup mayonnaise

$1/2$ teaspoon Tabasco

1 teaspoon minced garlic

2 tablespoons crumbled blue cheese

$1/4$ teaspoon salt

$1/4$ cup buttermilk

4 cups tender spring lettuces, chopped

1 cup cherry tomatoes

4 scallions, chopped

4 slices bacon, crumbled

Bottled vinaigrette

Shrimp with Spring Lettuces

- Wash, rinse, and pat dry deveined shrimp, leaving shells intact. Toss with 2 tablespoons of lemon juice and the lemon pepper.

- Make dressing with the remaining 1 tablespoon of lemon juice, the black pepper, mayonnaise, Tabasco, garlic, blue cheese, salt, and buttermilk.

- Divide the lettuce mixture evenly among six plates.

- Grill shrimp and serve on the lettuces with the tomatoes, scallions, bacon, and dressing.

A shrimp deveiner is specifically designed for deveining shrimp with their shells on and can be purchased at any kitchen supply store. Hold the shrimp back side up and place the deveiner under the tip of the shell. Gently slide the deveiner up the back of the shrimp, toward the tail, and remove the vein.

• • • • RECIPE VARIATION • • • •

Grilled Curried Shrimp Salad: Chop 1 pound grilled shrimp and mix with ½ cup mayonnaise, ½ cup plain yogurt, 3 tablespoons buttermilk, 2 teaspoons Madras or other good curry powder, 2 tablespoons chopped scallions, ½ teaspoon pepper, and ½ teaspoon seasoned salt. Serve on greens with sliced tomatoes, garnished with fresh cilantro.

Pick the Lettuces

- Lettuce of contrasting colors and shapes makes this dish particularly attractive.

- Brunia is a red oak-leaf loose-leaf type of lettuce notable for its pointed, bronze-tinged leaves and its fresh, crisp texture.

- With its bright green leaves and tender, sweet flavor, Black-seeded Simpson lettuce is excellent in this salad.

- The slightly bitter edge to Lollo Rosso lettuce contrasts nicely with the sweeter lettuces. Look for crisp copper-red leaves fading to bright green.

Prepare the Shrimp

- Preheat the grill to medium-high and lightly oil the grate.

- Thread the shrimp onto six 10- to 12-inch skewers and brush with bottled vinaigrette.

- Grill for about 5 minutes, turning halfway through cooking and basting frequently with the vinaigrette.

- The finished shrimp should be opaque on the inside and browned on the outside.

CAJUN TROUT WITH BROCCOLI RABE

Sharp, peppery broccoli rabe and Cajun-spiced blackened trout tickle the palate

Broccoli rabe, also known as Italian rapini, is a common vegetable with spiked leaves surrounding a green bud that resembles a small head of broccoli. Because of its slightly bitter flavor, broccoli rabe is somewhat of an acquired taste. It's thought to have descended from a wild herb related to the turnip that grew in either China or the Mediterranean. There's

a Chinese broccoli rabe that's considerably milder and more tender than its more pungent Italian relation.

This recipe tones down the strong flavor of the broccoli rabe with cherries, cooked shallots, and a little brown sugar. *Yield: 4 servings*

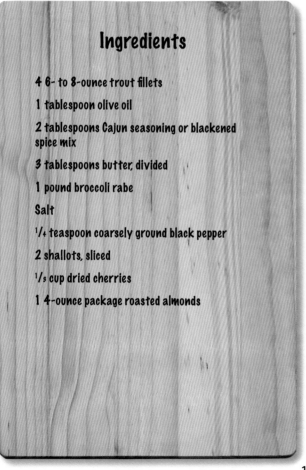

Ingredients

4 6- to 8-ounce trout fillets

1 tablespoon olive oil

2 tablespoons Cajun seasoning or blackened spice mix

3 tablespoons butter, divided

1 pound broccoli rabe

Salt

1/4 teaspoon coarsely ground black pepper

2 shallots, sliced

1/3 cup dried cherries

1 4-ounce package roasted almonds

Cajun Trout with Broccoli Rabe

- Rinse the fillets and pat dry. Lightly rub with olive oil and dredge the flesh side in the Cajun seasoning.

- In a large cast-iron skillet over high heat, cook the fillets, flesh side down, in the olive oil and 2 tablespoons butter turning after 3 minutes. Continue cook-

ing until the skin is crispy and the trout is firm to the touch.

- Prepare the broccoli rabe (see technique).

- Serve fish with the roasted broccoli rabe with shallots and cherries, garnished with the almonds.

It's easy to make your own blackened spice mix. Simply combine, in a small bowl, 1 tablespoon paprika, 1 teaspoon dried thyme, 1 teaspoon ground cumin, 1 teaspoon dry mustard powder, $\frac{1}{2}$ teaspoon cayenne pepper, and 1 teaspoon kosher salt.

Sautéed Broccoli Rabe with Mushrooms: In a large skillet, over medium heat, sauté 1 cup chopped onions and 6 ounces sliced fresh mushrooms until soft. Add 2 teaspoons chopped garlic and cook, 20 seconds. Stir in 1 pound cooked broccoli rabe, add ¾ teaspoon seasoned salt and ⅓ teaspoon lemon pepper, and sauté 10–15 minutes. Sprinkle with grated Romano cheese.

Prepare the Broccoli Rabe

- Fresh broccoli rabe has dark, spiky green leaves, small florets, and medium-size stalks.

- Trim the ends off the broccoli rabe, then toss it with olive oil, salt, and pepper until coated.

- Roast on a large baking sheet at 400°F for 8–12 minutes, or until the broccoli rabe is lightly browned and tender.

- Sauté the shallots in 1 tablespoon butter until soft. Add the cherries and cook for 1 minute. Add the broccoli rabe and cook 1 minute more.

Choose the Trout

- If you live in an area where fresh fish is plentiful, buy fresh trout. If not, use frozen, thawing it in the refrigerator.

- The fish's skin should have a metallic shine. Avoid dull-looking fish with discolored patches.

- If the head is intact, look for clear, bright eyes and rich red gills—no dull eyes or brick-colored gills.

- Fresh trout should smell like clean water. The only detectable odor should be slightly briny. If the trout smells fishy, it's over the hill.

VEGETABLES & SEAFOOD

BRAISED SEA BASS WITH FENNEL

Fresh fennel lends a fragrant sweetness to sea bass and tomato broth

Braising, the technique of searing or browning a main ingredient in fat and then simmering it in liquid over low heat in a covered pot, is generally associated with less expensive, tough cuts of meat. This recipe uses a tender cut of fish, browns it, and cooks it relatively quickly in a covered pan with some fennel-flavored tomato broth.

Serve braised sea bass with fennel as a soup with orzo or rice and hot, crusty peasant bread. *Yield: 4 servings*

Ingredients

2 tablespoons olive oil, divided

1 tablespoon butter

4 pieces (1 1/2 pounds) skin-on Chilean sea bass, rinsed and dried

1 fennel bulb

1 teaspoon chopped garlic

1/2 cup dry white wine

1/4 cup vermouth

1 cup chicken broth

1 1/2 cups diced fresh tomatoes

1/2 teaspoon seasoned salt

1/4 teaspoon freshly ground black pepper

2 tablespoons chopped fresh basil

Braised Sea Bass with Fennel

- Heat 1 tablespoon of the oil and the 1 tablespoon butter. Sear the fillets on each side until golden brown, then transfer to a plate.

- Cook the fennel in the remaining oil for 4–5 minutes. Add the garlic and brown 1 minute.

- Add the wine and vermouth, chicken broth, tomatoes, salt, pepper, and basil, cover the pan with a tight-fitting lid and simmer about 8 minutes.

- Return the sea bass to the pan and cook through, 4–5 minutes. Serve in shallow soup bowls with orzo.

164

Prepare the Fennel

- Since this recipe requires only the fennel bulb, trim the stalks that sprout at the top of the bulb, reserving the fragrant, frilly dill-like ends for garnish.

- Trim and discard a bit—not too much—of the bulb bottom.

- Cut the bulb in half lengthwise. If the core is small and white, keep it, but if it looks tough, core the fennel.

- With the cut side down, cut the bulb lengthwise again, and then cut it crosswise into thin slices.

Prepare the Sea Bass

- Rinse the fillets under cold water. Make sure they're completely dry before cooking so they'll brown and not steam.

- Season the fillets on both sides with salt and pepper.

- Sear the fish skin side up for 3–4 minutes. Flip with a spatula so as not to break the tender fillets, and cook the other side 3–4 minutes.

- Place the fillets in the broth skin side down and add any of the juices that remain on the plate for additional flavor.

VEGETABLES & SEAFOOD

VEGETABLE SEAFOOD NEWBURG

This classic seafood creation is even better with some zucchini, carrots, celery, and mushrooms thrown in

Lobster Newburg was created by a sea captain, Ben Wenberg, in 1876, who shared it with the owner of the famed Delmonico's Restaurant in New York, where it took a proud place on the menu as "Lobster a la Wenberg." But when Wenberg and Charles Delmonico had a spat, the dish was renamed lobster Newburg.

Wenberg or Newburg, it's one of the most delicious and richest dishes on the planet, its signature ingredients being lobster, butter, cream, cheese, cognac, and sherry. Seafood Newburg can include lobster, crab, shrimp, scallops, and other seafood, and the addition of fresh vegetables lessens the guilt of consumption. *Yield: 4–6 servings*

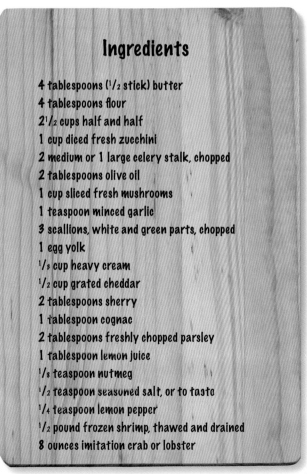

Ingredients

4 tablespoons (¹/₂ stick) butter
4 tablespoons flour
2¹/₂ cups half and half
1 cup diced fresh zucchini
2 medium or 1 large celery stalk, chopped
2 tablespoons olive oil
1 cup sliced fresh mushrooms
1 teaspoon minced garlic
3 scallions, white and green parts, chopped
1 egg yolk
¹/₃ cup heavy cream
¹/₂ cup grated cheddar
2 tablespoons sherry
1 tablespoon cognac
2 tablespoons freshly chopped parsley
1 tablespoon lemon juice
¹/₈ teaspoon nutmeg
¹/₂ teaspoon seasoned salt, or to taste
¹/₄ teaspoon lemon pepper
¹/₂ pound frozen shrimp, thawed and drained
8 ounces imitation crab or lobster

Vegetable Seafood Newburg

- Melt the butter in a saucepan over low heat. Whisk in the flour and then the half and half, stirring until thickened.

- In a 12-inch skillet, brown zucchini and celery in olive oil, 4–5 minutes. Add mushrooms, garlic, and scallions and cook 1 minute.

- Beat the egg yolk with the heavy cream and add to the sauce, stirring constantly.

- Add the cheese, sherry, cognac, parsley, lemon juice, nutmeg, seasoned salt, lemon pepper, seafood, and vegetables to the sauce and heat through.

If the Newburg sauce is too thick, add a little low-fat milk or chicken or vegetable broth until the consistency is smooth. You can also make a lower-calorie version by substituting a white sauce of 4 tablespoons "I Can't Believe It's Not Butter!," 4 tablespoons flour, 2 cups low-fat milk, and 1 cup chicken broth for the cream and half and half.

• • • • RECIPE VARIATION • • • •

Vegetable Seafood Newburg Casserole: Prepare the Vegetable Seafood Newburg as directed. Slightly undercook 8 ounces egg noodles and drain. In a large bowl, combine the Newburg and the noodles. Transfer mixture to a 2-quart casserole dish, top with crushed crackers or bread crumbs, and bake at 350°F 30–40 minutes until golden brown.

Choose the Seafood

- While fresh seafood is great, unless it's local and toxin-free, it isn't always healthier. Frozen is often a better choice.

- Use medium-size shelled and deveined frozen shrimp, which only require 2 minutes of defrosting under cold water.

- If you can afford fresh crab, which has the best flavor, go for it. Otherwise, use imitation crab or lobster—lots cheaper and quite tasty with other ingredients.

- Because of its inferior flavor and texture, never use canned seafood!

Serve the Newburg

- For appetizers or light luncheon entrees, Newburg is often served to great effect in patty shells, little bowls made of pastry dough or puff pastry.

- Bake the patty shells according to package directions and cool before adding the filling.

- For brunch, you can also serve the Newburg over toast squares. Simply toast the bread of your choice, cut into quarters, and top with the sauce. Or how about over waffles?

- For a main dish, serve the Newburg over rice, egg noodles, or hot biscuits.

VEGETABLES & SEAFOOD

CHICKEN CAPRESE

Fresh tomatoes and balsamic vinegar create an impressive and delicious chicken dish

The key to a caprese, a mixture of tomatoes, basil, and mozzarella that hails from the island of Capri, is the freshness of the ingredients. The tomatoes must be sweet and ripe but not too soft. The basil must, of course, be fresh and not dried. And the cheese must be buffalo mozzarella—a white, spongy ball of fresh mozzarella, not the aged or shredded variety.

While a caprese is something like the Italian version of pico de gallo, using fresh tomato, garlic and herbs, chicken caprese features a baked sauce and is delicious drizzled with balsmic reduction and served on a bed of baby spinach. *Yield: 4 servings*

Ingredients

4 skinless boneless chicken breasts, pounded to ¹/₂ inch thick

5 tablespoons olive oil, divided

2 tablespoons lemon juice

¹/₂ teaspoon seasoned salt

¹/₂ teaspoon lemon pepper

1¹/₂ cups Italian-seasoned bread crumbs

4 thin slices prosciutto

1 large fresh tomato, sliced into 4 pieces

4 thin slices fresh buffalo mozzarella

Balsamic reduction sauce

¹/₄ cup chopped fresh basil

2 cups fresh baby spinach

Chicken Caprese

- Toss the pounded chicken breasts in a mixture of 3 tablespoons olive oil, lemon juice, seasoned salt, and lemon pepper. Dredge in the bread crumbs.

- Sear the breasts in 2 tablespoons of heated olive oil until golden brown, about 2 minutes per side.

- Top the chicken with slices of prosciutto, tomato, and mozzarella and bake in a greased baking dish at 400°F for 7–8 minutes.

- Serve drizzled with balsamic reduction and garnished with chopped basil on a bed of baby spinach.

Tortellini Caprese: In a large, deep bowl, mix together 1½ pounds coarsely chopped fresh Roma tomatoes, 8 ounces cubed fresh buffalo mozzarella, 1 teaspoon chopped garlic, ½ cup chopped basil leaves, ⅓ cup chopped parsley, and 8 ounces cooked cheese tortellini. Toss with a good bottled balsamic vinaigrette.

Chicken Caprese Sandwiches: Prepare the caprese mixture as in Tortellini Caprese. Make the chicken breasts as in Chicken Caprese, omitting the tomato and mozzarella and baking just with the prosciutto. Slice 4 ciabatta rolls in half, spread with a little garlic and olive oil, and toast until lightly brown. Make sandwiches with the chicken breasts topped with the fresh caprese sauce.

Pound the Chicken Breasts

- Skinless boneless chicken breasts have a tapered shape and attached tenderloin, which can be removed as it usually falls off during pounding.

- Pounding gives the meat a uniform thickness and breaks it up to allow sauces to permeate quickly.

- Place the breast in a plastic bag, which will prevent the chicken from tearing.

- Starting at the thickest part of the breast, pound gently with a flat mallet, in a slight circular motion and outward to the edge of the meat.

Make the Reduction Sauce

- Aged balsamic vinegar can be expensive. Look for one that's reasonably priced.

- Pour 2 cups of vinegar into a pan. Whisk briskly over high heat, adding 3 ounces of butter in 3 chunks and continuing to whisk as the mixture boils to prevent burning.

- The vinegar naturally sweetens when reduced, but for a very sweet reduction, sprinkle in a tablespoon of sugar.

- Reduce the mixture by half, or until it takes on a syrupy quality.

CRUSTED CHICKEN WITH GREENS

Go south with fresh collard greens, pecan-crusted chicken, and sweet and spicy mustard sauce

You probably have to be born and bred down South to appreciate collard greens, or just "greens," as the traditional combination of boiled collard greens, kale, spinach, turnip greens, and mustard greens is known. A soul food staple, collard greens are usually cooked with smoked and salted meats like bacon, ham hocks, or pork necks and seasoned

with onion, vinegar, and crushed red pepper flakes.

Collard greens are a traditional New Year's Day dish, eaten with black-eyed peas and cornbread as a symbol for "greenbacks" and a harbinger of prosperity. This combination of collards, baked chicken, and pecans is already rich on its own. *Yield: 4 servings*

Ingredients

¹/₂ cup fresh bread crumbs

1 cup pecan pieces

¹/₄ cup chopped parsley

¹/₄ teaspoon lemon pepper

2 teaspoons paprika

¹/₂ teaspoon onion powder

¹/₂ teaspoon crushed red pepper flakes

2 teaspoons minced garlic, divided

1¹/₂ teaspoons seasoned salt, divided

4 skinless boneless chicken breasts

2 large eggs, beaten with ¹/₄ cup milk

2 pounds collard greens

4 slices bacon

1 medium yellow onion, chopped

2 tablespoons sesame oil

8 drops Tabasco

Sweet mustard sauce

Crusted Chicken with Greens

- In a blender, combine bread crumbs, pecan pieces, parsley, lemon pepper, paprika, onion powder, red pepper flakes, 1 teaspoon garlic, and ½ teaspoon seasoned salt. Pulse for 1 minute. Transfer to a shallow dish.

- Dip the chicken breasts in the beaten egg mixture.

- Dredge the breasts in the pecan mixture and transfer to a large, lightly greased baking dish. Bake at 375°F, turning once, until the crust is golden, 15–20 minutes.

- Serve over cooked collard greens, drizzled with mustard sauce.

GREEN ● LIGHT

To chop collard greens, begin by folding each leaf in half with the top side of the green folded inward. Cut along the stem and discard stem. Stack the greens in piles of 6–8 leaves, roll up the stacks, and chop into 1-inch strips.

• • • • RECIPE VARIATION • • • •

Good Ol' Southern Greens: Cook 3 smoked ham hocks and 3 cloves chopped garlic in 2 quarts boiling water with 2 teaspoons seasoned salt, ½ teaspoon red pepper flakes, and ½ cup cider vinegar until falling apart, about 3 hours. Add 3 pounds chopped collard greens and simmer until wilted, 30 minutes.

Prepare the Greens

- Wash and pat dry the greens. Discard the tough stems. Stack the leaves in small piles, roll up, and cut greens into 1-inch strips.

- In a large skillet with a tight-fitting cover, fry the bacon until crisp. Drain on paper towels, leaving the bacon fat in the skillet.

- Sauté the onion in the hot fat until soft, and add 1 teaspoon garlic, sautéing about 20 seconds.

- Mix in the greens, sesame oil, Tabasco, and 1 teaspoon seasoned salt and cook until tender, about 10 minutes.

Make the Mustard Sauce

- In a medium saucepan, combine 1 cup of spicy brown mustard with 1 cup of cider vinegar and ½ cup of apricot preserves.

- Heat on medium-high until mixture begins to bubble. Reduce heat.

- Stir in ¼ cup of brown sugar, 1 tablespoon Worcestershire sauce, 1 teaspoon black pepper, and ½ teaspoon seasoned salt.

- Simmer 25–30 minutes, then cool slightly. Drizzle to taste over the chicken and greens.

VEGETABLES & CHICKEN

CHICKEN WITH MORELS & MADEIRA

Chicken thighs play dress up in a fancy sauce of Madeira and white wine, cream, Gruyère cheese, and morel mushrooms

We rarely cook with morel mushrooms, because in the past they were not as easy to come by as the stardard white button mushrooms, being procured only by foraging in the wild. Today, however, you can find morels in most large supermarkets, and more and more people are becoming morel converts.

Morels have a unique earthy, nutty flavor that's both subtle and vibrant, which makes them a perfect companion to chicken in a Madeira cream sauce. Of course, you can use any kind of mushrooms for this dish, but if you can find morels, you won't be disappointed. *Yield: 4–6 servings*

Ingredients

8 skinless boneless chicken thighs

Salt and freshly ground pepper

Onion powder

1 cup flour

2 tablespoons olive oil

2 tablespoons butter

2 shallots, minced

³/₄ pound morel mushrooms

¹/₂ cup dry white wine

1 cup chicken stock or broth

¹/₂ cup heavy cream

¹/₃ cup Madeira

¹/₂ cup shredded Gruyère cheese

Chicken with Morels and Madeira

- Lightly sprinkle the chicken thighs with salt, pepper, and onion powder and dredge in flour.

- Brown the chicken in the olive oil and butter. Remove to a plate.

- Sauté the shallots and mushrooms 1 minute. Add the white wine and stock and reduce the sauce.

- Stir in the cream and Madeira and boil until thickened slightly. Add salt and pepper to taste. Return chicken to the skillet and heat through. Sprinkle with cheese and serve over noodles or rice.

Chicken with Mushrooms and Gruyère: Brown the floured chicken thighs as directed. Transfer to a 2-quart casserole dish. Add the sautéed morels and shallots, 1 cup chicken broth, ½ cup white wine, salt and pepper to taste, and the juice of 1 lemon. Top with shredded Gruyère cheese and bake at 350°F 45 minutes–1 hour, or until chicken is tender.

Creamy Chicken Mushroom Casserole: Brown the chicken as directed. Transfer to a casserole dish. Sauté the morels, shallots, and 1 cup chopped onion. Add the wine, broth, 2 cups fresh cream, salt, pepper, and 2 teaspoons paprika. Simmer 10–15 minutes. Pour over chicken and bake at 350°F 45 minutes–1 hour.

Clean the Morels

- Because the spongy texture of morels can trap sand, dirt, and even insects, the mushrooms must be thoroughly cleaned.

- After rinsing the morels, cut them in half lengthwise with a sharp knife. Make sure that each mushroom is hollow; this distinguishes real morels from poisonous mushrooms.

- Put the morels in a large bowl of water with 2 teaspoons salt, stirring slightly.

- Soak the morels overnight. After soaking, shake them to free any remaining debris.

Reduce the Sauce

- There should be some brown bits of chicken, known as "fond," left over in the pan. Cook the shallots in the fond.

- When adding the wine and stock, loosen any browned bits stuck to the pan and incorporate them into the sauce.

- Boil until the liquid is reduced by half. Reduce the heat to medium, add the Madeira and cream, and simmer until thickened.

- Stirring in 1 tablespoon of butter just before serving gives the sauce a nice sheen.

VEGETABLES & CHICKEN

COQ AU VIN MAGNIFIQUE

Here's a coq au vin that features fresh carrots, potatoes, mushrooms, and zucchini

The traditional master chef way of making this classic French dish is a big production, involving painstaking labor and daunting ingredients like lardoons and *beurre manie*.

When *Cook's Illustrated* triumphantly announced a "quick" coq au vin that takes only an hour and a half, I was amused because my "Coq au Vin Magnifique" has never taken more than that, from start to finish. With its fragrant herbs, deep rich wine sauce, and fresh vegetables, served in shallow bowls with crusty French or Italian bread, it makes a hearty one-dish meal. *Yield: 6–8 servings*

Ingredients

6 chicken thighs and 3 breast halves, washed and patted dry

Seasoned salt, pepper, and onion powder for seasoning the chicken

1 cup flour (for dredging)

1 medium zucchini

3 medium white or red potatoes

2 large or 3 medium carrots

4 slices bacon, cooked and diced, fat reserved

1 tablespoon olive oil

1 tablespoon butter

1 medium yellow onion, chopped

2 teaspoons chopped garlic

6 ounces fresh mushrooms, coarsely chopped

3 tablespoons tomato paste

2 cups dry red wine

2 tablespoons cognac or brandy

2 cups chicken stock or broth

3 sprigs fresh thyme

1 tablespoon chopped fresh parsley or 2 teaspoons dried parsley

3 sprigs fresh rosemary

2 bay leaves

1 teaspoon salt

$\frac{1}{2}$ teaspoon coarsely ground pepper

Coq au Vin Magnifique

- Season the chicken with seasoned salt, pepper and onion powder, and dredge in flour.

- Microwave the vegetables (**see technique**). Meanwhile, in a large skillet, brown the chicken pieces in the bacon fat and remove to a plate.

- Add the olive oil and butter to the skillet and sauté the onions, garlic, and mushrooms for 1 minute. Add the tomato paste, wine, brandy, stock, bacon, herbs, seasonings, and all vegetables.

- Cook on low heat for 1 hour. Finish the sauce (see technique) and serve.

········· GREEN ● LIGHT ·········

While coq au vin is most often made with red wine to create the rich brown sauce, it's also delicious with white wine, which gives it a lighter, more piquant edge. Just omit the brandy and substitute a full-flavored dry white wine such as Sauvignon Blanc for the red wine.

···· RECIPE VARIATION ····

Coq au Vin Fondue: In a fondue pot, heat 3½ cups of vegetable stock until simmering. Add ½ cup Burgundy, ½ cup sliced mushrooms, 1 tablespoon cognac, 1 tablespoon minced garlic, 2 chopped scallions, and salt and pepper to taste. Place individual pieces of chicken or vegetables on a fondue fork and cook through.

Microwave the Vegetables

- Wash and dry the zucchini, potatoes, and carrots. Do not peel the vegetables.

- Cut the zucchini into 1-inch chunks and the carrots into 2-inch slices. Quarter the potatoes.

- Place vegetables in a microwave-safe dish or small casserole and cover with wax paper. Add ⅓ cup of water.

- Microwave on high 4–5 minutes. You want the vegetables just slightly cooked, as they will finish on the stove.

Finish the Sauce

- When the chicken is tender, remove it from the pan and transfer it temporarily to a plate.

- Remove the bay leaves, thyme, and rosemary sprigs and discard.

- Bring the sauce to a high simmer, and boil until the sauce begins to thicken.

- Stir in 1 tablespoon of butter and add the chicken back to the pan. Heat through.

VEGETABLES & CHICKEN

THREE-PEPPER SIZZLING CHICKEN
This dish features a fresh pepper medley and chicken baked and stir-fried

This Asian dish is unique in that it comes in two parts. One involves a quick stir-fry of chicken breast strips and hot and mild peppers. The other takes place in the oven, where chicken thighs roast to browned perfection in a soy-teriyaki sauce. The two dishes meet and marry at the table, where they're joined together over rice. The flavors are dizzyingly good—the salt of the soy sauce blends with the fire of the hot chiles and a hint of sweetness from the teriyaki and bell peppers. *Yield: 6 servings*

Ingredients

6 chicken thighs

Lemon pepper and onion powder for seasoning chicken

$1/2$ cup soy sauce

$1/4$ cup teriyaki sauce

$1/3$ cup chicken broth

1 teaspoon Thai red chili paste

2 teaspoons minced garlic, divided

2 teaspoons grated fresh ginger

3 scallions, chopped

1 tablespoon butter, melted

4 skinless boneless chicken breasts, cut into 1-inch strips

2 hot chiles with seeds, chopped

1 small green bell pepper, cut into $1/4$-inch strips

1 small red bell pepper, cut into $1/4$-inch strips

2 tablespoons canola or vegetable oil

4 cups cooked rice

Three-Pepper Sizzling Chicken

- Season chicken thighs with the lemon pepper and onion powder and place in lightly greased baking dish

- Combine soy and teriyaki sauces, broth, chili paste, 1 teaspoon minced garlic, ginger, scallion, and melted butter.

- Brush the mixture over the chicken and bake at 350°F for 40–45 minutes, basting with sauce as needed.

- In a medium skillet, stir-fry the chicken strips, chiles, bell peppers, and remaining 1 teaspoon of garlic in hot oil until browned, 2 minutes. Serve.

Three-Pepper Asian Chicken Salad: Sauté the chicken breast strips and peppers as directed. Cool. Toss with 1 head chopped iceberg lettuce, 1 cup grated cabbage, 1 cup grated carrots, 1 cup chopped cucumber, 3 chopped scallions, 1 10-ounce can Chinese fried noodles, and bottled raspberry or pomegranate vinaigrette.

Three-Pepper Sizzling Chicken Wraps: Place 2 tablespoons of the chicken strips and peppers in the center of a 10-inch (small burrito size) flour tortilla. Add some chopped bok choy (Chinese cabbage), grated carrots, and chopped scallions. Drizzle with soy sauce. Repeat with more tortillas until you run out of filling. Heat finished wraps for 20 seconds in the microwave.

Handling the Hot Peppers

Bake the Chicken Thighs

- Serrano or jalapeño peppers are good for this dish.

- When buying hot chile peppers, make sure that they're firm to the touch and the skin is smooth. Once they wrinkle, their crisp texture and fresh flavor are gone.

- When handling very hot peppers, wear rubber gloves. The peppers contain capsaicin, a highly irritating oil that can cause burns and can seep through latex.

- After chopping the peppers, always wash your hands, even if you've worn gloves, and don't rub your nose or eyes.

- Brush the chicken with the soy sauce mixture every 15 minutes or so.

- Add water or chicken broth to the bottom of the baking dish to keep the soy sauce from burning.

- After 30 minutes, turn the oven up to 450°F and bake the chicken 10–15 more minutes, until the skin is crispy and dark brown.

- Spoon the sauce in the baking dish over both types of chicken when serving.

VEGETABLES & CHICKEN

177

ZUCCHINI-STUFFED CHICKEN LEGS

A vegetable-cheese-bread stuffing is placed under the skin of chicken leg quarters

Stuffed whole chicken, stuffed chicken breasts . . . stuffed chicken legs? You may never have made them, but they are simple to prepare and gratifyingly good. You just loosen the skin from the flesh and fill the pouch with whatever you like. In this case, shredded zucchini is combined with onions, croutons, and ricotta and Romano cheeses to create a savory,

moist stuffing. The chicken is brushed with herb butter and baked atop a bed of sliced potatoes cooked in the juices. How good does that sound? *Yield: 4–6 servings*

Ingredients

4 medium potatoes, thinly sliced

Seasoned salt and pepper

1/2 cup chopped yellow onion

2 tablespoons butter

1 teaspoon minced garlic

1 pound zucchini, shredded

1 1/2 cups seasoned croutons

2/3 cup ricotta cheese

2 tablespoons grated Romano cheese

1 egg, beaten

6 chicken leg quarters

1 cup herb butter, melted

Zucchini-Stuffed Chicken Legs

- Line a lightly greased 13 x 9 x 2-inch baking dish with 2 layers of sliced potatoes and sprinkle with salt and pepper.

- Sauté the onion in butter in a medium skillet until soft. Brown the garlic. Add the zucchini and cook 3 minutes.

- Remove from heat and mix well with the croutons, ricotta, Romano cheese, and egg.

- Stuff the chicken legs and place skin side up on top of the potatoes. Brush the chicken with the herb butter and bake at 375°F for 1 hour, basting every 15 minutes.

178

GREEN ● LIGHT

Because it has a high degree of moisture, shredded zucchini needs to "sweat." Spread the zucchini on paper towels, sprinkle with salt, and let it sit for 15 minutes, blotting it with more towels to remove excess water.

• • • • RECIPE VARIATION • • • •

Zucchini Carrot Pistachio Stuffing: In 2 tablespoons olive oil, sauté ½ cup finely chopped onion, 6 ounces sliced fresh mushrooms, 1 tablespoon chopped shallots, ½ cup grated zucchini, and ½ cup grated carrots. Combine 3 cups whole grain bread crumbs, 1 cup shelled pistachio nuts, 1 cup chicken stock, and ½ cup melted butter. Add to skillet and season with salt and pepper.

Stuff the Chicken Legs

- Starting at the thigh end, loosen the top skin of the leg to create a small pouch over the thigh portion. Make sure to leave the skin attached at one side.

- Fill pouch with stuffing and pull the skin back to its original position.

- To prevent the skin from shrinking when cooking, pierce it with the tip of a knife between the pouch and leg bone.

- Secure the skin with toothpicks.

Make the Herb Butter

- Bring 1½ sticks of unsalted butter to room temperature.

- Finely chop 1 tablespoon of fresh parsley, 1 teaspoon fresh basil, and 1 teaspoon fresh chives.

- In a small mixing bowl, add the fresh herbs and 1 teaspoon dried tarragon, ½ teaspoon salt, and ½ teaspoon fresh lemon juice to the butter.

- Combine the ingredients with a spoon or hand mixer until well blended.

VEGETABLES & CHICKEN

SPIKED BABY CARROTS WITH PORK
Orange liqueur and a cinnamon stick add a wonderful kick to baby carrots

Everybody knows that pork chops and fruit were born to be together. Apples, cranberries, apricots, and pineapple, cooked as sauces or made into a glaze, are common accessories to pork. But vegetables can do the job as well. Tender, sweet baby carrots drizzled with a simple sauce of orange juice, butter, honey, and orange liqueur combine vegetable and fruit into an ideal side dish for pork chops fried in an herbed Parmesan breading. Add some garlic mashed potatoes or parsley potatoes in herb butter to the plate and you've got a memorable meal. *Yield: 4 servings*

Ingredients

2 bunches baby carrots

$1/2$ cup orange juice

2 tablespoons honey

$1/2$ cinnamon stick

1 tablespoon butter

1 tablespoon Grand Marnier or other orange liqueur

3 eggs, lightly beaten

3 tablespoons milk

$1 1/2$ cups Italian-seasoned bread crumbs

$1/2$ cup grated Parmesan

2 tablespoons dried parsley

4 cloves garlic, chopped

2 tablespoons olive oil

4 pork chops, cut $1 1/4$-inch thick

Spiked Baby Carrots with Pork

- Cook the carrots, then combine orange juice, honey, cinnamon stick, butter, and liqueur and simmer for 3–5 minutes. Remove cinnamon stick.

- Preheat oven to 325°F. Beat together eggs and milk. In a separate bowl, combine bread crumbs, Parmesan, and parsley. Sauté garlic in olive oil in an ovenproof skillet until lightly browned. Remove from pan.

- Dip pork chops in egg mixture and then into the bread crumb mixture, coating evenly. Brown in oil 5 minutes per side, then bake in skillet for 25–30 minutes.

Cook the Carrots

Prepare the Pork Chops

- Choose bright, crisp carrots with healthy green leaves. If the leaves are wilted or the carrots aren't firm, avoid them.

- Baby carrots don't need to be peeled, just buffed with a vegetable brush.

- Place the carrots in a steamer insert and steam for 12–15 minutes. Or microwave them with 2–3 tablespoons of water on high for 8 minutes.

- Arrange the cooked carrots on a platter around the chops and drizzle the liqueur sauce over them. Garnish with parsley.

- Rib chops are preferable to loin chops because they have a little more fat and won't tend to dry out during cooking.

- Place the bread crumb mixture on a sheet of wax paper and put the egg-dipped chops into the crumbs, turning several times to coat well.

- Brown the chops over medium-high heat without overcooking the inside, which toughens them.

- The baked pork chop should be crisp on the outside and tender, not dry, on the inside.

SPRING VEGETABLES WITH LAMB

Delicate early spring vegetables, fresh herbs, wine, and lamb make a delicious stew

There are many kinds of lamb stew. The Irish version layers chunks of lamb in a pot with potatoes, turnips, and carrots, covered with water or chicken stock, seasoned only with salt and pepper, and cooked until tender. Lamb navarin, a French peasant dish, features baby carrots, new potatoes, and young squash. Greek lamb stew uses a variety of spices, from bay

leaf, thyme, and rosemary to oregano and cinnamon, and may include tomatoes, olives, potatoes, chickpeas, and other vegetables.

This lamb stew is a combination of different cuisines—the root vegetables of Ireland, the early spring vegetables of France, and the seasoning of Greece. *Yield: 6 servings*

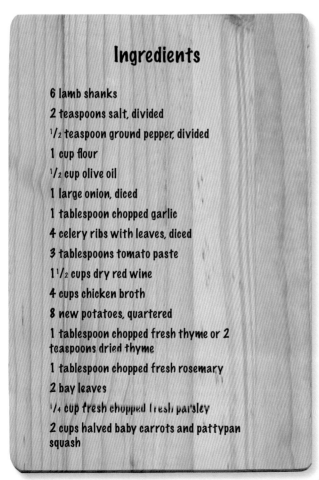

Ingredients

6 lamb shanks

2 teaspoons salt, divided

1/2 teaspoon ground pepper, divided

1 cup flour

1/2 cup olive oil

1 large onion, diced

1 tablespoon chopped garlic

4 celery ribs with leaves, diced

3 tablespoons tomato paste

1 1/2 cups dry red wine

4 cups chicken broth

8 new potatoes, quartered

1 tablespoon chopped fresh thyme or 2 teaspoons dried thyme

1 tablespoon chopped fresh rosemary

2 bay leaves

1/4 cup fresh chopped fresh parsley

2 cups halved baby carrots and pattypan squash

Spring Vegetables with Lamb

- Coat lamb shanks with mixture of 1 teaspoon salt, 1/4 teaspoon pepper, and flour. Brown in hot oil in a large skillet or Dutch oven. Transfer to plate.

- Sauté onion, garlic, and celery for 3 minutes. Add tomato paste, wine, and broth, stirring well.

- Add lamb back to the pot with the potatoes, herbs, and remaining salt and pepper. Simmer, covered, for 45 minutes.

- Blanch spring vegetables and add to pot. Simmer 30 minutes more.

Blanching is an easy technique that many cooks use to keep vegetables crisp and tender. By boiling vegetables briefly, chilling them in ice water, and then reheating them slowly, blanching preserves texture, color, and flavor.

• • • • RECIPE VARIATION • • • •

Irish Lamb Stew: Brown the lamb shanks as directed. In a large stew pot, place a layer of the quartered new potatoes, carrots, onion, celery, and squash. Season with salt, pepper, and half the herbs. Place half the shanks on top and pour half the broth over all. Repeat. Cover and cook on low heat 1 hour, or until lamb is tender.

Prepare the Squash

- Pattypan squash gets its name from its flying saucer shape. Because of its scalloped edges, it's also known as scalloped squash.

- For best taste and texture, choose the smallest ones available, making sure they're regularly shaped and free of nicks.

- Wash and dry the squashes. Trim away any blemishes and any woody areas at the stem end.

- Because the pattypans are so small to begin with, you need only cut them in half for this recipe.

Blanch the Vegetables

- Bring a large pot of salted water to a rapid boil over high heat.

- While the water heats, fill a medium bowl about ¾ full with ice. Add enough cold water to cover the ice.

- Cook the baby carrots and squash in the boiling water, 3–4 minutes.

- Quickly remove the vegetables and submerge them in the ice bath to stop the cooking process. Remove as soon as they're just cooled.

GREEN BEAN & BEEF STIR-FRY
Crunchy browned green beans are a great addition to any stir-fry

Stir-frying is one of the fastest and best ways to cook vegetables. You can mix and match them with beef, pork, poultry, and seafood, or whip up mixed vegetable stir-fries resplendent with color, texture, and flavor. Stir-frying is a particularly good cooking method for vegetables like green beans, which usually must be cooked and blanched ahead of time so that they don't overcook in a sauce. Stir-frying eliminates

the step of cooking the beans separately, allowing for an easy one-skillet dish which, when served over jasmine rice, is particularly tasty. *Yield: 4 servings*

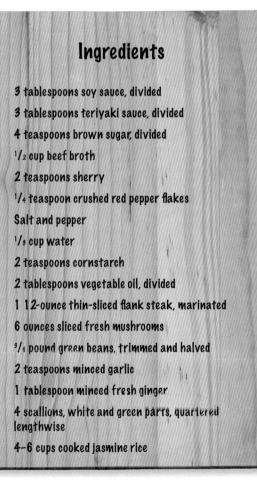

Ingredients

3 tablespoons soy sauce, divided

3 tablespoons teriyaki sauce, divided

4 teaspoons brown sugar, divided

$1/2$ cup beef broth

2 teaspoons sherry

$1/4$ teaspoon crushed red pepper flakes

Salt and pepper

$1/3$ cup water

2 teaspoons cornstarch

2 tablespoons vegetable oil, divided

1 12-ounce thin-sliced flank steak, marinated

6 ounces sliced fresh mushrooms

$3/4$ pound green beans, trimmed and halved

2 teaspoons minced garlic

1 tablespoon minced fresh ginger

4 scallions, white and green parts, quartered lengthwise

4–6 cups cooked jasmine rice

Green Bean and Beef Stir-Fry

- In a medium bowl, whisk together 1 tablespoon each soy and teriyaki sauce, 2 teaspoons brown sugar, broth, sherry, pepper flakes, salt, pepper, water, and cornstarch.

- Heat 1 tablespoon oil in a nonstick skillet. Brown the beef and transfer to a bowl.

- Add remaining oil and brown the mushrooms. Add the green beans and cook until spotty brown, 3–4 minutes. Push the vegetables to the side and brown the garlic and ginger. Add the beef, scallions, vegetables, and sauce and simmer 1 minute. Serve over jasmine rice.

• • • • RECIPE VARIATION • • • •

Other Stir-Fry Possibilities: In place of the beef in this recipe, try: cubed firm tofu; chicken breast strips; pork strips; Chinese red sausage, or lap cheong; shrimp; scallops; or firm fish fillets, such as cod, haddock, turbot, or snapper.

Prepare the Beef

- Cut across the grain so the meat won't be tough. The slices should be ¼ inch thick. For easier slicing, freeze the beef for 20–30 minutes beforehand.

- Marinate the sliced beef for 15 minutes to 1 hour in 2 tablespoons each soy and teriyaki sauce and 2 teaspoons of brown sugar.

- Drain well after marinating, as any excess liquid will prevent proper searing.

- Cook the beef in batches; cooking it all at once causes it to steam in its own liquid and become chewy and dry.

Use the Right Pan

- While woks are the traditional stir-fry pan, their actual searing surface is small.

- A slope-sided stir-fry pan is shallower than a flat-bottomed wok, but lacks enough room for quick stirring and pushing aside ingredients.

- A flat-bottomed stir-fry pan is a better alternative to the wok but not as efficient as a large nonstick pan.

- Because of its ample frying surface, a nonstick skillet measuring at least 12 inches across the top is best for this dish.

185

CORNED BEEF & CABBAGE

The old St. Patty's Day staple makes stars out of simple cabbage and potatoes

Corning is a process of curing and preserving meat that has been around at least since the ninth century A.D. For corned beef, the meat is placed in a large crock and covered with large rock-salt kernels that were known as "corns" of salt. The Irish have long been associated with corned beef because, until the early nineteenth century, they were the biggest exporters of that product. Contrary to popular belief, corned beef and cabbage is not a traditional Irish dish, but corned beef is. Nonetheless, Irish and non-Irish folks alike enjoy this tempting combination of tender corned beef, cabbage, and potatoes boiled in a spiced pot liquor. *Yield: 8 servings*

Ingredients

1 3-pound corned beef brisket (uncooked), in brine

4 quarts cold water

2 teaspoons black peppercorns

2 bay leaves

4 whole allspice berries

2 whole cloves

$^1/_2$ medium head green cabbage

24 small new potatoes, halved

2 tablespoons butter

$^1/_4$ cup chopped fresh parsley

Seasoned salt and pepper

Corned Beef and Cabbage

- Rinse the corned beef in a colander under cold water and place in a Dutch oven with a tight-fitting lid.

- Add the water, peppercorns, and herbs and spices. Bring to a boil uncovered, skimming off any scum that rises to the surface. Cover, transfer the pot to the oven, and braise at 300°F for 3 hours and 45 minutes.

- Remove the corned beef to a cutting board and cover with foil.

- Simmer the cabbage and potatoes in the cooking liquid until tender, about 15 minutes.

• • • • RECIPE VARIATIONS • • • •

Sweet and Sour Corned Beef and Cabbage: When adding the cabbage and potatoes to the broth, add 1 16-ounce can sauerkraut, 3 grated carrots, ½ cup Piesporter Riesling or another semisweet white wine, 2 tablespoons cider vinegar, 2 teaspoons Dijon mustard, ¼ cup ketchup, and ¼ cup brown sugar. Mix well and simmer 15–20 minutes.

Bubble and Squeak:. Brown 3 slices diced bacon. Add one thinly sliced onion and cook until soft. Add 1 cup of the cooked corned beef, 1 tablespoon butter, 3 cups of the cooked cabbage and potatoes, 2 teaspoons paprika, salt, and coarsely ground pepper. Brown on both sides. Serve with eggs as a breakfast entrée, or as a dinner side dish.

Prepare the Cabbage

- With a paring knife, cut a small piece off the end of the cabbage opposite to the core. Rest the cabbage on this end, making sure it's steady.

- Using a chef's knife, cut the cabbage head in half.

- Lay down one half of the cabbage, cut side down, and switch to the paring knife to cut around the core and remove it.

- Cut the cored cabbage into 8 thick wedges and tie each wedge with kitchen string like a package.

Plate the Dish

- Transfer the cooked cabbage to a large platter with a slotted spoon. Remove the string.

- Slice the corned beef across the grain into thin slices. Lay the slices over the cabbage and surround with the potatoes.

- Dress the potatoes with 2 tablespoons butter, fresh chopped parsley, and a little seasoned salt and pepper.

- Ladle some of the broth over the corned beef, adding salt and pepper to taste, and serve with mustard or horseradish sauce.

SHEPHERD'S PIE

This meat and vegetable casserole topped with cheesy mashed potatoes was made for cold winter nights

Shepherd's pie, also known as cottage pie, is an English meat pie topped with mashed potatoes. The term "cottage pie" dates back to the eighteenth century, when the rural poor, who lived in modest cottages, were introduced to the affordable potato. Although the original dish may have been made in a pie crust, the typical shepherd's pie is not really a pie at all, but rather a casserole. Shepherd's pie can be made with ground or cubed meat and vegetables, and it is a tasty, economical, and filling way of reinventing leftovers. *Yield: 6 servings*

Ingredients

¹/₂ cup chopped celery

1 tablespoon canola, corn, or vegetable oil

1 small yellow onion, chopped

1¹/₂ cups sliced fresh mushrooms

1¹/₂ pounds ground or diced meat of choice

3 medium carrots, cut crosswise into 1-inch slices

8 ounces frozen peas, slightly thawed

1 can cream of tomato soup

1 cup milk

¹/₂ teaspoon dried basil

Seasoned salt and coarsely ground pepper

¹/₂ teaspoon onion powder

6 medium potatoes, quartered and boiled

2 tablespoons butter

¹/₂ cup sour cream

¹/₃ cup half and half

¹/₂ teaspoon garlic powder

1 16-ounce can French fried onion rings

1 8-ounce package shredded sharp cheddar

Shepherd's Pie

- In a large skillet, sauté the celery in the oil until soft. Add the onion and mushrooms and cook 2 minutes.

- Combine the meat, carrots, peas, sautéed vegetables, tomato soup, milk, basil, ¹/₂ teaspoon seasoned salt, ¹/₂ teaspoon pepper, and ¹/₂ teaspoon onion powder.

Transfer to a 2-quart casserole dish.

- Mash potatoes (see technique) and mound onto the casserole, spreading out like a frosting. Top with onion rings and cheese and bake uncovered at 350°F for 30 minutes or until lightly browned and bubbling.

GREEN ● LIGHT

Try different meats for shepherd's pie, such as ground or diced cooked lamb or turkey, chopped ham, or ground country sausage. Or omit the cream of tomato soup and make the pie the way they do in England, Canada, and Australia, with creamed corn. For a vegetarian shepherd's pie, substitute 2 cups of cooked lentils for the meat.

• • • • RECIPE VARIATION • • • •

Shepherd's Pie Hash: Combine 2 cups cooked ground or chopped beef, 2 cups mashed potatoes, 1 medium chopped onion, 1 chopped green pepper, 1 teaspoon dry mustard, 1 teaspoon chopped garlic, ½ teaspoon seasoned salt, ½ teaspoon coarsely ground pepper, and 1½ cups beef broth. Bake in a greased shallow baking dish at 350°F for 35–45 minutes.

Select the Meat

- Shepherd's pie is adaptable to all sorts of meats, especially leftovers.

- Brown uncooked ground meats like beef, lamb, or turkey in the skillet with the celery, onions, and mushrooms.

- If using cooked lamb or beef, cut it into 1-inch chunks.

- For lots of extra flavor, add several slices of chopped cooked bacon with its drippings to the casserole.

Prepare the Mashed Potatoes

- In a saucepan, cover the raw potato quarters with salted water and bring to a boil.

- Reduce heat and simmer until tender, about 15 minutes.

- In a large bowl, mash the potatoes with the butter, sour cream, half and half, 1 teaspoon seasoned salt, garlic powder, and ¼–½ teaspoon coarsely ground pepper.

- Whip with a wooden spoon or hand mixer until fluffy.

CREAMED SPINACH WITH VEAL

Creamed spinach is a perfect accompaniment to savory Viennese veal cutlets

Wienerschnitzel, or breaded and fried veal cutlets, have found their way into many ethnic cuisines. In Italy and Argentina, they're called *milanesa;* in Portugal, *bife panado.* Finland's *Wieninleike* uses pork instead of veal. The Iranians have a spicy breaded chicken cutlet called *shenitsel,* while Israeli shnitsel is made from chicken or turkey breast.

For a delicate, even bland dish like creamed spinach, there is no substitute for freshly ground nutmeg. Grate the whole nutmeg nut or seed on a Microplane just prior to use to release its flavor. *Yield: 4 servings*

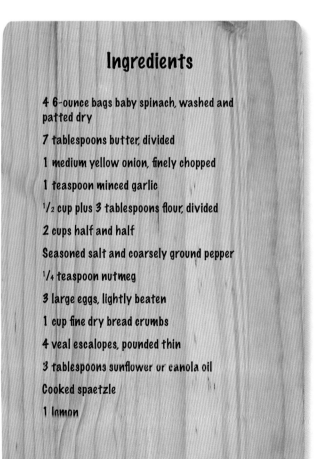

Ingredients

4 6-ounce bags baby spinach, washed and patted dry

7 tablespoons butter, divided

1 medium yellow onion, finely chopped

1 teaspoon minced garlic

½ cup plus 3 tablespoons flour, divided

2 cups half and half

Seasoned salt and coarsely ground pepper

¼ teaspoon nutmeg

3 large eggs, lightly beaten

1 cup fine dry bread crumbs

4 veal escalopes, pounded thin

3 tablespoons sunflower or canola oil

Cooked spaetzle

1 lemon

Creamed Spinach with Veal

- Make the creamed spinach (see technique).

- Place ½ cup of flour, beaten eggs, and bread crumbs in 3 individual shallow dishes.

- Season the veal cutlets with seasoned salt and pepper. Dredge each cutlet in the flour, coat with the egg mixture, and dredge in the bread crumbs.

- Heat the oil and 2 tablespoons butter in a large skillet. Brown cutlets, one at a time, on both sides, about 2 minutes per side. Drain on paper towels and serve with the spinach, spaetzle, and lemon wedges.

190

• • • • RECIPE VARIATION • • • •

Fresh Tomatoes with Creamed Spinach: Slice off the tops of 6 medium tomatoes and reserve them. Carefully scoop out the seeds and turn tomatoes upside down to drain. Sprinkle them with salt and pepper and chill. Fill the chilled tomatoes with creamed spinach and put the tops back on like little lids. Serve while the spinach is still hot.

Make the Creamed Spinach

- In a large skillet, sauté the spinach in 2 tablespoons of butter until it cooks down.

- In a 2-quart saucepan, melt 3 tablespoons butter and sauté the onion until soft. Add the garlic and brown 1 minute.

- Whisk in 3 tablespoons flour to make a roux, and gradually add the half and half, whisking constantly over medium heat until sauce thickens. Add 1 teaspoon salt, ¼–½ teaspoon freshly ground pepper, and the nutmeg.

- Fold spinach into white sauce and keep warm.

Make the Spaetzle

- Beat 4 eggs and gradually add 4 cups of flour, 1 teaspoon salt, and ½ cup water to make a stiff, smooth batter. If batter is too stiff, add a little more water.

- Push the batter through a spaetzle press or small colander onto a plate.

- Drop the dumplings into boiling water and boil gently until they rise to the top.

- Scoop the spaetzle out with a slotted spoon and transfer to a serving bowl. Toss with melted butter, a little salt, and chopped fresh parsley.

STUFFED EGGPLANT BARQUETTES

Eggplants stuffed with vegetables, meat, and cheese are found in cooking traditions around the world

Stuffed eggplant looks like more work than it's worth, but that really isn't the case. It basically involves halving and hollowing out the eggplant; chopping up the pulp and cooking it with a mixture of onion, garlic, mushrooms, ground meat, bread crumbs, and cheese; filling the eggplant halves with the mixture; and baking them until brown and bubbly. The result is a tender, delicious vegetable dish that can be served as a side or a main course.

The American eggplant, also referred to as the Western or globe eggplant, is available all year round, but its local availability is late summer to early fall, with August and September being its peak season. *Yield: 6 servings*

Ingredients

3 medium globe eggplants, halved and hollowed out, pulp reserved

6 ounces fresh mushrooms, chopped

1 medium yellow onion, finely chopped

¼ cup olive oil

1 teaspoon minced garlic

1 pound ground sausage

1 cup crumbled goat cheese or ricotta cheese

1 large egg

⅓ cup minced fresh parsley

½–1 teaspoon kosher salt

¼–½ teaspoon coarsely ground pepper

⅓ cup Italian-seasoned bread crumbs

½ cup shredded Gruyère cheese

Stuffed Eggplant Barquettes

- Chop the eggplant pulp into small cubes and mix with the mushrooms.

- Sauté the onion in 1 tablespoon of the olive oil until soft. Add garlic and brown. Add the remaining olive oil, stir in mushrooms and eggplant pulp and sauté 4 minutes. Mix vegetables with sausage, bread crumbs, and goat cheese or ricotta. Beat in egg and add parsley, salt, and pepper.

- Stuff the eggplant shells with the mixture. Top with Gruyère and bake in a lightly greased baking dish at 375°F until cheese is golden brown, about 30 minutes.

• • • • RECIPE VARIATIONS • • • •

Other Stuffings: For a Greek twist, use ground lamb, add a little cinnamon and oregano, and mix the filling with a béchamel sauce (see Chapter 9) and voila— you've got a stuffed eggplant moussaka! A Creole stuffing might include green pepper, tomatoes, celery, bacon, and rice.

Stuffed Eggplant Appetizers: Make the stuffing for Stuffed Eggplant, omitting the Gruyére. Bake the stuffing in a casserole dish for 20–30 minutes. Spread 20–30 warm pita rounds with the stuffing mixture and top with a spoonful of hummus. Garnish with fresh parsley and serve immediately.

Prepare the Eggplant

- Cut washed, stemmed eggplants in half lengthwise.

- Arrange the halves on paper towels, cut side up. Sprinkle with salt and drain for 30 minutes. Wash and wipe them dry.

- With a serrated spoon, scoop out the pulp, being careful not to pierce the skins and leaving ½-inch-thick shells.

- Blanch the shells for 3–4 minutes in boiling water and plunge them into an ice water bath for several more minutes. Drain, dry, and cool before filling.

Make the Filling

- Because the eggplant pulp is slightly rubbery, chop it with a very sharp or serrated knife.

- Almost any meat will work for the stuffing. Some people use sausages, others ground or cooked turkey or ham. Combining the meat with crumbled bacon adds even more flavor.

- You can also try a seafood-stuffed eggplant using chopped shrimp, crab, scallops, or lobster.

- Start with ⅓ cup of bread crumbs and add a little more if the mixture needs more binding.

POTATO & VEAL STUFFED PUMPKIN
This savory stuffed pumpkin dish is perfect for a Halloween supper

Most people I know have never heard of stuffed pumpkin, let alone made it. Yet *poitron farci*, as it is known in France, is a popular dish that blends the sweetness of the squash with savory ingredients like veal, potatoes, carrots, celery, and tomatoes, in an autumn-spiced white wine broth.

Pumpkin may also be filled with fruits and spices and served as a dessert dish over gingerbread or pumpkin bread with plenty of whipped cream. Either way, stuffed pumpkin is an impressive culinary creation, a feast for both the stomach and the eyes. *Yield: 6 servings*

Ingredients

2 tablespoons butter

1 large celery stalk, chopped

1 small yellow onion, chopped

1 large carrot, grated

1 1/2 teaspoons minced garlic

2 pounds veal, cut into 1-inch cubes and dusted with flour

4 ounces dry white wine

1 1/2 cups diced fresh tomatoes

2 cloves

1/4 teaspoon nutmeg

1/4 teaspoon ground allspice

1 teaspoon seasoned salt

1/4-1/2 teaspoon freshly ground pepper

1 good-sized pumpkin, hollowed out and parboiled

Reserved pumpkin flesh, cut into 1-inch cubes

3 medium white or red potatoes, diced

Shredded or grated Parmesan

Potato and Veal Stuffed Pumpkin

- In a heavy skillet, melt the butter and brown the celery, onion, and carrot. Add the garlic and brown for 15 seconds.

- Add the veal and brown for 5 minutes. Add the wine and cook down by 1/3. Add the diced tomatoes and seasonings.

- Mix in the cubed pumpkin and potatoes and cook over low heat for 30 minutes.

- Stuff the pumpkin with the filling, sprinkle with the cheese, and bake at 450°F for 15 minutes, until browned on top. Serve with the top on, removing it at the table.

· · · · RECIPE VARIATION · · · ·

Sweet and Spicy Stuffing: Stuff pumpkin with a mixture of 6 chopped apples, 1 cup chopped walnuts, 1 16-ounce can whole-berry cranberry sauce, 1 20-ounce can drained pineapple chunks, ¾ cup brown sugar, ½ cup dried currants, and ½ cup rum. Add 2 teaspoons fresh minced ginger, ½ teaspoon nutmeg, and ½ teaspoon cinnamon.

Prepare the Pumpkin

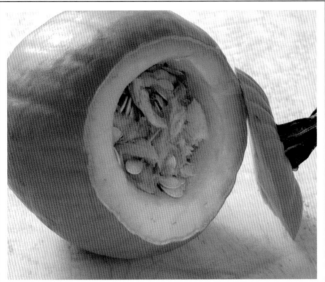

Roast the Seeds

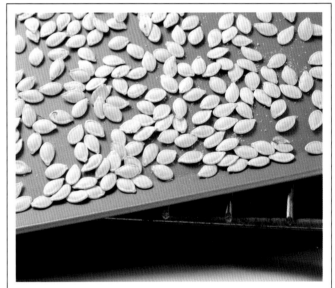

- Cut a 1-inch top off the pumpkin and set aside.

- With a pointed or serrated spoon, scoop out the stringy membrane and seeds, leaving a ½-Inch thick shell. Reserve the seeds.

- Parboil the pumpkin and top in a large pot of gently boiling water for 15 minutes.

- Drain the pumpkin by placing it upside down on paper towels or in a colander. Cool before stuffing.

- Rinse the seeds under cold water and pick out pulp and strings. Do this just after you've cleaned out the pumpkin, before the pulp has dried.

- Let the seeds dry out and scatter them in a single layer on an oiled baking sheet.

- Sprinkle with salt or a mixture of sweet and savory spices and bake at 325°F until toasted.

- Cool and store in an airtight container.

STUFFED ARTICHOKES

Artichokes are stuffed with meat, cheese, and rice, drizzled with white wine, and baked to delectable perfection

These stuffed artichokes make a perfect luncheon entree. You might serve them with French onion soup, a tossed green salad, rolls, and a light dessert. For dinner, the stately old *Gourmet's Menu Cookbook* from 1963 suggests the following menu: "Minestrone, Bread Sticks, Veal Scallops with Lemon, Stuffed Artichokes and Plum Milk Sherbet." Ooh la la!

The stuffed artichokes can be prepared in advance and reheated before serving. Leftover stuffing keeps for up to two weeks in the refrigerator and longer in the freezer. *Yield: 6 servings*

Ingredients

2 tablespoons butter

1 small yellow onion, chopped

2 teaspoons chopped garlic

³/₄ cup diced ham

³/₄ cup chopped sausage meat

6 ounces sliced fresh mushrooms

6 fresh Roma or similar-size tomatoes, diced

¹/₂ teaspoon seasoned salt

¹/₄ teaspoon coarsely ground pepper

Juice of 1 lemon

1¹/₂ cups cooked rice

¹/₂ cup grated Gruyère or Emmental cheese

1 tablespoon chopped fresh basil

2 tablespoons chopped fresh parsley

6 medium artichokes, chokes removed

Dry white wine

3 slices uncooked bacon

Stuffed Artichokes

- Melt the butter in a large skillet. Lightly brown the onion and garlic followed by the ham, sausage, and mushrooms.

- Add the tomatoes, salt, pepper, and lemon juice and cook over medium heat, stirring often, until liquid has cooked down.

- Remove from the heat and mix well with the rice, cheese, basil, and parsley.

- Stuff the cooled parboiled artichokes, drizzle with white wine, top each with half a bacon slice, and bake in a buttered glass baking dish at 400°F for 30–40 minutes.

• • • • RECIPE VARIATIONS • • • •

Stuffed Artichokes Italiano: Stuff artichokes with the following mixture: 1 pound ground beef, 1 pound ground Italian sausage, ½ teaspoon each garlic and onion powder, 1 cup Italian bread crumbs, ½ cup grated Romano, 1 beaten egg, ½ cup milk, and salt and pepper to taste. Stand them up in a Dutch oven, cover with marinara sauce and simmer 40 minutes.

Vegetarian Artichoke Salad: Combine 1 cup cooked pearl barley; 1 teaspoon seasoned salt; ⅓ cup each chopped cucumber, bell pepper, chopped scallions, and chopped pecans; ¼ cup olive oil; 1 tablespoon balsamic vinegar; 1 tablespoon Dijon mustard; and 1 teaspoon sugar. Refrigerate and stuff cold artichokes with mixture.

Prepare the Artichokes

- Wash the artichokes and drain upside down to dry. Cut the stems straight across, leaving a level base so the artichokes will stand upright.

- Remove the tough outer leaves at the base and cut about ½ inch off the tips of the remaining leaves.

- With a sharp knife, slice the top of the artichokes straight across, taking off about 1 inch.

- Parboil the artichokes for 15–20 minutes. Remove from heat, rinse under cold water, drain in a colander, and cool before stuffing.

Stuff the Artichokes

- Pull out and discard the yellow prickly leaves in the center of the artichokes and scrape out the hairy choke.

- Spread the leaves and place enough filling in the center to be gently mounded. Tuck some filling between the spread leaves as well.

- Drizzle some dry white wine over the filling to moisten it.

- Close the leaves gently and arrange the artichokes close together in the baking dish.

197

SPINACH-STUFFED MUSHROOMS

Crab meets spinach meets cheese in these betcha-can't-eat-just-one 'shrooms

I've made these stuffed mushrooms many times for catered affairs as well as my own parties, and there's only one bad thing about them: There are never any left for me to enjoy the next day. People snap them up, and no wonder. Hot out of the oven, the tender, juicy mushrooms and crabmeat-spinach-cheese filling melt in your mouth, seducing you

into grabbing just one more. These stuffed mushrooms are, of course, designed as appetizers. Fill the big, flying saucer portobellos, though, and you've got a splendid entree. *Yield: 24 appetizers*

Ingredients

24 smaller-sized portobello mushrooms, cleaned and stemmed

2 tablespoons minced scallions

1 cup diced cooked or imitation crabmeat

1/2 cup garlic and herb cream cheese

10 ounces cooked spinach, chopped (12 ounces fresh)

2 tablespoons butter

Juice of half a lemon

1 cup Italian-seasoned bread crumbs

1 egg, beaten

1 teaspoon dried dill weed

1/2 teaspoon seasoned salt

1/4 teaspoon lemon pepper

1/3 cup dry white wine

1 cup shredded Parmesan

Spinach-Stuffed Mushrooms

- Prepare the mushrooms (see technique). Sauté scallions with the chopped mushroom, 2–3 minutes. Remove from heat and cool.

- In a small mixing bowl, combine the mushroom mixture with the crabmeat, cream cheese, cooled spinach, and all other ingredients except for the shredded cheese.

- Stuff the mushroom caps with the mixture. Top with the cheese and arrange the mushrooms in a 13 x 9 x 2-inch glass baking dish sprayed with nonstick cooking spray. Bake at 375°F for 20 minutes, until browned.

When hollowing out mushrooms, be extremely gentle. Those fragile caps can tear just like that, rendering the mushroom unusable for stuffing. And because the biggest mistake people make with this dish is choosing mushrooms that are too small to stuff adequately, avoid the small button mushrooms and be sure to use portobellos or criminis.

Nacho Stuffed Mushrooms: Stuff and bake the mushrooms with the following mixture: 1 pound cooked ground beef, browned with 1 cup diced onion and 1 teaspoon chopped garlic, 1 cup bread crumbs, 1 6-ounce can diced chiles, ½ teaspoon seasoned salt, ⅓ teaspoon lemon pepper, and 1 12-ounce jar salsa con queso.

Prepare the Mushrooms

- Brush the dirt off the mushrooms with a mushroom brush (a toothbrush works in a pinch) or place the mushrooms in a colander, rinse, and rub clean with paper towels.

- Carefully pull out stems; if they don't pull out easily, cut them off close to the cap.

- Using a grapefruit spoon or a small melon baller, gently scoop out the mushroom meat, leaving caps intact.

- Finely chop the stems and mushroom pieces.

Cook the Spinach

- You can use either frozen or fresh spinach for the stuffing.

- If using fresh, microwave around 12 ounces on high with ¼ cup of water until wilted, about 6 minutes.

- Allow the spinach to cool to the touch. Then wring the excess moisture out of the spinach with your hands as you would a wet rag. Note: You'll have half the volume of spinach you started with.

- If the spinach isn't the frozen chopped variety, chop it before adding it to the stuffing.

ATHENIAN CABBAGE ROLLS

Cinnamon, oregano, and lemon juice are the signature seasonings in this recipe from Greece

I grew up on Jewish stuffed cabbage rolls, enticing parcels of cabbage leaves filled with ground meat, rice, and seasonings and cooked in a sweet and sour tomato sauce. It wasn't until many years later, after I developed a fascination with world cuisine, that I discovered that stuffed cabbage is a universal phenomenon that takes many forms. Polish, Hungarian,

Italian, Cuban, Creole—there's a stuffed cabbage for every ethnicity, with both similar and unique ingredients.

These Greek stuffed cabbage rolls take some time to prepare, but they'll definitely wow a dinner crowd. Serve garnished with yogurt and fresh mint. *Yield: 4–6 servings*

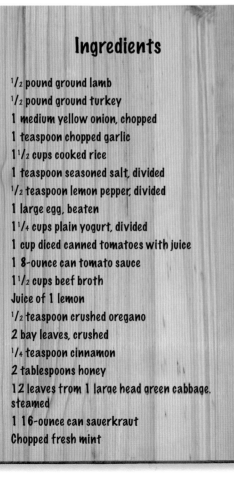

Ingredients

¹/₂ pound ground lamb

¹/₂ pound ground turkey

1 medium yellow onion, chopped

1 teaspoon chopped garlic

1¹/₂ cups cooked rice

1 teaspoon seasoned salt, divided

¹/₂ teaspoon lemon pepper, divided

1 large egg, beaten

1¹/₄ cups plain yogurt, divided

1 cup diced canned tomatoes with juice

1 8-ounce can tomato sauce

1¹/₂ cups beef broth

Juice of 1 lemon

¹/₂ teaspoon crushed oregano

2 bay leaves, crushed

¹/₄ teaspoon cinnamon

2 tablespoons honey

12 leaves from 1 large head green cabbage, steamed

1 16-ounce can sauerkraut

Chopped fresh mint

Athenian Cabbage Rolls

- In a bowl, combine meats, onion, garlic, rice, ¹/₂ teaspoon seasoned salt, ¹/₄ teaspoon lemon pepper, egg, and ¹/₂ cup of yogurt.

- In another bowl, combine tomatoes and juice, tomato sauce, broth, lemon juice, oregano, bay leaves, cinnamon, remaining salt and pepper, and honey. Make cabbage rolls (see technique) and layer them in a Dutch oven over broken cabbage leaves and sauerkraut.

- Cover with half the tomato sauce and repeat. Cover and simmer 1 hour. Serve with yogurt and mint.

Core a whole cabbage by slicing a small piece off the end opposite the core and resting the cabbage on this end. Now, holding the head in place with one hand, use the other hand to cut into the cabbage around the core with a paring knife. Once the knife circles the entire core, use the tip to gently dislodge it. Pull the core out.

• • • • RECIPE VARIATION • • • •

Stuffed Cabbage Soup: Omit the beaten egg and yogurt in Athenian Cabbage Rolls. In a large pot, brown the ground beef, onion, and garlic in oil. Coarsely chop the cabbage and add to the pot with the rest of the ingredients. Add 3 cups water and an additional 3 cups beef broth and simmer 45 minutes.

Prepare the Cabbage

- Place the cored cabbage head under running water and peel off 12 large leaves. Save any leaves that break.

- Steam the leaves in a covered Dutch oven in 1 inch of boiling water for 10 minutes, or until limp. Drain and rinse in cold water.

- Chop up 3–4 cups of the rest of the cabbage.

- Place any broken cabbage leaves on the bottom of the Dutch oven.

Make the Rolls

- Lay out a cooked cooled cabbage leaf and spoon in ¼ cup of filling.

- Tuck in the sides of the leaf about an inch

- Tightly roll the leaf until it resembles a burrito or an egg roll.

- Secure with 2 toothpicks.

CHRISTMAS STUFFED PEPPERS

Stuffed red and green bell peppers topped with mashed potato "hats" enliven a Christmas table

Some years ago, I was fortunate enough to be invited to the annual family Christmas dinner of a retired Swiss master chef, Hans Lutenauer, where I learned the art of food presentation. Bright green blanched broccoli was served on a large platter in the shape of a Christmas tree, with cherry tomatoes for ornaments and blue cheese dressing for flocking. Whole poached fish was encircled by a wreath of fresh parsley, rosemary, and cranberries. This inspired me to create Christmas stuffed bell peppers, with mashed potato snow and hats. I think Hans would approve. *Yield: 6 servings*

Ingredients

1 16-ounce can diced tomotoes with juice

$1/_2$ pound sweet Italian sausage

1 cup cooked ham

1 medium yellow onion, finely chopped

2 large eggs, lightly beaten

$1/_3$–$1/_2$ cup milk

$1/_4$ teaspoon ground nutmeg, preferably fresh

1 teaspoon seasoned salt

$1/_4$–$1/_2$ teaspoon coarsely ground pepper

$1/_3$ cup grated Romano or Parmesan cheese, divided

1 cup fine dry bread crumbs, divided

3 red bell peppers, seeded and parboiled

3 green bell peppers, seeded and parboiled

Christmas Stuffed Peppers

- In a mixing bowl, mash the sausage meat with the ham, onion, tomatoes and juice. If using sausage in a casing, cut the end and squeeze the meat out.

- Blend in the eggs, milk, seasonings, half the cheese, and half the bread crumbs.

- Stuff the peppers with the filling, sprinkle with the remaining cheese and bread crumbs.

- Bake in a greased gratin dish at 375°F for 30 minutes or until nicely browned.

Prepare the Peppers

- Wash the peppers and slice off the top quarters.

- With a paring knife, go around the inside of the pepper, loosening the membrane.

- Pull the membrane and seeds out of the pepper, leaving the shell intact.

- Parboil the peppers for 5 minutes, remove from the pot, and submerge in ice water until they're no longer warm. Drain and dry upside down on paper towels or in a large colander. Cool before filling.

Decorate the Peppers

- You'll need a pastry bag with a ½-inch fluted tip and about 3 cups of mashed potatoes.

- Transfer the potatoes to the bag and pipe a decorative swirl on top of the baked peppers to resemble a tiny elf's hat. On the tip of the hat, place a piece of pimiento like a bell.

- Arrange the peppers on a Christmas platter and pipe more potatoes all around them, to simulate snow. Sprinkle with chopped fresh parsley.

- Congratulations! You are now a food artiste.

CORN FRITTERS WITH CHILE RELISH

Crisp corn fritters are topped with tangy chile relish and cool sour cream

In addition to yams mousseline (see Chapter 11), no Southern Thanksgiving would be complete without corn fritters. These simple delicacies, traditionally made with corn kernels, eggs, flour, milk, and melted butter, are either shallow- or deep-fried and are served with jam, fruit, honey, maple syrup, or cream. This savory recipe for corn fritters is a more elaborate affair that includes cream-style corn, buttermilk, cornmeal, and mild green chiles, along with a sweet hot chile relish.

For deep-frying, choose a cooking oil with a high smoke point, meaning that it doesn't break down at deep-frying temperatures. Peanut, safflower, sunflower, and canola oil are good choices. *Yield: 4–6 servings*

Ingredients

1 cup cooking oil

1 15-ounce can cream-style corn

2 large eggs, beaten

$\frac{1}{2}$ cup sour milk or buttermilk

1 cup flour

1 cup yellow cornmeal

$\frac{1}{2}$ cup sugar

1 teaspoon salt

1 teaspoon baking soda

1 teaspoon baking powder

Sour cream

For relish:

2 celery stalks, trimmed

$\frac{1}{4}$ cup red bell pepper

1 cucumber, peeled

$\frac{1}{4}$ cup scallions

$\frac{1}{4}$ cup balsamic vinegar

$\frac{1}{2}$ teaspoon dried mustard

$\frac{1}{4}$ cup jalapeño pepper jelly

1 6-ounce can mild diced green chiles

$\frac{1}{4}$ teaspoon seasoned salt

1 16-ounce can sweet corn, drained

Corn Fritters with Chile Relish

- Place a deep, heavy skillet on the stove over medium-heat and add the oil.

- Empty the cream-style corn into a medium mixing bowl and stir in the beaten eggs and sour milk.

- Add the flour, cornmeal, $\frac{1}{4}$ cup sugar, and salt. When the oil is hot enough, add the baking soda and baking powder to the flour mixture.

- Fry the fritters until golden brown. Drain and serve topped with sweet chile relish and sour cream.

- **Green Chile and Cheese Corn Fritters:** To the fritter ingredients, add ½ cup chopped green chiles and ½ cup shredded sharp cheddar cheese. Serve the fritters topped with sour cream, chopped fresh cilantro and chopped green onion, or with guacamole and chopped tomato.
- **Baked Corn Fritters:** Line two baking sheets with parchment paper and grease the paper with canola oil. Drop rounded tablespoons of the batter onto the baking sheets, leaving at least 1 inch between each fritter. Bake on the middle rack in a 425°F oven for 10 minutes; the fritters will be golden brown on the bottom. Remove the pans, flip over the fritters, and return the pans to the oven, baking 8–10 more minutes.

Make the Relish

- Wash and pat dry the celery and red pepper.

- Finely chop the cucumber, scallions, celery, and pepper.

- In a large bowl, combine the vinegar, mustard, ¼ cup sugar, jalapeño jelly, chiles, and seasoned salt.

- Add the chopped vegetables and corn and toss. Transfer to a covered container and chill several hours. Toss once more before serving.

Fry the Fritters

- When adding the oil to the skillet, leave a safety margin of 2 inches for the oil to bubble.

- Heat the oil to 350–375°F. The oil is ready when a 1-inch cube of white bread dropped into it browns in 60 seconds.

- Drop the fritter batter by tablespoons into the hot oil and fry until golden brown, watching carefully, as the process is fast.

- Remove fritters with a slotted spoon and drain on paper towels.

PANCAKES & FRITTERS

INDIAN VEGETABLE FRITTERS
These savory and spicy fritters are a staple of Indian cuisine

Pakoras are fried vegetable fritters common throughout South Asia and, particularly, India and Pakistan, where they are sold on the street and eaten as snacks. They are something like the Indian version of tempura: a variety of vegetables are chopped and mixed into a batter of chickpea and rice flour and deep-fried until light, fluffy, and golden brown. They may be dipped in a *raita,* or yogurt sauce, or eaten with chutney.

Try this recipe with different vegetables, such as mushrooms, artichokes, carrots, sweet potato, or broccoli. *Yield: 4 servings*

Ingredients

1 cup chickpea flour

3 tablespoons rice flour

³/₄ cup water, or as needed

1 teaspoon coarsely ground coriander seeds

2 tablespoons fresh cilantro

2 hot chiles

1 small potato

1 small to medium zucchini

¹/₂ pound cauliflower

1 teaspoon whole cumin

1 teaspoon chopped garlic

1 teaspoon salt

¹/₄ teaspoon coarsely ground pepper

Vegetable oil (for frying)

Fruit chutney and yogurt sauce

Indian Vegetable Fritters

- Mix both flours with the water, until the consistency resembles pancake batter. Allow to rest 10 minutes.

- Crush the coriander seeds, and finely chop the cilantro, chiles, and vegetables.

- Toast cumin in a hot skillet (no oil) for 10–15 seconds.

Remove and add to batter, along with vegetables, cilantro, chiles, garlic, salt, and pepper.

- Drop the batter by tablespoons into the hot (350–375°F) oil and fry until golden brown. Drain on paper towels. Serve with sauce.

Spicy Cabbage Pakoras: In a medium bowl, combine 1 cup shredded cabbage, ¼ cup chickpea flour, 2 tablespoons rice flour, 1 teaspoon red chili powder, ½ teaspoon ground turmeric, ½ teaspoon cumin seeds, ½ teaspoon grated ginger, ½ teaspoon salt, and 5 tablespoons water. The batter should be thick and just coat the cabbage. Fry as described below.

Serve with cool yogurt sauce.
Honey Mint Chutney: In a blender or food processor, combine 3 cups mint leaves, 2 coarsely chopped green chile peppers, 2 tablespoons lime juice, 2 tablespoons honey, and 2 tablespoons water. Grind into a fine paste, adding more water if necessary. Add salt to taste. Serve with Indian Vegetable Fritters.

Find the Chickpea Flour

- Chickpea flour is simply chickpeas that are ground into flour.

- You can find chickpea flour—also known as besan, gram flour, and garbanzo bean flour—in Indian and Middle Eastern groceries, health-food stores, specialty markets, and online.

- Make your own chickpea flour by toasting 2 cups of dried chickpeas in a 450°F. oven for 5–10 minutes, until they are golden brown. Then grind like flour.

- Adding a little rice flour to the chickpea flour makes the fritters extra crisp.

Make the Yogurt Sauce

- Indian yogurt sauce, or raita, is similar to Greek tzatziki, but with different spices.

- There are many different kinds of raitas, including cucumber, mint, tomato, carrot, and even banana.

- To make an all-purpose raita, combine 1½ cups of plain yogurt with ⅓ cup mayonnaise, 1 finely chopped medium cucumber, 1 teaspoon chopped garlic, 2 chopped scallions, 2 teaspoons grated fresh ginger, the juice of 1 lemon, 1 teaspoon toasted cumin seeds, and salt and pepper to taste. Chill for 1 hour.

PANCAKES & FRITTERS

SWEET POTATO–CARROT CROQUETTES

Celebrate fall with fried sweet potato–carrot croquettes and warm cranberry sauce

In France, fast food existed long before Burger King and McDonald's, in the form of croquettes. Invented, so to speak, around 1700, croquettes—from the French *croquer,* or "to crunch"—are a small fried food consisting of minced meat, mashed potatoes, soaked white bread, egg, milk, wine, and seasonings. The mixture was formed into patties, balls, or cylinders and deep-fried for a quick snack.

These sweet potato–carrot croquettes are a creative alternative to mashed sweet potatoes or yams, and they make a great addition to the Thanksgiving table. Serve them with homemade spiced cranberry sauce, which is almost as easy to make as opening a can of cranberry sauce. *Yield: 6 servings*

Ingredients

2 large sweet potatoes, peeled and diced

2 medium red potatoes, peeled and diced

1 cup carrots, thinly sliced

2 tablespoons butter

3 cups milk

2 egg yolks, beaten

1 tablespoon brown sugar

1 tablespoon maple syrup

¼ teaspoon salt

¼ teaspoon cinnamon

¼ teaspoon nutmeg

½ cup flour

1 egg, beaten

1 cup plain bread crumbs

Oil (for frying)

Cranberry sauce

Sweet Potato–Carrot Croquettes

- Cook the sweet potatoes, red potatoes, and carrots until they're fork-tender.

- Drain the potatoes and carrots in a colander and transfer them to a large mixing bowl. Mash with the butter, milk, egg yolks, brown sugar, maple syrup, salt, and spices. Chill for 1 hour.

- Form the mixture into patties. Dredge the patties in flour, dip in beaten egg, dredge in bread crumbs, and fry in ½ inch of hot oil until golden brown. Drain on paper towels.

- Serve with warm cranberry sauce.

The ratio of solids to liquids is very important in croquettes. The solids should never be watery—always well drained—and enough sauce should be added to them to bind them well. For easy handling and shaping, it's essential to chill the croquette mixture before forming the croquettes.

• • • • RECIPE VARIATION • • • •

Cajun Carrot Croquettes: Mix well: 2 cups mashed cooked carrots, 1 cup flour, 1 teaspoon baking powder, 2 beaten eggs, ½ cup sugar, and 1 teaspoon cinnamon. Drop by tablespoons into oil no hotter than 350°F; otherwise the insides won't cook. Fry one croquette for 2 minutes to test for doneness.

Make the Croquettes

Make the Cranberry Sauce

- Croquettes are much easier to shape when they're very cold, so chill the mixture in the refrigerator for at least an hour.

- You can form the croquettes into various shapes, like balls, cones, or patties. The balls and cones will require more oil to deep-fry.

- Don't make the croquettes too large or they may brown too much or have a cold spot inside.

- Make sure the oil is at least 350°F, as croquettes will break in oil that isn't sufficiently hot.

- Bring 1 cup of water to a boil. Add a 12-ounce bag of whole cranberries and cook on medium-low heat, stirring occasionally, until they burst open, about 10 minutes

- Peel an orange and cut it into chunks, reserving juice.

- Add the orange, juice, ½ cup each brown and white sugar, 2 tablespoons candied ginger, and 2 tablespoons apricot jam to the sauce.

- Stir until thick and remove from heat.

ZUCCHINI LATKES

The potato pancakes that are a Chanukah tradition get a boost with the addition of grated zucchini

Chanukah, the Jewish festival of lights, is inextricably linked with latkes, potato pancakes fried in oil to commemorate the tiny bit of oil that burned for eight miraculous days in the temple that the Maccabees won back from the Greeks during the Ptolemaic Empire.

Most people don't know, however, that "latke" and "potato"

are not necessarily synonymous. Latke is actually the Ukrainian word for "pancake." Jewish cookbooks have sour milk latkes, buttermilk latkes, and blueberry latkes, too.

Potato latkes with zucchini are a Romanian Jewish delicacy. Serve them topped with sour cream, cinnamon sugar, or applesauce. *Yield: Approximately 24 2½-inch latkes*

Ingredients

2 medium zucchini, grated

4 large potatoes, peeled and grated

½ cup fine bread crumbs

2 tablespoons flour

3–4 tablespoons grated yellow onion

1 teaspoon chopped garlic

1 teaspoon seasoned salt

½ teaspoon coarsely ground pepper

4 eggs, beaten

Vegetable oil (for frying)

Applesauce, sour cream, and cinnamon sugar

Zucchini Latkes

- In a large mixing bowl, combine all the ingredients except the eggs, applesauce, sour cream, and cinnamon sugar.

- Add the eggs and blend into a thick batter, adding more flour if the mixture is too runny.

- Heat ¼ inch of vegetable oil in a large, heavy skillet to 350–375°F.

- Fry the latkes until golden brown and crisp. Serve hot with applesauce, sour cream, and cinnamon sugar toppings.

You want your ingredients dry for latkes. Wet potatoes and zucchini undergo an unpleasant alchemical transformation when fried, resulting in soggy, greasy latkes that fall apart in the pan. So make sure to squeeze as much moisture as possible from the grated vegetables.

•••• RECIPE VARIATION ••••

Sweet Potato Zucchini Latkes: Replace the regular potatoes with 2 large sweet potatoes. Omit the onion and garlic and add 1 tablespoon brown sugar, 1 tablespoon white sugar, 1 teaspoon ground cloves, 1 teaspoon ground cinnamon, and ½ teaspoon nutmeg.

Grate the Vegetables

Fry the Latkes

- Grate the zucchini and potatoes in a food processor fitted with a fine grating disk or with a good old-fashioned hand grater.

- For lacy latkes with rough, crispy edges, shred the potatoes coarsely. For denser latkes with smooth edges, use the fine side of the grater.

- Wring out the grated vegetables either with a cheesecloth or your hands, extracting as much moisture as possible.

- Grate the onion with a hand grater and add to the zucchini and potatoes.

- Test the temperature of the oil by dropping a small amount of latke mixture into the pan. If it turns golden brown within 1 minute, the oil is ready.

- Carefully drop spoonfuls of the mixture into the hot oil and flatten the mounds with a spatula.

- Fry until nicely browned on both sides.

- While making batches, transfer the finished latkes to a 200°F oven, in a single layer and uncovered, to keep them warm and crispy until ready to serve.

EGGPLANT PANCAKES MILANESE
Savory eggplant pancakes are topped with toasted bread crumbs and Parmesan

Savory pancakes are to lunch and dinner what hotcakes and syrup are to breakfast. Yet too few people ever make them. With the exception of egg foo young, which we call a Chinese pancake, but which is really an omelet, savory batter-based pancakes generally belong in the category of the great unknown.

So get to know them. A good place to begin is with this recipe, a delicious pancake made with chopped roasted eggplant, shallots, garlic, and fresh herbs and topped with toasted bread crumbs and Parmesan. *Yield: 4 servings*

Ingredients

2 teaspoons minced garlic

1 tablespoon minced shallots

$1/3$ cup olive oil, divided

4 Japanese eggplants, roasted, peeled, seeded, and chopped

$1/3$ cup plus 4 tablespoons flour

$1/2$ teaspoon baking powder

2 beaten eggs

$1/2$ cup vegetable broth

2 tablespoons chopped fresh parsley

1 tablespoon chopped fresh basil or 1 teaspoon dried basil

1 teaspoon salt

$1/2$ teaspoon coarsely ground pepper

For the topping

1 tablespoon butter

1 cup bread crumbs

$1/4$ cup parmesan

Salt and lemon pepper to taste

Eggplant Pancakes Milanese

- In a large, heavy skillet, brown garlic and shallots in 1 tablespoon olive oil.

- Combine the roasted chopped eggplant, garlic and shallots, flour, baking powder, eggs, broth, and seasonings.

- Coat the skillet with more olive oil. Heat to medium and add the batter ¼ cup at a time. Cook pancake on each side until bubbles form on the surface and the bottom has browned.

- Sprinkle the pancakes with topping (see technique) and serve with lemon wedges.

The Asian eggplant varieties, particularly Japanese and Chinese, have thinner skins, a more delicate flavor than the American globe, and fewer of the seeds that tend to make eggplants bitter. Use them in this dish, as they are best for a light pancake with delicate seasonings.

···· RECIPE VARIATION ····

Florentine Eggplant Pancake Topping: Over medium heat, toast ¼ cup pine nuts in a skillet until golden. Add 2 teaspoons chopped garlic and sauté 30 seconds. Add 4 cups baby spinach, 1 16-ounce can diced tomatoes, 2 tablespoons chopped fresh basil, ½ teaspoon salt, and ¼ teaspoon freshly ground pepper. Cook 2–3 minutes.

Roast the Eggplant

- Pierce the eggplants in several places with the tines of a fork and place them on a baking sheet.

- Broil the eggplants until the skin buckles, about 5 minutes. Turn them over and repeat on the other side, 3–5 minutes.

- Remove from the oven and cool completely. For quick cooling, place them in a paper bag in the refrigerator.

- Strip off the skin, scoop out the seeds, and chop the pulp.

Make the Topping

- Heat 1 tablespoon butter in a medium skillet.

- When the foam subsides, add 1 cup of fine plain or Italian-seasoned bread crumbs.

- Sauté the bread crumbs over medium heat until brown and toasty, about 1–2 minutes.

- Add grated Parmesan and mix well with a little salt and lemon pepper.

PANCAKES & FRITTERS

MUSHROOM & SPINACH CREPES

These tender crepes are filled with a mixture of mushrooms, spinach, shallots, feta cheese, and cream

These very thin pancakes are the national dish of France, and their preparation is both a skill and an art. We're all familiar with the sight of the accomplished chef swirling the crepe batter around in a special crepe pan, flipping the crepe at just the right moment, turning it out on a plate and filling it with a delectable entree or dessert concoction. And we

doubt that we could ever do the same. After all, it all looks so . . . French.

It really doesn't take long, though, to learn how to make crepes, and once you do, the sky's the limit when it comes to the fillings. Mushroom and spinach crepes are a great brunch, lunch, or light dinner entree. *Yield: Approximately 16 crepes*

Ingredients

6 ounces fresh mushrooms, sliced and chopped

1 tablespoon minced shallots

2 tablespoons olive oil, divided

2 6-ounce packages fresh baby spinach, cooked, drained, and chopped

³/₄ teaspoon seasoned salt

¹/₄ teaspoon lemon pepper

¹/₃ cup heavy cream

¹/₃ cup crumbled feta cheese

1¹/₂ cups flour

¹/₈ teaspoon salt

3 eggs

1¹/₂ cups milk

2 tablespoons unsalted butter, melted

Grated sharp cheddar

Mushroom and Spinach Crepes

- In a medium skillet, brown the mushrooms and shallots in 1 tablespoon olive oil. Stir in the spinach, seasonings, cream, and feta. Remove from heat and cool.

- Whisk the flour, salt, eggs, milk, and butter in a bowl until blended into a thin batter.

- Fry the crepes in a crepe pan or 8-inch diameter non-stick skillet and turn out on a plate in a stack.

- Fill the crepes, fold, and sprinkle with grated cheddar. Heat in a 325°F oven just until the cheese melts, about 3 minutes. Serve immediately.

ZOOM

The traditional crepe pan is a shallow steel frying pan, or a flat griddle. It heats rapidly and cooks the crepe quickly. An "upside down" crepe pan is extremely handy for making crepes as thin as possible. The underside is actually the top flat surface, with rounded sides, on which the crepe cooks.

• • • • RECIPE VARIATION • • • •

Crab Mushroom Crepes: Prepare 8–10 crepes. Sauté 1 pound crabmeat and ½ pound sliced mushrooms in 1 tablespoon butter for 2 minutes. Add 1 tablespoon chopped parsley, 1 teaspoon seafood seasoning, ¼ teaspoon freshly ground pepper, and ¼ teaspoon dry mustard. Fill crepes with the mixture and pour béchamel sauce over the crepes.

Make the Crepes

Fill the Crepes

- Heat 1 tablespoon of oil in a crepe pan and then tip it out, just coating the surface.

- Pouring in 2–3 tablespoons of batter with one hand, lift the pan above the burner with your other hand.

- Tilt the pan in all directions, quickly swirling the batter until it covers the pan in a very thin layer.

- Return to burner and brown over medium-high heat. Slide a knife under the crepe to loosen, carefully turn with a spatula, and brown the other side for just a few seconds.

- Crepes have an inside and an outside. The side that cooks first is the outside because it looks more attractive.

- With the outside facing down, place the mushroom filling in a line down the center of the crepe.

- Fold the right side just past the middle and then do the same with the left.

- The filling should show at the ends.

215

ZUCCHINI BREAD

A wonderfully moist, sweet bread that's good for you and tastes good too!

Around the end of summer, when gardens are overflowing with zucchini and everybody's trying to pawn some off on everybody else, you tend to start seeing a lot of zucchini bread. That's not so bad: Although you might get sick of zucchini, who ever gets sick of this delicious quick bread, which is really more like a rich, dense cake? The grated zucchini makes it extra moist and nutritious. Have it for breakfast as well as dessert. *Yield: 2 loaves*

Ingredients

3 eggs

1 cup vegetable oil

1 teaspoon lemon juice

1/3 cup water

2 teaspoons vanilla extract

2 cups grated zucchini, moisture extracted

3 cups flour

1 cup white sugar

1 cup brown sugar

1 teaspoon baking soda

1/4 teaspoon baking powder

1 teaspoon ground cinnamon

1 teaspoon ground nutmeg

1 teaspoon salt

1/2 cup chopped walnuts or pecans

1/2 cup raisins

Powdered sugar

Zucchini Bread

- In a medium bowl, beat the eggs until light and frothy. Mix in the oil, lemon juice, water, and vanilla extract. Stir in zucchini.

- In a large bowl, combine the flour, sugar, baking soda, baking powder, spices, and salt.

- Mix the wet ingredients into the dry until smooth. Fold in the nuts and raisins.

- Divide batter into two greased and floured loaf pans and bake on the middle rack at 350°F for 45 minutes to 1 hour. Remove from the oven, cool, and dust with powdered sugar.

Because the zucchini bread will continue to cook even after it's removed from the oven, slightly underbaking it ensures a moist loaf. Check the bread after 45 minutes by inserting a knife in the center. If it comes out with a lot of batter, bake the bread at least 10 minutes more. If only a slight amount of batter sticks to it, remove the loaves.

RECIPE VARIATION

Chocolate Zucchini Bread: Omit the raisins, and lemon juice. Reduce the sugar to ¾ cups each white and brown. Add ¾ cup mini chocolate chips, 6 tablespoons unsweetened cocoa powder, and the zest of 1 orange. Top loaves with a mixture of 2 tablespoons brown sugar, 2 tablespoons white sugar, and ½ teaspoon cinnamon. Bake at 350°F, 45–50 minutes.

Prepare the Zucchini in Advance

- It's always good to have frozen shredded zucchini on hand.

- Store fresh zucchini at room temperature for no more than 4 days. Refrigeration can speed up ripening.

- To freeze, peel the zucchini and shred the pulp.

- Measure out 2 cups of pulp and place in a ziptop bag. Squeeze the air out of the bag and seal.

- When ready to use, thaw zucchini and squeeze out all excess moisture (as in the Zucchini Latkes, Chapter 18).

Prepare to Bake the Bread

- Lining the loaf pans with parchment sheets, leaving a couple inches hanging over the pan, makes for easy removal after baking.

- Avoid overmixing the batter. It should be thick and moist, something like a buttercream frosting.

- Level the batter in the pans by running a spatula over the top of each loaf.

- Once it's baked, cool the bread in the pans for 10 minutes. Then turn out onto wire racks. If left in their pans, the loaves will get sweaty.

TOMATO HERB BREAD

Buttermilk, tomatoes, fresh herbs, and Parmesan give this bread fantastic flavor and texture.

Fresh herb bread is generally considered a luxury far beyond the reaches of the average pocketbook. If you buy it in a bakery, it can run anywhere from $5 to $8 per loaf. Yet herb breads are not only easy and fairly inexpensive to make—they can be used in many different, budget-friendly ways. This tomato herb bread makes wonderful appetizers, sandwiches, or little

pizzas. Cut it into cubes and sauté it in olive oil with some salt, pepper, and fresh garlic and you have smashing croutons for Caesar salad or French onion soup. Spread a little olive oil and garlic on toasted tomato herb bread and top it with scrambled eggs and shredded mozzarella for breakfast. Or just enjoy it hot out of the oven, all by itself. *Yield: 2 loaves*

Ingredients

2 envelopes active dry yeast

$\frac{1}{2}$ cup warm water

$1\frac{1}{2}$ cups warm buttermilk

$\frac{1}{2}$ cup grated Parmesan

1 egg

2 tablespoons vegetable oil

5 tablespoons sun-dried tomatoes, chopped

1 tablespoon chopped fresh rosemary

1 tablespoon chopped fresh basil

2 teaspoons crushed red pepper flakes

1 teaspoon salt

3 cups all-purpose flour

2 cups whole wheat flour

Tomato Herb Bread

- In a large bowl, sprinkle yeast over warm water and let stand 10 minutes. Stir in buttermilk, Parmesan, egg, oil, tomatoes, herbs, pepper flakes, and salt.

- With a wooden spoon, mix in 2 cups of flour. Add remaining flour ½ cup at a time. Knead and let the

- dough rise several times (see technique).

- Divide dough into two loaves and bake in greased and floured loaf pans at 350°F until golden brown, 20–30 minutes. Tap the loaves on the bottom. If they sound hollow, they're done.

Tomato Herb Bread Sandwiches: Spread 8 thin slices of tomato herb bread with garlic and herb cream cheese. Layer with watercress and thinly sliced salami. Top with 8 more bread slices, cut each sandwich in half, and serve with Roasted Tomato & Barley Soup (see page 78).

Tomato Herb Bread Pizzas: Cut a loaf of tomato herb bread into 1-inch slices. Spread each slice with pizza sauce. Add a layer of crumbled buffalo mozzarella. Top with chopped fresh mushrooms, onions, garlic, fire-roasted red peppers, and ham. Sprinkle with freshly grated Romano cheese, place on baking sheets, and bake at 400°F for 10–15 minutes.

Prepare the Dough

- Take the dough from the bowl and knead on a floured surface for 6–8 minutes.

- Place in a greased bowl and turn to coat. Cover with a cloth and let it rise in a warm place until doubled in size.

- Divide the dough into two pieces, form into tight loaves, and place in two greased and floured 8 x 4-inch loaf pans.

- Let the dough rise again for about an hour, until your finger leaves a mark when lightly pressed into it.

Select the Tomatoes

- Sun-dried tomatoes are ripe tomatoes that have been placed in the sun to remove most of the water.

- You can use sun-dried tomatoes packed in olive oil or the dehydrated product for this recipe.

- If using dehydrated tomatoes, soak them in warm water for 30 minutes, until soft and pliable.

- Drain, pat dry, and snip the tomatoes into ¼-inch pieces with scissors.

BREADS & DESSERTS

219

CHILE CHEESE CORN MUFFINS

Cheddar cheese and diced green chiles add flavor and personality to sweet corn muffins

Corn bread is a quick and tasty way to use pantry staples and make meals a little snappier. It's a great alternative to plain old bread and rolls, and who could eat chili without it?

Some people bake their corn bread in a pan. Others do it the old-fashioned Southern way, in a cast-iron skillet. Sweet corn bread is a Northern favorite, while Southerners tend to

like it drier and saltier, preferring to add honey or syrup at the table. This recipe turns your basic corn bread into muffins that are simultaneously sweet and savory and that can be prepared in a jiffy—even if you don't use that Jiffy corn muffin mix! *Yield: 12 muffins*

Ingredients

¹/₂ cup buttermilk

2 large eggs

¹/₃ cup sour cream

1 4-ounce can diced green chiles

¹/₂ cup canned cream-style corn

1 cup all-purpose flour

1 tablespoon baking powder

1 teaspoon salt

¹/₂ cup light brown sugar

1 cup yellow cornmeal

¹/₂ cup (1 stick) butter, melted

1 cup shredded cheddar

Chile Cheese Corn Muffins

- In a medium bowl, whisk together the buttermilk, eggs, sour cream, chiles, and cream-style corn.

- In a large bowl, combine the dry ingredients.

- Fold the buttermilk mixture into the dry mixture with a rubber spatula. When well blended, fold in the melted butter and the cheese.

- Bake in a muffin tin at 350°F until golden brown and a toothpick inserted into the center comes out clean, 30–35 minutes.

• • • • RECIPE VARIATION • • • •

Broccoli Cheese Corn Muffins: Replace the chiles in Chile Cheese Corn Muffins with 10 ounces cooked, drained and cooled chopped broccoli. Sauté 1 chopped yellow onion and add to recipe. Use a combination of ½ cup grated sharp cheddar and ½ cup grated Pepper Jack cheeses. Make the muffins as directed.

Make the Muffins

- Use a good-quality nonstick muffin tin.

- Spray each muffin cup with nonstick cooking spray or with a paper towel dipped in shortening.

- If muffin cups are filled more than ¾ full, there

won't be enough room for the muffins to puff up and they'll end up with flat tops.

- If baked muffins stick to the bottoms of the muffin cups, place the hot muffin tin on a wet towel for a couple of minutes to loosen them.

Substitute a Cornbread Mix

- Although many people prefer muffins from scratch, there's nothing wrong with using a packaged corn muffin mix.

- Omit all ingredients in the above recipe except for the chiles and cheese and add milk and egg according to package directions.

- Instead of ½ cup cream-style corn, add 1 14- to 16-ounce can.

- Blend in the cheese and chiles. Because of the added ingredients, bake longer than the package directions indicate (30–35 minutes).

BREADS & DESSERTS

221

WINTER SQUASH COGNAC PIE

Fresh squash replaces pumpkin in this rich, melt-in-your-mouth spiced pie with a little kick

The holidays aren't the holidays without pumpkin pie. This age-old classic is usually made with canned pumpkin, although if you've already scooped out your jack-o-lantern, you can always reserve the innards and cook them up. While canned pumpkin makes a perfectly acceptable pie, cooked squash or pumpkin is a whole different experience—much more flavorful, delicately textured, and buttery.

For an interesting variation on this recipe, try squash or pumpkin eggnog pie. Just omit the nutmeg and substitute a good-quality eggnog for the heavy cream. *Yield: One 9-inch pie*

Ingredients

$^{1}/_{2}$ cup white sugar

$^{1}/_{2}$ cup light brown sugar

$^{1}/_{4}$ teaspoon salt

$^{1}/_{2}$ teaspoon ground ginger

$^{1}/_{8}$ teaspoon ground cinnamon

$^{1}/_{8}$ teaspoon ground nutmeg

$^{1}/_{8}$ teaspoon ground allspice

$1^{1}/_{2}$ cups heavy cream

2 cups mashed cooked butternut squash

3 eggs, beaten

$^{1}/_{2}$ cup evaporated milk

2 tablespoons cognac

2 tablespoons maple syrup

1 tablespoon butter, melted

1 9-inch ginger-cookie pie crust

Whipped cream

Winter Squash Cognac Pie

- Mix sugars, salt, and spices. Blend in cream, squash, eggs, evaporated milk, cognac, maple syrup, and butter.

- Pour filling into the ginger-cookie crust and bake 15 minutes at 425°F.

- Reduce oven temperature to 350°F and bake 40–50 minutes longer, until pie is creamy-firm in center.

- Cool and serve topped with fresh whipped cream and cinnamon.

222

Prepare the Squash

- Peel, seed, and cube 2 pounds of butternut squash, or use prepeeled and cubed fresh squash, which you can usually find in the produce section of the supermarket.

- In a small saucepan, cover the squash cubes with water. Bring to a boil and cook until tender, about 15 minutes.

- Drain, cool, and mash the squash.

- Measure out 2 cups of mashed squash and refrigerate leftovers.

Make the Crust

- Crush about 20 ginger cookies in a plastic ziptop bag. Thin crisps like Anna's Ginger Thins are perfect.

- In a small bowl, combine the crushed cookies with ¼ cup (½ stick) melted unsalted butter, cooled.

- Press into a lightly greased 9-inch glass pie dish.

- Bake at 375° for 8–10 minutes, or until golden brown, making sure not to let the crust get too dark. Cool before filling.

BREADS & DESSERTS

CREAM-FILLED PUMPKIN ROLL
Delicate ginger cream makes a luscious filling for this light roll cake

A roll cake, or jelly roll cake, is simply a flat square or rectangular cake, baked very thin in a baking sheet and then spread with filling and rolled into a log. Roll cakes taste great, but who wants to go to the trouble of making one when you can buy them ready-made at the supermarket? Well, as soon as you've tasted a homemade one—you will.

Those supermarket roll cakes are loaded with chemicals and preservatives, giving them a fake taste. Plus, they're always sickly sweet. Making your own roll cake is actually very simple, and it's so much fresher tasting and healthier. With its rich, moist texture and light ginger cream filling, this spiced pumpkin roll is a dessert dream. *Yield: 1 roll cake*

Ingredients

1 cup flour

$^1/_2$ teaspoon baking soda

$^3/_4$ teaspoon baking powder

$^1/_4$ teaspoon salt

1 teaspoon cinnamon

$^1/_2$ teaspoon ground allspice

$^1/_2$ teaspoon ground ginger

$^1/_2$ teaspoon ground nutmeg

2 eggs, separated

$^1/_2$ cup sugar

$^1/_2$ cup dark brown sugar

1 teaspoon vanilla

$^3/_4$ cup canned pumpkin

2 tablespoons milk

Ginger cream

$^1/_4$ cup powdered sugar

Cream-Filled Pumpkin Roll

- Grease and flour a 15 x 10 x 1-inch jelly roll pan.

- In a small bowl, combine the flour, baking soda, baking powder, salt and spices. In a large bowl, combine egg yolks, sugars, and vanilla. Beat until thick and add pumpkin and milk. Blend in the flour mixture.

- Beat egg whites until stiff and gently fold into batter; don't overmix.

- Spread into pan and bake at 375°F for 12–14 minutes. Roll cake when it's hot, allow to cool, then unroll, fill with ginger cream, roll again and dust with powdered sugar.

• • • • RECIPE VARIATION • • • •

Mocha Cream Filling: Cream 9 tablespoons butter and ¾ cup superfine sugar until well blended. In a double boiler, melt 3 ounces semisweet chocolate in 2 tablespoons strong coffee, stirring constantly. Cool. Add to the butter mixture and blend well. Beat in 2 eggs until very smooth and light. Cool and spread over cooled unrolled cake.

Make the Cake Roll

Make the Ginger Cream

- Sprinkle powdered sugar over a clean, thin towel that's slightly larger than the cake.

- Loosen cake from the pan and invert onto the towel. Trim rough edges.

- Roll the cake while it is hot to ensure pliability when cooled.

- Roll the cake and towel into a 10-inch long roll. Place seam side down on a wire rack and cool completely.

- Unroll the cake and set towel aside. Spread filling over the surface, leaving a ¼-inch border on the sides, and roll back up.

- Chill a large bowl. In another large bowl, beat 6 ounces cream cheese with a hand mixer until light and fluffy.

- Add 1 tablespoon rum and 1 teaspoon vanilla.

- Beat in 1½ cups powdered sugar and ¼–½ teaspoon ground ginger until smooth.

- In the chilled bowl, beat 1 cup heavy cream until stiff. Gently fold into the cream cheese mixture. Cover and chill 1 hour.

BREADS & DESSERTS

OH MY GOD CARROT CAKE

A moist, fruity cake emboldened by crushed pineapple, orange juice, and a maple sugar–currant icing

Many things carrot became popular during World War II, when meat and sugar were among the staples at the top of the rationing list. People came to rely more and more on vegetables and vegetarian dishes, and carrots were highly prized, especially in the dessert category, because a carrot cake or bread required less sugar.

A lot of people avoid making carrot cakes because of the necessary grating, which seems to require a lot of time and elbow grease. But it doesn't really take all that long, and if you're really lazy, there's always the food processor. *Yield: 1 Bundt cake*

Ingredients

1 cup white sugar

1 cup dark brown sugar

2 cups flour

2 teaspoons baking soda

2 teaspoons baking powder

2 teaspoons ground cloves

1 teaspoon nutmeg

1 teaspoon cinnamon

1 teaspoon salt

1 teaspoon vanilla

5 tablespoons orange juice

4 eggs

1½ cups oil

3 cups grated carrots

1 8- to 9-ounce can crushed pineapple

½ cup chopped walnuts or pecans

Currant walnut icing

Oh My God Carrot Cake

- In a large bowl, combine sugars, flour, baking soda, baking powder, spices, salt, vanilla, and orange juice.

- Add the eggs to the mixture one at a time, followed by the oil.

- Fold in the carrots, pineapple, and nuts.

- Pour the batter into a Bundt pan sprayed thoroughly with nonstick cooking spray and dusted with flour. Bake at 325°F for 1 hour and 15 minutes, or until golden brown. Cool 10 minutes in the pan, invert onto a plate, and frost with currant walnut icing.

···· RECIPE VARIATION ····

Oh My God Carrot Cake with Coconut: Try adding 1 cup coconut to this tropics-inspired recipe. Not only does it add extra sweetness, but it also adds texture and flavor and will help keep the cake moist in the refrigerator for a longer period.

Grate the Carrots

- You want fresh, sweet carrots for this recipe. Packaged grated carrots are usually dry, thick, and tasteless.

- Hand-grating the carrots, while a little time consuming, yields a nice, finely grated result that's great for soft batter.

- If you hate hand-grating, chop the carrots into 1-inch slices and put them in a food processor with a sharp blade or grater attachment.

- Pulse for a few seconds at a time until the carrots are the consistency you want.

Make the Icing

- Soften 8 ounces of cream cheese and ¼ cup (½ stick) unsalted butter to room temperature. Cream together in a medium mixing bowl.

- Beat in 3 cups of powdered sugar, 2 tablespoons evaporated milk, 1 tablespoon vanilla, and ¼ cup maple syrup.

- Plump ⅓ cup of currants by soaking in ⅓ cup of water for 5 minutes. Drain well.

- Fold the currants and ⅓ cup chopped walnuts into the icing. Spread over the cooled Bundt cake.

RESOURCES
A complete guide for all your vegetable cooking needs

Even the most accomplished chefs use cooking resources. While this book gives you the basics of vegetable cooking, you'll want to expand your knowledge on a regular basis. There are many ways to do this, from books and magazines to cooking shows and videos, cooking Web sites, hotlines, and helplines, and product and equipment Web sites.

Use the following resource guide to find answers to your farmers' market directories, cooking tips, recipe ideas, places to buy equipment and ingredients, vegetable cooking questions, and much more.

Another resource that you might never have noticed: free super market recipe cards. You can find them in the produce section of most large and specialty markets, and they feature many quick and delicious ways to use fresh vegetables.

FARMERS' MARKETS, CSAs & VEGETABLE FESTIVALS

Where to find fresh and organic produce, community supported agriculture, and vegetable events near you

Farmers' Markets and CSAs

Alternative Farming Systems Information Center
http://afsic.nal.usda.gov
Absolutely everything you want to know about alternative farming, from CSAs and organic farming to education and research, alternative marketing, eco–pest control, and more. You can search for your local CSAs here.

Farmer Net
www.farmernet.com
Lists all the farmers' markets in Southern California, with locations and times, along with a "What's Fresh" guide.

Farmer's Market Search
http//apps.ams.usda.gov/FarmersMarkets
U.S. government Web site has listings of farmers' markets by state and city.

Local Harvest
www.localharvest.org
Where to find locally grown produce anywhere in the country. Comprehensive map locates farmers' markets, family farms, CSAs, farm stands, and u-pick produce in your area.

The Original Farmers Market
www.farmersmarketla.com
Website for the original Los Angeles Farmers Market, in operation since 1934. Has a handy "Market Meals" section featuring weekly recipes.

Vegetable Festivals

The National Asparagus Festival
www.nationalasparagusfestival.org
Web site for the annual festival celebrating asparagus in Michigan's Oceana County.

Party Guide: Vegetable & Spice Festivals
www.partyguideonline.com/foodndrink/vegetable.html
A countrywide guide to pumpkin festivals, asparagus festivals, corn festivals, garlic festivals, herb festivals, pickle festivals, potato festivals . . . you name it, it's here.

PickYourOwn.org
www.pickyourown.org
Includes a guide to finding fruit and vegetable festivals near you.

Vegetablebuzz.com
www.vegetablebuzz.com
Provides a directory and information about asparagus festivals around the world.

Wikipedia List of Festivals in the United States
http://en.wikipedia.org/wiki/List_of_festivals_in_the_United_States#Food.2C_harvest_and_wild_game_festivals
Provides a wide-ranging list of food festivals, including a sampling of vegetable festivals such as the Circleville, Ohio Pumpkin Festival; The Reynoldsburg Tomato Festival in Reynoldsburg, Ohio; Sycamore Pumpkin Festival in Sycamore, Illinois, and others.

BOOKS & MAGAZINES

This is just a small sample of the many books and magazines available that will help and inspire you on your vegetable cooking journey

Books

Chesman, Andrea. *The Roasted Vegetable*. Harvard Common Press, 2002.
Probably the best book out there on roasting every kind of vegetable, with sections on sandwiches, main dishes, side dishes, soups, pasta, grains, and more.

Jaffrey, Madhur. *Madhur Jaffrey's World-of-the-East Vegetarian Cooking*. Knopf, 1981.
You'll find a wonderful variety of Indian- and Asian-influenced vegetable dishes here.

Katzen, Mollie. *The Enchanted Broccoli Forest*. Ten Speed Press, 1982.
A classic in the vegetable field, by the author of *The Moosewood Cookbook*. Offers engaging and thorough tips and instructions for vegetarian dishes and menus.

Katzen, Mollie. *The Vegetable Dishes I Can't Live Without*. Hyperion, 2007.
The Queen Victoria of vegetable cookery—yes, she's been on the throne almost that long—offers her personal favorites in yet another delightful cookbook.

Miller, Robin. *Quick Fix Meals*. Taunton Press, 2007.
Lots of good ideas for vegetables, with spin-off recipes to take you through the week.

Palazzi, Antonella. *The Great Book of Vegetables*. Simon and Schuster, 1991.
The ultimate vegetable encyclopedia, with instructions on how to buy and prepare fresh vegetables, cooking methods, and hundreds of recipes.

Sedaker, Cheryl. *365 Ways to Cook Chicken*. Harper and Row, 1984.
A great source of ideas for ways to cook vegetables and chicken.

Tanner, Lisa. *The Potato Experience*. Ten Speed Press, 1986.
Clam fondue skins? Egg foo young skins? Chicken liver stroganoff skins? They're all here, along with soufflés, fritters, salads, biscuits, and whatever other forms potatoes can come in.

Magazines

Body + Soul
www.wholeliving.com
A Martha Stewart publication offering a wealth of good info on healthy living and eating, with easy gourmet vegetable recipes in every issue.

Bon Appétit
www.bonappetit.com
Always features a variety of vegetable and vegetarian dishes with unique spin on everyday ingredients.

Cooking Light
www.cookinglight.com
A great place to find vegetable recipes and recipes for vegetables and meat, poultry, and fish, with a complete recipe index.

Cook's Illustrated
www.cooksillustrated.com
The magazine for serious and novice cooks alike. Ingredient and equipment tips, detailed instructions on vegetable cooking, invaluable "kitchen notes," and more.

Fine Cooking
www.finecooking.com
Features recipes, in-depth articles, test kitchen with equipment tips, quick meals, and book reviews.

Real Simple
www.realsimple.com
A magazine about keeping things simple, in and out of the kitchen, with recipes for light, elegant vegetable sides, salads, and entrees in every issue.

Vegetarian Times
www.vegetariantimes.com
Excellent vegetable recipes feature really creative tips on vegetable cooking, along with menus for healthy eating.

COOKING SHOWS, VIDEOS & WEB SITES

Watch the experts prepare tempting vegetable dishes and join discussion groups

Cooking Shows

America's Test Kitchen on PBS
www.americastestkitchentv.com
The chefs and editors of *Cook's Illustrated* offer innovative ways to prepare everything, including vegetables.

Delicious TV Totally Vegetarian on PBS
www.delicioustv.com
A vegetarian cooking show hosted by Toni Fiore, author of *Totally Vegetarian: Easy, Fast, Comforting Cooking for Every Kind of Vegetarian* (Da Capo Press, 2008).

Everyday Food on PBS
www.pbs.org/everydayfood
Sarah, Lucinda, Anna, and John offer "quick, easy and practical solutions to the challenges of everyday cooking."

Everyday Italian on the Food Network
www.foodnetwork.com/everyday-italian
Host Giada De Laurentiis shares favorite recipes from her Italian upbringing, including many healthy, creative ways of serving vegetables. Maybe that's how she stays so skinny!

Healthy Appetite with Ellie Krieger on the Food Network
www.foodnetwork.com/healthy-appetite-with-ellie-krieger
The renowned dietitian and *New York Times* bestselling author shows you how to eat smart and tasty. You can also find her videos here.

Videos

Best Cooking Videos on the Net
www.bestcookvideos.com
An infinite variety of vegetable recipes prepared on video.

Get Cooking with Mollie Katzen
http://get-cooking.com
Mollie and friends in all-new, beautifully produced videos that demonstrate basic cooking techniques and share invaluable tips o everything from chopping vegetables to choosing the best cookin equipment.

ifood.tv
www.ifood.tv
Recipes for delicious vegetable entrees, soups, sides, and more, wit video instructions.

Khana Pakana
www.khanapakana.com
Indian vegetarian and vegan recipes, plus tips on eating healthy an vegetarian.

Raw Life
www.rawlife.com
Get ideas and instruction on the art of raw vegetable preparation.

Recipe Web Sites

Allrecipes.com
www.allrecipes.com
And they do mean all. If it isn't in here, it probably doesn't exist. The Seattle-based site bills itself as "the world's largest social network of food and entertaining enthusiasts."

Cook & Eat
www.cookandeat.com
Great Web site featuring "tasty photos and recipes," many of them vegetable-oriented.

Cooks.com
www.cooks.com
Any and all recipes, vegetable and otherwise, along with many tips, nutrition facts, and forums.

Epicurious
www.epicurious.com
Find virtually any vegetable recipe here, with helpful slideshows and commentary.

Scented Nectar
www.scentednectar.com
Features a directory of more than 700 vegetarian recipe sites.

Vegetarian Times
www.vegetariantimes.com
Online offshoot of the magazine offers "the world's largest collection of vegetarian recipes."

FIND INGREDIENTS

Some places you can visit to find fresh, ethnic, and regional ingredients, as well as more exotic fare

Cajun Grocer
www.cajungrocer.com
Premium authentic Cajun foods and ingredients at value prices.

Cajun Supermarket
www.cajunsupermarket.com
The most extensive online Louisiana Cajun and Creole retailer.

Eden Organic
www.edenfoods.com
One of the best places to find organic products and ingredients.

eFoodDepot.com
www.efooddepot.com
Thai, Japanese, Chinese, Indian, and Indonesian sauces and ingredients can be purchased here.

ImportFood.com
www.importfood.com
Find Thai recipes, ingredients, and cookware.

Peapod
www.peapod.com
Offers online grocery shopping and delivery.

Whole Foods Market
www.wholefoodsmarket.com
The Web site for this nationwide natural and organic grocery feature recipes, tips on buying locally grown produce, a directory of stores i your area, and more.

FIND COOKWARE & ACCESSORIES
Learning about and buying the best and most reasonably priced cooking equipment

Calphalon
www.calphalon.com
One of the best manufacturers of cookware—the kind chefs love. Get recipes, video instruction, and cooking tips here, too.

Cooking.com
www.cooking.com
Great one-stop place for deals on name-brand cookware, with rating scale and extensive buying guide.

Cookware.com
www.cookware.com
All brands of cookware at discount prices.

Cookware & More
www.cookwarenmore.com
The All-Clad outlet since 1984, offering deep discounts on All-Clad irregulars.

Crate and Barrel
www.crateandbarrel.com
Lots of kitchen appliances and gadgets, plus an outlet store.

Gourmet Food at About.com
http://gourmetfood.about.com
Offers advice on where to purchase cookware and kitchen tools and do your gourmet shopping.

ManPans
www.manpans.com
This eco-friendly "Made in the USA" manufacturer offers a large selection of cookware, woks, fry pans, sauté pans, and accessories.

Williams-Sonoma
www.williams-sonoma.com
It's high end, but if you've got the bucks, you'll find the best of everything you need for your kitchen.

COOKING HOTLINES & HELP SITES

Got a problem? Need a good recipe idea? Help is just a click away

Ask
www.ask.com
Tips, forums, recipes, troubleshooting—it's all here.

Betty Crocker
www.bettycrocker.com
You don't have to use Betty's products to get cooking help and ideas from her.

ChefsLine
www.chefsline.com
(800) 977-1224
Chefs offer kitchen coaching and expert cooking tips. Small fee involved.

Home Chef Cooking Tips
http://homechefcookingtips.com
A good place for information on ingredients, recipes, equipment, healthy kids' meals, and more.

Recipe Zaar Kitchen Help Live
www.recipezaar.com/chat
A 24-hour kitchen help chat forum.

METRIC CONVERSION TABLES

Approximate U.S. Metric Equivalents

Liquid Ingredients

U.S. MEASURES	METRIC	U.S. MEASURES	METRIC
1/4 TSP.	1.23 ML	2 TBSP.	29.57 ML
1/2 TSP.	2.36 ML	3 TBSP.	44.36 ML
3/4 TSP.	3.70 ML	1/4 CUP	59.15 ML
1 TSP.	4.93 ML	1/2 CUP	118.30 ML
1 1/4 TSP.	6.16 ML	1 CUP	236.59 ML
1 1/2 TSP.	7.39 ML	2 CUPS OR 1 PT.	473.18 ML
1 3/4 TSP.	8.63 ML	3 CUPS	709.77 ML
2 TSP.	9.86 ML	4 CUPS OR 1 QT.	946.36 ML
1 TBSP.	14.79 ML	4 QTS. OR 1 GAL.	3.79 L

Dry Ingredients

U.S. MEASURES	METRIC	U.S. MEASURES		METRIC
1/16 OZ.	2 (1.8) G	2 4/5 OZ.		80 G
1/8 OZ.	3 1/2 (3.5) G	3 OZ.		85 (84.9) G
1/4 OZ.	7 (7.1) G	3 1/2 OZ.		100 G
1/2 OZ.	15 (14.2) G	4 OZ.		115 (113.2) G
3/4 OZ.	21 (21.3) G	4 1/2 OZ.		125 G
7/8 OZ.	25 G	5 1/4 OZ.		150 G
1 OZ.	30 (28.3) G	8 7/8 OZ.		250 G
1 3/4 OZ.	50 G	16 OZ.	1 LB.	454 G
2 OZ.	60 (56.6) G	17 3/5 OZ.	1 LIVRE	500 G

GLOSSARY

Here's a handy reference guide to some basic cooking terminology

Aioli: A garlic mayonnaise made in France's Provence region, used as a condiment or sauce.

Blanch: To plunge food into boiling water, partially cooking it, and then plunge it into an ice bath to set it.

Braise: To brown foods in fat and then cook them in a covered casserole or skillet with a small amount of liquid.

Chop: To cut food into very small pieces with a chef's knife, food processor, or blender.

Deep-fry: To cook quickly in a large quantity of oil heated to at least 350°F, in a deep pot or deep fryer. As opposed to shallow-frying, in which the food is fried in a few inches of hot oil in a skillet or frying pan.

Dice: To cut food into cubes the shape of dice, usually about 1/4-inch thick.

Fold: To blend a fragile mixture, such as beaten egg whites, delicately into a heavier mixture, such as a soufflé base or a cake batter.

Frittata: An open-faced omelet with other ingredients, such as meat or vegetables, cooked first in a skillet and then finished under the broiler.

Gratin: A casserole dish with a topping of bread crumbs, grated cheese, and dots of butter, broiled or baked until light brown.

Grill pan: A skillet with ridges, used on the stovetop to simulate grilling.

Julienne: To cut into thin strips, as in julienned carrots.

Microplane grater: A perforated steel tool for grating and grinding ingredients, such as nutmeg seeds and ginger root, or for zesting citrus fruit.

Pan-fry: To cook quickly in a small quantity of very hot fat in a shallow saucepan or skillet.

Reduce: To boil down a liquid, reducing it in quantity and concentrating its taste, as for sauces.

Roux: A cooked mixture of butter or oil and flour, whisked into a paste and used as a base for thickening sauces.

Sauté: A cooking method whereby food is browned quickly in a small quantity of very hot oil or butter. The sauté pan is frequently shaken so that the food moves around quickly and doesn't burn. From the French *sauter,* meaning "to jump."

Scallop: A layered dish, usually of potatoes or another vegetable, baked in a white sauce, often with cheese and bread crumbs.

Smoke point: The stage at which heated fat begins to emit smoke and acrid odors and impart an unpleasant flavor to foods. The higher its smoke point, the better suited a fat is for frying.

Soufflé: A light, fluffy baked dish made with egg yolks and beaten egg whites combined with various other ingredients and served as a main dish or dessert.

Steam: To cook food by setting it over boiling liquid, in a wire basket or steamer. Steaming can also be done with very little water in a microwave.

Stir-fry: To cook food quickly by browning it in hot fat in a wok or skillet and moving it constantly with a spatula or wooden spoon.

Tagine: A two-part casserole dish used in North African cooking, most commonly in Morocco, consisting of a bottom plate and a removable conical-shaped lid.

Tian: A French casserole or gratin dish.

Timbale: A custard-like dish of eggs, cheese, chicken, fish, or vegetables baked in a drum-shaped pastry mold of the same name.

Toss: To mix lightly, as with salad ingredients or in coating vegetables with oil before roasting, or to flip food in a skillet or sauté pan by tossing the pan.

Whisk: A tool made of wire loops used to stir or whip a mixture briskly until smooth. Also refers to the act of whisking.

INDEX

A

Alfredo Sauce, 99
appetizers, 36–47, 193
artichokes, 153, 197
Artichoke Avocado Caesar Salad, 48–49
Asian Pork Pitas, 85
asparagus, 60, 72–73
Asparagus Potato Salad, 52–53
Asparagus Salade Niçoise, 53
Asparagus Scallop Wraps, 157
Asparagus Tempura, 40–41
Asparagus Timbales, 150–51
Athenian Cabbage Rolls, 200–201

B

Baby Artichokes with Aioli, 36–37
Bacon Hollandaise Asparagus, 60–61
Baked Corn Fritters, 205
Baked Eggs with Artichokes, 152–53
Becker, Marion Rombauer, 22
beef, 45, 184–89, 201
Beet Salad, 69
Best Borscht Ever, 74–75
books and magazines, 230–31
Braised Sea Bass with Fennel, 164–65
Brandy Yams Mousseline, 130–31
breads and muffins, 216–21
Broccoli and Bacon Breakfast Burritos, 149
Broccoli and Bacon Quiche, 148–49
Broccoli Carrot Potato Burritos, 90–91
Broccoli Cheese Corn Muffins, 221
Broccoli Mashed Potato Bake, 122–23
Broccoli Mushroom Alfredo, 98–99
Broccoli Potato Breakfast Cakes, 123
broccoli rabe, 163
Bruschetta Burgers, 45
Bubble and Squeak, 187
bulgur, 119
burritos, 90–91
Buttermilk Ranch Dressing, 26
Butternut Cream Cheese Soup, 83

C

Cabbage and Chicken Egg Foo Young, 154–55
Caesar Cobb Salad Wrap, 93
Cajun Carrot Croquettes, 209
Cajun Trout with Broccoli Rabe, 162–63
Cardini, Caesar, 48
Carrot and Parsnip Gratin, 70–71
carrot juice, 33
Carrot Orange Soup, 77
carrots, 181
Carrot Salad, 43
Cashew Pea Salad, 51
Casserole of Spring Vegetables, 132–33
cast-iron grills, 57
Cauliflower and Broccoli Skins with Swiss Cheese, 125
cheeses, 91, 95, 149
Cheest Asparagus Soup, 73
Cheesy Spinach Squares, 46–47
chicken, 85, 107, 147, 154–55, 168–79
Chicken and Corn Soufflé, 147
chicken broth, 79
Chicken Caesar, Caesar Niçoise, and Western Caesar, 49
Chicken Caprese, 168–69
Chicken Caprese Sandwiches, 169
Chicken Flatbread Gyros, 85
Chicken with Morels and Madeira, 172–73
Chicken with Mushrooms and Gruyére, 173
chickpea flour, 207
chiles, 157
Chili Cheese Corn Muffins, 220
Chinmoy, Sri, ix–x
Chipotle Pecadillo Wontons, 39
Chocolate Zucchini Bread, 217
Choucroute Rouge, 67
Christmas Stuffed Peppers, 202–3
coconut milk, 139
Coconutty Sweet Potatoes, 126–27
Coconutty Sweet Potato Pancakes, 127

Coconutty Sweet Potato Pudding, 127
Coconut Vegetable Curry, 138–39
cole slaw, 35, 67
collard greens, 171
community supported agriculture (CSA), 3, 236
cooking hotlines and help sites, 229
cooking shows, videos and recipe web sites, 232–33
cookware and accesories, 235
Coq au Vin Fondue, 175
Coq au Vin Magnifique, 174–75
Cordon Bleu Pasta Salad, 107
corncob smoking, 93
Corned Beef and Cabbage, 186–87
Corn Fritters with Chile Relish, 204–5
Crab and Mushroom Timbales, 151
Crab Mushroom Crepes, 215
Crab Rangoons, 39
Cranberry-Ginger Yams Mousseline, 131
Cream of Tomato Soup, 79
Creamed Spinach with Veal, 190
Cream-Filled Pumpkin Roll, 224–25
Creamy Carrot Ginger Soup, 76–77
Creamy Chicken Mushroom Casserole, 173
Creamy Polish Beet Borscht, 75
Creamy Thyme Asparagus Soup, 72–73
Creamy Veggie Pasta Salad, 106–7
Crème Fraiche, 77
crepes and crepe pans, 214–15
croquettes, 208–9
Crunchy Garden Salad Tacos, 34
Crusted Chicken with Greens, 170–71
Cucumber and Pork Pitas, 84–85
Cucumber Sandwiches, 43
Curried Butternut Squash Soup, 82–83
Curried Pasta Salad with Crabmeat and Peas, 107
curry powder, 83

D

desserts, 222–27

E

eggplant, 57
Eggplant Pancakes Milanese, 212–13
Eggplant Parmesan Casserole, 135
Eggplant Parmesan Lasagna, 135
eggs, 144–55
Eggs Baked in Green Peppers, 153
Eggs Benedict with Artichokes and
    Tomatoes, 153
Environmental Working Group (EWG), 31
Escarole with Bacon, 133
Exotic Three-Bean Salad, 55

F

Family Vegetarian Cookbook, x
farmers' markets, 2, 236
Fennel, Tomato, and Chicory Salad, 35
Fettuccine Alfredo alla Spinaci, 99
Filo Tartlets, 47
Florentine Eggplant Pancake Topping, 213
French-Cut Green Beans with Cashews and
    Ham, 63
Fresh Tomatoes with Creamed Spinach, 191
frittatas, 144–45
fritters, 204–7
Fruity Veggie Salad with Bacon, 35

G

Garlic Sweet Potatoes, 129
Ginger Citrus Slaw, 35
Gnocchi in Butter and Herb Sauce, 105
Gnocchi with Chestnut Béchamel, 105
Gnocchi with Spinach Béchamel, 104–5
Good Ol' Southern Greens, 171
Goulash, 63
grape leaves, 119
Green Bean and Beef Stir-Fry, 184–85
Green Beans Paprikash, 62–63
Green Beans with Salmon, 158–59
Green Chile and Cheese Corn Fritters, 205
Grilled Asparagus with Balsamic
    Vinaigrette, 61

Grilled Curried Shrimp Salad, 161
Grilled Green Beans in Vinaigrette, 159
Grilled Mediterranean Salad, 56–57
Grilled Portobellos, 87
Grilled Vegetable Pockets, 57

H

ham, 61, 107, 202–3
Homemade Enchilada Sauce, 91
Honey Mint Chutney, 207
Honeyed Carrots and Parsnips, 71

I

Indian Vegetable Fritters, 206–7
ingredients and where to find, 234

International Egg Foo Young, 155
Irish Lamb Stew, 183

J

juicing and juicers, 32–33

K

Kicked-Up Mushroom Leek Soup, 80–81

L

lamb, 85, 182–83, 200–201
latkes, 210–11
lettuces, 161
Lettuce with Mushrooms and Rice, 133

M

Madeira wine, 81
metric conversion tables, 237
Mexican Rice, 111
Mexican Scalloped Potatoes, 120–21
Mixed Vegetable Soufflé, 146–47
Mocha Cream Filling, 225
Mushroom and Spinach Crepes, 214–15
Mushroom Leek Soup with Other
     Vegetables, 81
Mushroom Noodles Romanoff, 137
mushrooms, 81, 86, 117, 137, 172–73, 199
Mushroom Stroganoff, 136–37
Mustard Sauce, 171

N

No-Noodle Vegetable Kugel, 101
Nacho Stuffed Mushrooms, 199

O

Oh My God Carrot Cake, 226–27
Oh My God Carrot Cake with Coconut, 227
oils for cooking, 22
olives, 59
orzo, 115
Other Stir-Fry Possibilities, 185
Other Timbale Suggestions, 151
Oyster and Vegetable Po'boys, 89

P

pancakes, 127, 210–13
Pan-Seared Chilean Sea Bass with
     Asparagus, 165
paprika, 63
pasta and noodles, 37, 51, 96–107, 135–37,
     142–43, 169
Pasta with Roasted Baby Artichokes, 37
Pea and Mushroom Tortellini, 96–97
Pea and Radish Spring Salad, 50–51
Pea Pasta Salad, 51
peas, early spring, 97
Pecan Sweet Potato Pie, 223
peppers, 29, 177
pesticides, 31
Pesto Bruschetta, 44–45

Pilaf-Stuffed Acorn Squash, 115
Pineapple Fried Rice, 109
pitas, 84–85
pizzas, 94–95, 219
pork, 84–85, 180–81
Portobello Ciabattas, 86–87
Potato and Veal Stuffed Pumpkin, 194–95
potatoes, 52–53, 69, 71, 120–33, 194–95,
     208–9, 211
pumpkin seeds, 195
Pumpkin Spiced Squash Soup, 83

R

radishes, 51
Red Cabbage with Bacon and Wine, 66–67
Red Pepper Eggplant Parmesan, 134–35

Red Slaw, 67
resources, 228–36
rice, 59, 108–17, 138–39
Risotto Milanese, 113
Risotto with Summer Squash, 112–13
roadside stands, 1
Roasted Asparagus and Prosciutto
     Roll-ups, 61
Roasted Green Bean Salad, 58–59
Roasted Green Beans with Shallots and
     Pecans, 59
Roasted Teriyaki Sweet Potatoes, 128–29
Roasted Tomatillo Guacamole, 141
Roasted Tomato and Barley Soup, 78–79
Roasted Tomato and Eggplant Bisque, 79

S

salads
    Artichoke Avocado Caesar Salad, 48–49
    Asparagus Potato Salad, 52–53
    Asparagus Salad Niçoise, 53
    Beet Salad, 69
    Carrot Salad, 43
    Cashew Pea Salad, 51
    Chicken Caesar, Caesar Niçoise, and
        Western Caesar, 49
    Cordon Bleu Pasta Salad, 107
    Creamy Veggie Pasta Salad, 106–7
    Curried Pasta Salad with Crabmeat and
        Peas, 107
    Exotic Three-Bean Salad, 55
    Fennel, Tomato, and Chicory Salad, 35
    Grilled Mediterranean Salad, 56–57
    Pea and Radish Spring Salad, 50–51
    Pea Pasta Salad, 51
    Roasted Green Bean Salad, 58–59
    Salmon, Tomato, and Vege Salad, 34
    Spicy Vegetable and Peanut Noodle
        Salad, 143
    Sweet Potato Tropical Fruit Salad, 129
    Tailgate Three-Bean Salad, 54–55
    Three-Bean Salad Italiano, 55
    Tuna Pasta with Tortellini and Peas, 97
    Unbeetable Potato Salad, 69
    Vegetarian Artichoke Salad, 197
Salmon, Tomato, and Vege Salad, 34
sandwiches, 43, 57, 84–89, 92–93, 169, 219
sausages and keilbasas, 74–75, 192–93,
    196–97, 202–3
Sautéed Baby Artichokes, 37
Sautéed Broccoli Rabe with Mushrooms, 163
Scalloped Potatoes Lorraine, 121
seafood
    Asparagus Scallop Wraps, 157
    Braised Sea Bass with Fennel, 164–65
    Cajun Trout with Broccoli Rabe, 162–63
    Crab and Mushroom Timbales, 151
    Crab Mushroom Crepes, 215
    Curried Pasta Salad with Crabmeat and
        Peas, 107
    Green Beans with Salmon, 158–59
    Grilled Curried Shrimp Salad, 161

    Pan-Seared Chilean Sea Bass with
        Asparagus, 165
    Salmon, Tomato, and Vege Salad, 34
    Seafood Zucchini Boats, 65
    Shrimp with Spring Lettuces, 160–61
    Spinach-Stuffed Mushrooms, 198–99
    Thai Asparagus & Scallops, 156–57
    Vegetable Seafood Newburg, 166–67
Seafood Zucchini Boats, 65
Seared Portobellos in Wine, 87
Shepherd's Pie Hash, 189
Shepherd's Pie (with beef or meat of choice),
    188–89
Sherried Vegetable Potato Skins, 124–25
Shiitake and Wild Rice Casserole, 116–17
shrimp deveiner, 161
Shrimp with Spring Lettuces, 160–61
side dishes, 60–71
Some Non-Veggie Additions, 139
soufflés, 146–47
soups, 31, 72–83, 133
spaetzle, 191
Spanish Bruschetta, 45
Spanish Rice with Green Beans, 110–11
Spicy Cabbage Pakoras, 207
Spicy Vegetable and Peanut Noodle
    Salad, 143
Spiked Baby Carrots with Pork, 180–81
Spinach and Leek Frittata, 144–45
Spinach and Potato Frittata, 145
Spinach Crust, 149
Spinach Lasagna, 102–3
Spinach Moussaka, 47
Spinach-Stuffed Mushrooms, 198–99
Spring Vegetables with Lamb, 182–83
The Sri Chinmoy Vegetarian Cookbook
    (Chinmoy), ix–x
Stuffed Artichokes, 196–97
Stuffed Artichokes Italiano, 197
Stuffed Cabbage Soup, 201
Stuffed Eggplant Appetizers, 191
Stuffed Eggplant Barquettes, 192–93
Stuffed Eggplant Moussaka, 193
Stuffed Peppers with Herbed Cottage
    Cheese, 203
sugar snap peas, 51

Super-sized Layered Veggie Salad with
    Bacon, 35
Sweet and Sour Corned Beef and
    Cabbage, 187
Sweet and Sour Roasted Beets, 68–69
Sweet and Spicy Stuffing, 195
Sweet Potato-Carrot Croquettes, 208–9
Sweet Potato Tropical Fruit Salad, 129
Sweet Potato Zucchini Latkes, 211

T

Tabbouleh, 118–19
tacos, 34
Tailgate Three-Bean Salad, 54–55
Tempura Dipping Sauce, 41
teriyaki sauce, 129
Thai Asparagus and Scallops, 156–57
Three-Bean Salad Italiano, 55
Three-Pepper Asian Chicken Salad, 177
Three-Pepper Sizzling Chicken, 176–77
Three-Pepper Sizzling Chicken Wraps, 177
tofu, 143
Tomatillo Enchilada Pie, 140–41
Tomatillo Ranch Dressing, 141
Tomato Carrot Rice Pilaf, 114–15
tomatoes, 45, 219
Tomato Herb Bread, 218–19
Tomato Herb Bread Pizzas, 219
Tomato Herb Bread Sandwiches, 219
Tortellini Caprese, 169
tortillas and tortilla pies, 140–41
tostadas, 91
Tuna Pasta with Tortellini and Peas, 97
turkey, 200–201
Tzatziki, 85

U

Unbeetable Potato Salad, 69

V

veal, 190–91, 194–95
Vegetable Bacon Caesar Wraps, 92–93
vegetable festivals, 3, 236
Vegetable Fried Rice, 108–9
Vegetable Noodle Kugel, 100–101
Vegetable Po'Boys, 88–89

INDEX

243

vegetables
    blanching, 14–15, 183
    braising, 164
    buying local, 2–3
    canned and canned substitutes, 8–9
    freezing, 5
    and freshness, xii–1
    frozen and frozen alternatives, 8, 9
    frying, 22–23
    grilling, 18–19
    organic, 30–31
    prepackaged and bulk bagged, 1
    raw, 24–35
    roasting, 16–17
    sautéing, 20–21
    seasonal, 10–11
    steaming, 12–13
    stir-frying, 21, 184–85
    storing, 4–5
    stuffed, 192–203
    washing, 6–7
Vegetable Seafood Newburg, 166–67
Vegetable Seafood Newburg
    Casserole, 167
Vegetable Spread Supreme, 42–43
Vegetables with Tofu and Spinach, 139
Vegetable Tofu Lo Mein, 142–43
Vegetable Tostadas, 91
Vegetable Wontons, 38–39
Vegetarian Artichoke Salad, 197
vegetarian entrees, 132–43
Veggie Medley Pesto Pizza, 94–95
Veggie Smoothie, 33

W
White Spinach Lasagna with Clams, 103
White Vegetable and Clam Pesto Pizza, 95
Wild Rice Stuffing, 117
wines, 81, 137
Winter Squash Cognac Pie, 222–23
wraps, 92–93

Y
Yams in Apricot Sauce, 131

Z
Zucchini Boats Provençal, 64–65
Zucchini Bread, 216–17
Zucchini Latkes, 210–11
Zucchini-Stuffed Chicken Legs, 178–79

INDEX